BERNARD BERGONZI, author of several
books on twentieth-century literature, has recently completed an edition of critical pieces
on the *Four Quartets*. He is professor of
English at the University of Warwick.

MASTERS OF WORLD LITERATURE

T. S. Eliot

MASTERS OF WORLD LITERATURE SERIES

LOUIS KRONENBERGER, GENERAL EDITOR

T. S. Eliot

✦✦

by

Bernard Bergonzi

The Macmillan Company, New York, New York

The Macmillan Company
866 Third Avenue, New York, N.Y. 10022
Collier-Macmillan Canada Ltd., Toronto, Ontario

Library of Congress Catalog Card Number: 78–162337

FIRST PRINTING

Printed in the United States of America

F O R

Benet, Clarissa, and Lucy

Contents

Preface

Toward the end of T. S. Eliot's life a friend asked him if he could say more about some lines from "Little Gidding":

> And what the dead had no speech for, when living,
> They can tell you, being dead: the communication
> Of the dead is tongued with fire beyond the language
> of the living.

Eliot replied that we cannot fully understand a person's life, and grasp the totality of his being, until he is dead: "Once he is dead, the acts of his life fall into their proper perspective and we can see what he was tending toward." These words have been in my mind while writing this book, some five years after Eliot's death; I have felt that it is now possible, however imperfectly, to see the life and the work as an achieved whole, a completed pattern. One says "pattern" advisedly; as many readers have noticed, certain themes and images persist throughout Eliot's work, both in prose and verse, recurring in different forms during the fifty years of his literary career. The figure in the carpet is both pronounced and intricate, and this fact has encouraged critics to treat the whole of Eliot's *oeuvre* as a single timeless entity, so that a phrase from 1910 can be juxtaposed with one from 1940, as though nothing had happened between them. The way in which Eliot's mind developed and altered over half a century is often lost sight of;

Eliot himself complained that writers who quoted his critical opinions seldom added, "this is what Mr. Eliot thought (or felt) in 1933," or whenever, and were disinclined to allow that the critic might since have changed his mind.

A major lesson of Eliot's criticism was that literature must be read synchronically, with past and present coexisting and mutually interacting, and the strategy of his poetry was always concerned with the need to circumvent time. The lesson may have been learned too well: the ease with which Eliot's work lent itself to synchronic readings encouraged critics to see its pattern in too static a fashion.

I have been conscious throughout of the pattern, the figure in the carpet, but I have also felt the need to tell a story which moves forward in time: its remote origins lay in Somerset three centuries ago, though it properly began in St. Louis, Missouri, toward the end of the last century. It unfolds in Gloucester and Cambridge, Massachusetts, and in Paris and Munich; it continues in London during two world wars and the depressed years between, with episodes in Canterbury and Virginia, Huntingdonshire and New York. "In my end is my beginning": at length the circle ended where it began, and Eliot's ashes were buried in East Coker's parish church. The characters of the story come equally from the present and the past: Ezra Pound, Irving Babbitt, and Charles Maurras; Arnaut Daniel, Lancelot Andrewes, and Charles Baudelaire; Ben Jonson, Marie Lloyd, and Groucho Marx.

I have used the format of the critical biography in order to tell this story; I have concentrated on the public details of Eliot's literary career—dates, encounters, publications—and have thought the task worth doing, if only because so much misinformation, particularly about his early life, has been circulated. I have relied almost entirely on printed sources; the only exception was information kindly provided by Mrs. Valerie Eliot, concerning the composition of *The Waste Land* and Vivien Eliot's contributions to *The Criterion*. I have not discussed Eliot's personal life, apart from those aspects of it which were generally known to his acquaintances, and with so reticent a man these occasions were infrequent. And although I think it valid, if requiring much tact, to treat poems as a source of biographical information, I have, I hope, avoided the romantic error of using poems as material for a biography and then interpreting the poems in the light of the biography. I have generally confined my critical discussion of the poetry to a separate section of each chapter. The biographical element in this book is, in fact, no more than a framework, or skeleton, intended to relate the different phases of Eliot's life as economically and accurately as possible; I expect this outline to be supplanted as more information becomes available, and particularly when Eliot's letters are published.

I have respected, and indeed I accept implicitly, Eliot's insistence that "poetry is itself and not another thing." But he also believed that poetry did not exist in isolation from other forms of human activity: although the poem arose from the poet's lonely creative struggle, it also expressed the fears and aspirations of its age, though in a far more profound sense than that indicated by callow demands for "contemporary relevance." I find wholly admirable Eliot's assumption that the poet, though both learned and dedicated to his craft, should participate in a wide range of the pursuits common to civilized men; that he should read Dante and frequent music halls, and be interested in philosophy and religion, sociology and politics, the ballet and education. Indeed, Eliot wrote on more subjects than most readers, or the present writer, feel at home with; I have done my best to give some account of his work in all its aspects, relying, where necessary, on the assistance of commentators more expert than myself. Eliot's career presents, I think, an example of heroism on two planes. As a creative artist he courageously made poetry out of his personal suffering; as a man of letters his constant devotion to the life of the mind and civilized values—often pursued in the face of extreme fatigue, ill-health, and many private troubles—remains a noble example, whatever mistakes and errors of judgment he made in his political and cultural stances.

I never met Eliot, though I once saw him at a public gathering, but I have been intimate with his poetry ever since 1946 when I bought the thin wartime Faber edition of his *Collected Poems 1909–1935*, which I still possess, now heavily annotated. He bewildered me as an adolescent but he totally captured my mind, and I have never escaped that captivity, nor wanted to, despite

many hours spent discussing his poetry with students and tem-
porary phases of staleness. When I began writing this book I
thought I knew his poetry as well as anyone could; I have since
discovered how wrong I was. Indeed, its capacity constantly to
renew itself, to reveal fresh and unsuspected aspects, is, to my
mind, one of the marks of Eliot's greatness as a poet. That my
admiration is tempered by an awareness of the places where he
fails to achieve greatness will also be apparent. In his best criticism Eliot offers the inspiriting example of an adult intelligence
that expects to be argued with, and there are many occasions
when I have accepted that invitation.

I

St. Louis, Harvard, Paris

1888–1914

T. S. ELIOT'S first American ancestor was Andrew Eliot, who left East Coker in Somerset in about 1670 to settle in Massachusetts, and founded a distinguished Boston family. In 1834 the Reverend William Greenleaf Eliot, a recent graduate of the Harvard Divinity School, moved to St. Louis, where he became a leading citizen. He established the first Unitarian church and founded Washington University; in addition to a life of active public service he wrote extensively on ethical and philosophical questions. William Greenleaf Eliot's second son, Henry Ware Eliot, graduated from Washington University in 1863 and went into business in St. Louis. He married Charlotte Stearns, who came from another celebrated New England family: Thomas Stearns Eliot, their seventh and youngest child, was born on September 26, 1888.

He grew up in a prosperous and cultivated Unitarian home. Although William Greenleaf Eliot died before T. S. Eliot was born, his influence was still pervasive: "I was brought up to be very much aware of him: so much so, that as a child I thought of him as still the head of the family—a ruler for whom *in absentia* my grandmother stood as vicegerent." W. G. Eliot's code of behavior was regarded almost like the tablets brought down from the mountain by Moses, though it contained more injunctions than prohibitions. One of the most pressing was the law of public service, which T. S. Eliot thought had left him throughout his life with "an uncomfortable and very inconvenient obligation to serve upon committees."

In 1917 Eliot wrote, "a writer's art must be racial—which means, in plain words, that it must be based on the accumulated sensations of the first twenty-one years." One needs to bear these words in mind in discussing Eliot's American origins, however much he may have seemed in later years to have transformed himself into an Englishman. What we know of his childhood reveals the source of certain insistent images in his poetry. Next to the family house in St. Louis was a school called Mary Institute, founded by Eliot's grandfather and named after an aunt who died in girlhood; it was attended by his sisters, and he preserved a vivid memory of it: "a high brick wall . . . concealed our back garden from the schoolyard and also concealed the schoolyard from our back garden. There was a door in this wall and there was a key to this door." From the garden he could hear the children playing in the yard, and after school he would play in the empty schoolyard himself and occasionally even venture into the school. Here we have a source in Eliot's early experience for the laughter of hidden children that recurs in his poetry. In Helen Gardner's words, "this intensely moving symbol of the laughter and excited business of children heard playing was not only a symbol of a happiness that the childless Eliot was never to know, but a memory of a childish loneliness, hearing the 'others' playing and laughing, and longing to be 'one of them.'" Such loneliness could well be experienced by the youngest child of a large family.

In 1897 Henry Ware Eliot built a summer home for his family by the sea at Gloucester, Massachusetts, and here Eliot was to spend summer vacations for the rest of his boyhood. Memories of the sea pervade his poetry:

> From the wide window towards the granite shore
> The white sails still fly seaward, seaward flying
> Unbroken wings.

He became expert at sailing:

> The boat responded
> Gaily, to the hand expert with sail and oar.

And there were other seaside memories of a more particular and curious kind. Amid the philosophical abstractions of Eliot's Harvard dissertation on F. H. Bradley there occurs this gnomic sentence: "The sea-anemone which accepts or rejects a proffered morsel is thereby relating an idea to the sea-anemone's world." Twenty years later Eliot returned to this image in talking about the possible sources of poems:

There might be the experience of a child of ten, a small boy peering through sea-water in a rock pool, and finding a sea-anemone for the first time: the simple experience (not so simple, for an exceptional child, as it looks) might lie dormant in his mind for twenty years, and re-appear transformed in some verse-context charged with great imaginative pressure.[1]

St. Louis itself, with its fogs and "the sunsets and the dooryards and the sprinkled streets," is the setting of "Prufrock." In his fifties Eliot revived in "The Dry Salvages" his early memories of the Mississippi, "a strong brown god—sullen, untamed and intractable." He regarded his birthplace with some affection: in 1953 he told a St. Louis audience, "I think I was fortunate to have been born here, rather than in Boston, or New York, or London." In the middle decades of the nineteenth century it was a prosperous and rapidly developing city, which offered a rich field for the socially active Unitarianism of William Greenleaf Eliot. There was a strong Germanic influence in its civic life and a high-minded interest in philosophical debate. But in 1880 St. Louis suffered the humiliation of being surpassed in size by Chicago, and in the early 1900s there came shattering disclosures of municipal corruption and boss-dominated local politics.

Eliot received his early education at Smith Academy, to which he has paid appropriate tribute; it provided a good grounding in what he regarded as the essentials: "Latin and Greek, together with Greek and Roman history, English and American history, elementary mathematics, French and German. Also English! I am happy to remember that in those days English composition was still called Rhetoric!" As a small boy he had a taste for such vig-

---

[1] *The Use of Poetry and the Use of Criticism* (New York: Barnes & Noble, 1955; London: Faber & Faber, 1964), pp. 78–79.

orous and extroverted poetry as "Horatius," "The Burial of Sir
John Moore," "Bannockburn," Tennyson's "Revenge," and some of
the border ballads. "The only pleasure that I got from Shakespeare was the pleasure of being commended for reading him;
had I been a child of more independent mind I should have refused to read him at all." But at about the age of fourteen he
picked up a copy of FitzGerald's *Omar Khayyám* which affected
him like a sudden conversion, making the world appear painted
with "bright, delicious and painful colours." Eliot recalls writing
"some very gloomy quatrains in the form of the *Rubáiyát*." He
then went on and took "the usual adolescent course with Byron,
Shelley, Keats, Rossetti, Swinburne." His earliest surviving literary exercises in verse and prose were published in the *Smith
Academy Record* when he was sixteen. One of them, "A Lyric,"
was written as an exercise in the manner of Ben Jonson. His
mother, herself a minor poet who took her writing with some
seriousness, said that she thought this poem was better than anything she had written herself: "I knew what her verse meant to
her. We did not discuss the matter further."

In 1905 Eliot left St. Louis for Massachusetts. He spent a year
at Milton Academy, then entered Harvard, where he was to remain—apart from a year in Paris—until 1914. Since the Eliots
were originally a New England family, and Eliot spent so long in
Cambridge and so thoroughly absorbed its prevailing style, the
assumption is often made that he was an essential New Englander, that his early life in Missouri can be dismissed as an
irrelevance. But this was not the way Eliot saw the matter himself. He was very aware of his mixed background—particularly
as he regarded St. Louis as a Southern city—so that for him what
Henry James called the "complex fate" of being an American was
unusually complex, even before he began to make a European
identity for himself. On St. George's Day (April 23), 1928, he
wrote in a letter to the late Sir Herbert Read:

Some day I want to write an essay about the point of view of an American who wasn't an American, because he was born in the South and
went to school in New England as a small boy with a nigger drawl, but
who wasn't a southerner in the South because his people were north-
erners in a border state and looked down on all southerners and Vir-

ginians, and who so was never anything anywhere and who therefore felt himself to be more a Frenchman than an American and more an Englishman than a Frenchman and yet felt that the USA up to a hundred years ago was a family extension.[2]

Cambridge in the 1900s, as Conrad Aiken remembered it forty years later, was still in many respects a village, at least in the parts around Harvard:

Lilacs and white picket fences under elms, horse-drawn watering-carts to lay the dust in the blindingly dusty streets of summer, board-walks put down on the pavements every winter and taken up again every spring, sleighs and pungs in the snow, and the dreadful college bell reverberant over all.[3]

When Eliot entered Harvard in 1906, its president, Charles William Eliot, a distant relation of the St. Louis Eliots, was near the end of a long and active period of office. C. W. Eliot was a vigorous exponent of the American concept of democratic education and had introduced the elective system of taking courses. The mature T. S. Eliot would certainly not have approved of President Eliot's liberal-democratic activism and Unitarian ethos, and he has recorded his suspicions of the elective system. Nevertheless, as an undergraduate he took advantage of it to pursue the studies he had begun at Smith Academy, particularly in Greek and Latin, which even then were not very popular at Harvard. He continued, too, with French and German and took courses in medieval history and comparative literature. George Santayana's popular "History of Modern Philosophy" course led to the four years of intense philosophical study that Eliot pursued as a graduate student between 1911 and 1915. At Harvard there was a well-established tradition of Dante studies, and in 1910 Eliot first read the *Divine Comedy,* puzzling out the meaning with the help of a prose translation. The influence of Dante was to be of lifelong importance, not only for his poetry, but for his whole intellectual development.

[2] Allen Tate, ed., *T. S. Eliot: The Man and His Work* (New York: Delacorte Press, 1966; London: Chatto & Windus, 1967), p. 15.
[3] Richard March and Tambimuttu, eds., *T. S. Eliot: A Symposium* (London: Poetry London, 1948; Chicago: Henry Regnery Co., 1949), p. 20.

We owe to Eliot's friend Conrad Aiken our first impressions of him as an undergraduate. He was "a singularly attractive, tall and rather dapper young man, with a somewhat Lamian smile." He was painfully shy but made deliberate efforts to overcome his shyness by plunging into Cambridge social life and attending dances and parties and even, somewhat later, by taking boxing lessons. He took his A.B. in 1909 and enrolled for the M.A. in English literature. One of the M.A. courses he took was not in English but in French, and it introduced him to a teacher who was deeply to affect Eliot's values and attitudes. This was Irving Babbitt, whose course was called "Literary Criticism in France with Special Reference to the Nineteenth Century." Babbitt was a man wholly at odds with President Eliot's progressivism. He was a deeply conservative thinker who was opposed to almost all aspects of modern civilization, whether democracy or industrialism or literary romanticism. Eliot has said of him: "His outspoken contempt for methods of teaching in vogue had given him a reputation for unpopularity which attracted to him some discerning graduates and undergraduates." Eliot's account of Babbitt's disorganized but persuasive way of lecturing suggests that he was one of those effective but dangerous teachers who simultaneously stimulate their pupils' interests and indoctrinate them with their own prejudices:

Somehow or other one read a number of books, Aristotle's *Politics* or Lafontaine's *Fables*, just because Babbitt assumed that any educated man had already read them. What held the lectures or talks together was his intellectual passion, one might say intellectual fury; what made them cohere was the constant recurrence of his dominant ideas; what gave them delight was their informality, the demand which they made upon one's mental agility, and the frankness with which he discussed the things that he disliked, and which his pupils came to dislike too.[4]

From Babbitt, Eliot first conceived the importance of "classicism" and "tradition," notions which were later to be reinforced by the influence of Charles Maurras and the French neoclassical movement. Yet Eliot was never a wholehearted disciple of Babbitt, who admired his pupil's criticism but not his poetry. (Eliot's dual

[4] *The Criterion,* October 1933.

reputation, as a "revolutionary" in poetry and a "traditionalist" in criticism, involved him in some paradoxical situations.) In later years Eliot found himself disagreeing with Babbitt's purely humanistic ethical scheme and his tendency to prefer Confucianism to Christianity. Babbitt, on his part, was irritated that his pupil's expressions of affection and admiration were inevitably followed by sharp criticisms of his views. In the late twenties he told F. W. Bateson that Eliot had been "a very poor student"; the incapacity, if it existed, must have arisen from a phase of indolence rather than lack of intellectual ability.

At the same time that Eliot was absorbing the importance of the classical virtues from Babbitt, his own poetry was exhibiting quite other qualities. Between 1907 and 1909 he contributed a few poems to the *Harvard Advocate* which were technically adroit and heavily *fin de siècle* in flavor. They exhibit a marked preoccupation with flower imagery. The dominant influences on these early poems are Tennyson and Swinburne. Eliot also read with respectful interest, as did other young men at Harvard at that time, the English poets of the eighteen-nineties, such as John Davidson, Ernest Dowson, and Arthur Symons. But they hardly represented a living tradition to an ambitious young American poet who was conscious, like many American writers, of the need to make a language for himself, and who so far had found no one to help him. The solution came suddenly, and not from an English or American source.

In December 1908 Eliot discovered in the library of the Harvard Union, Arthur Symons's *The Symbolist Movement in Literature,* an important work of criticism, first published in 1899, which had introduced to the English-speaking world some of the most significant French poets of the age. This book Eliot subsequently described as "one of those which have affected the course of my life." Symons introduced him directly to Laforgue and Rimbaud and Verlaine, and indirectly to Corbière. And of these poets, Laforgue was the one who had most immediately to offer Eliot, who "was the first to teach me how to speak, to teach me the poetic possibilities of my own idiom of speech." From Laforgue, Eliot learned the possibility of an ironic, self-deprecating diction which offered scope for subtler expression than anything currently available to him in English. Laforgue also showed a shy and sensitive young poet the means of distancing and presenting for sardonic contemplation experiences too painful to encounter more intimately. The impact of Laforgue transformed Eliot's poetry, as is apparent from three poems published in the *Harvard Advocate* between November 1909 and January 1910—"Nocturne," "Humouresque," and "Spleen"—and a fourth, "Conversation Galante," written in 1909 but not published until 1916.

These four poems are, of course, derivative and minor, and of little absolute importance in Eliot's *oeuvre*. But they indicate his remarkable grasp of the possibilities of literary cross-fertilization, showing to what extent the poetic resources of one language can be carried over into another. Such transferences have always been important in English poetry—as in Chaucer or Spenser or Milton—but by the early twentieth century the principle had been overshadowed by the Romantic stress on direct self-expression. Here and there in these Laforguian exercises there are motifs which are picked up in Eliot's later poems. For instance, the final stanza of "Spleen" presents an image which is transformed and elaborated in the slightly later and far superior "The Love Song of J. Alfred Prufrock":

> And Life, a little bald and gray,
> Languid, fastidious, and bland,
> Waits, hat and gloves in hand,
> Punctilious of tie and suit
> (Somewhat impatient of delay)
> On the doorstep of the Absolute.

Many people are to be found waiting, impatiently or irresolutely, on doorsteps or the tops of stairs in Eliot's poetry. This stanza also exhibits some of the characteristic Laforguian properties that Eliot found appealing, for it was not merely the particular formal and verbal devices of Laforgue's poetry that attracted Eliot but something in his total poetic personality. Arthur Symons wrote of Laforgue in words that seem to point directly to Prufrock or the protagonist of "Portrait of a Lady":

He has invented a new manner of being René or Werther: an inflexible politeness towards man, woman, and destiny. He composes love-poems hat in hand, and smiles with an exasperating tolerance before all the transformations of the eternal feminine. He is very conscious of death, but his *blague* of death is, above all things, gentlemanly. He will not permit, at any moment, the luxury of dropping the mask: not at any moment.

The direct influence of Laforgue on Eliot's poetry did not last beyond 1912, and was to be much less profound than that of Dante or indeed of Baudelaire, whom he also read at Harvard, but whose implications he does not seem to have realized until much later.

Yet there is a sense in which Eliot may have borne a Laforguian impress on his personality all his life. Symons quotes a description of Laforgue by a friend which refers to his formal demeanor, his tall top hat, his sober necktie, his English jacket, his clerical overcoat, and the umbrella always under one arm. Apart from the top hat, these attributes are curiously reminiscent of those visible in Eliot himself in later years (even allowing for the spirit of sober dandyism that was prevalent at Harvard in his time). It is, in fact, very likely that Eliot experienced a certain psychological identification with the young Frenchman whose poems had offered him such liberating possibilities. In 1919 Eliot wrote in *The Egoist* about a "feeling of profound kinship, or rather of a peculiar personal intimacy, with another, probably a dead author . . . It is a cause of development, like personal relations in life. Like personal intimacies in life, it may and probably will pass, but it will be ineffacable."

In 1910 Eliot moved into a new and more mature phase of poetic activity. He wrote the first two "Preludes," "Portrait of a Lady," and the first part of "Prufrock," which was completed in 1911, when he also wrote the third and fourth "Preludes," "Rhapsody on a Windy Night," and, probably, "La Figlia che Piange." I shall discuss these poems in a separate section of this chapter. In the autumn of 1910 Eliot, after taking his M.A., went to Paris to spend an academic year studying French literature and philosophy at the Sorbonne. It was, as he subsequently wrote, a very good time for an intellectually alert young man to discover Paris. The air was full of ideas: the *Nouvelle Revue Française* was still new, and Péguy was publishing his influential *Cahiers de la Quinzaine;* one might catch sight of Anatole France walking by the Seine, and one could buy the latest books of Gide or Claudel on publication day. And, in Eliot's words, "over all swung the spider-like figure of Bergson. His metaphysic was said to throw some light upon the new ways of painting, and discussion of Bergson was apt to be involved with discussion of Matisse and Picasso." To have truly felt *la ferveur bergsonienne,* Eliot said, one must have attended his weekly lectures in an overflowing hall at the Collège de France. In order to find a place it was necessary to arrive more than an hour early, which ensured a large captive audience for the immediately preceding lecture on statistics. Eliot's references to Bergson as a philosopher have always been unenthusiastic, but Philip Le Brun has suggested that Eliot's debt to him may be greater than is generally realized.

Eliot's principal acquaintance in French literary circles was the young novelist Alain-Fournier, with whom he had lessons in French conversation, and who made him read Dostoyevsky. He also met Alain-Fournier's brother-in-law, the critic Jacques Rivière, later editor of the *Nouvelle Revue Française.* An important intellectual influence that Eliot first encountered in Paris was Charles Maurras and the *Action Française,* which sowed the seed of a development that eighteen years later was to culminate in Eliot's rash public claim of an adherence to classicism in literature and royalism in politics. In a more purely literary way, his interest was aroused by the novels about Parisian low-life of Charles-Louis Philippe, some of whose imagery quickly found its way into his poems. A more shadowy figure from Eliot's period in Paris is the friend whom he remembered in 1934, "coming across the Luxembourg Gardens in the late afternoon, waving a branch of lilac, a friend who was later (so far as I could find out) to be mixed with the mud of Gallipoli." This, no doubt, was Jean Verdenal, *mort aux Dardanelles,* to whose memory *Prufrock and Other Observations* was dedicated. In the summer of 1911 Eliot traveled in Europe, visiting Northern Italy and Munich, where he finished "Prufrock" and, perhaps, received impressions, crystalized ten years later in *The Waste Land,* of rain over the Starnbergersee and sunlight in the Hofgarten. In September Eliot was back at Harvard.

2

With the poems written between 1910 and 1912—"Portrait of a Lady," "The Love Song of J. Alfred Prufrock," "Preludes," "Rhapsody on a Windy Night," and "La Figlia che Piange"—Eliot attained an astonishing creative maturity and, in effect, invented modern poetry in English. That is to say, he had succeeded, seemingly without effort, in assimilating into English poetry the achievements of French Symbolism, which was something that the talented minor poets of the eighteen-nineties had wanted to do but failed to accomplish. In these poems one finds a genuine literary equivalent to the refashioning of form and sensibility achieved in painting and music by the European *avant-garde* of the 1900s: Eliot proved himself a fitting contemporary of Picasso and Stravinsky, though it was to be several more years before anyone realized it. When Eliot was writing these poems, Ezra Pound was pursuing a comparable modernity in London and becoming well-known as a poet and an entrepreneur of new artistic movements. But if one considers the poems Pound wrote at that time and compares them with Eliot's work, it is evident at once that Pound, for all his exquisite ear and sense of rhythm, was still unadventurous in diction, still close in feeling to the *fin de siècle,* and, compared with Eliot, remote from the contemporary urban world. The point has to be firmly made since Eliot and Pound are often presented as a kind of literary partnership, with Eliot as the junior member. It is certainly true that in later years Eliot allowed himself to be much influenced by Pound: nevertheless, he wrote some of his finest poems long before they met. Furthermore, the work of 1910–1912 represents a level of intense creative activity and achievement that did not occur again in Eliot's career until he wrote *The Waste Land* in 1921. He wrote these poems in almost complete intellectual isolation, without access to that "current of ideas" which, he argued in *The Sacred Wood,* was so desirable for the first-order mind engaged in creation. It was his remarkable achievement to grasp, by himself, the possibilities for a poet writing in English first of Laforgue (and after his year in Paris, of other French writers), and then of Laforgue combined with the late-Elizabethan and Jacobean dramatists. "I do not know anyone who started from exactly that point," Eliot remarked in 1928, and it is true that no one else had (although Arthur Symons, who imitated Laforgue and knew the Elizabethans well, might have made the connection twenty years earlier, but failed to).

"Portrait of a Lady" and "Prufrock" are dramatic monologues where the drifting, invertebrate reflections of Laforgue's *Dernier Vers* are given a certain stiffening and verbal energy by the influence of late-Elizabethan and Jacobean dramatic verse. "Portrait of a Lady," written when Eliot was twenty-one, is his first important poem and one which remains impressive; it is in no sense a piece of apprentice work. It is more immediately approachable than "Prufrock" and makes the best possible introduction to the study of Eliot's poetic *oeuvre*. The title recalls Henry James, and though there is nothing of Isabel Archer in the poem, the situation and atmosphere have some of the quality of a James short story dealing in muted desperation and polite betrayal. Conrad Aiken has referred to its source in Eliot's socializing in Boston and Cambridge: "our dear deplorable friend, Miss X, the *précieuse ridicule* to end all preciosity, serving tea so exquisitely among her bric-a-brac, was to be pinned like a butterfly to a page in 'Portrait of a Lady.'" There is little in the poem that will seem strange to a reader familiar with Browning's dramatic monologues; though it makes an immediate contrast with the typical form of the latter, in which an articulate, even garrulous, speaker steadily reveals himself in his remarks to an interlocutor whose own remarks are never heard. In Eliot's poem, which might be called a "dramatic interior monologue," the lady does most of the talking and the young man silently ruminates, pursuing the aimless reflections that flicker through his consciousness. There is a carefully composed time scheme, with episodes in December, April, and October, providing an early example of Eliot's lifelong preoccupation with times and seasons. The characters emerge from their broken and unsatisfactory encounters with a fair degree of solidity and identity; they exist in a world which, however precarious it may be, has a certain coherence. The lady's speeches combine the formal and the colloquial with an impelling nervous energy. They indicate the presence of the potential dramatist in Eliot in a way that does not reappear until "A Game of Chess" in *The Waste Land;* there is a remarkable virtuosity in the counterpointing of the marked yet wavering rhythm, the tones of the speaking voice, and the intricate syntax.

In one respect, "Portrait of a Lady" is as much novelistic as it is dramatic. We never know the situation "as it is," but through the consciousness of the young man who not only renders what happened but tries, however inadequately, to justify his attitudes and at the same time unconsciously reveals his own moral hollowness. This device is known to the critics of fiction as the "corrupt" or "deluded" narrator, and James's *Aspern Papers* offers a good example of it. In Eliot's poem the narrator's consciousness is at all times on the verge of dissolution: his attempts to engage in polite drawing-room conversation are interfered with by the grotesque musical sounds going on inside his head. (Eliot may be parodying the symbolist insistence that music is the highest of the arts.) He makes an effort literally to compose himself but his impressions remain as fragmentary and disjunctive as the items in a daily paper, though his consciousness is haunted by possibilities of aesthetic and moral significance that remain beyond him:

> I take my hat: how can I make a cowardly amends
> For what she has said to me?
> You will see me any morning in the park
> Reading the comics and the sporting page.
> Particularly I remark
> An English countess goes upon the stage.
> A Greek was murdered at a Polish dance,
> Another bank defaulter has confessed.
> I keep my countenance,
> I remain self-possessed
> Except when a street-piano, mechanical and tired
> Reiterates some worn-out common song
> With the smell of hyacinths across the garden
> Recalling things that other people have desired.
> Are these ideas right or wrong?

F. R. Leavis has rightly praised these lines, remarking that "the play of tone and inflection mean the possibility of a kind of strong and subtle thinking in poetry"; they show to what extent Eliot was an innovative force in the poetry of 1910. They also point to elements in his later poetry, such as the drifting cosmopolitans of "Gerontion" and *The Waste Land,* and the wistful eroticism symbolized by the Hyacinth Girl.

In the third section of "Portrait of a Lady" the narrator seems reduced, even in his own estimation, to a state of subhuman absurdity: "I mount the stairs and turn the handle of the door / And feel as if I had mounted on my hands and knees." The possibility of disintegration becomes palpable. In the closing lines the possibility of the lady's death presents him with an image of significance that he can neither fully grasp nor brush aside, though the act of contemplating it at least restores his consciousness to a momentary coherence. (The line, "Well! and what if she should die some afternoon," shows Eliot boldly enlarging on a Laforguian source, "Enfin, si, par un soir, elle meurt dans mes livres. . .")

There are obvious things in common between "Portrait of a Lady" and "The Love Song of J. Alfred Prufrock"; both, for example, employ the Laforguian dramatic monologue, unfolding the fragmentary consciousness of a male narrator who recoils from or is otherwise unable to accomplish a possible sexual encounter. Yet "Prufrock" is considerably more radical. If "Portrait of a Lady" is like a painting that, though stylized, is basically representational, "Prufrock" is like a cubist version of a similar subject. The time, place, and identity which were genuinely if precariously present in the earlier poem have all been dissolved.

The name "Prufrock," which occurs only in the title, is derived, as Hugh Kenner has pointed out, from a firm of furniture wholesalers in St. Louis in the early years of the century. Like so many other fragments of casual experience it remained lodged in Eliot's memory until it could be put to some good use. In the full title of the poem, the conventional expectations of "Love Song" are instantly and sharply counteracted by the absurd proper name that follows. It is an effective example in miniature of Eliot's method which has several times given a strange ghostly identity to bare, unqualified names. The poem's epigraph is from Dante, the first of many such quotations and allusions in Eliot's work; it is hard to exaggerate Eliot's indebtedness, and the extent to which he has aspired to identify himself with Dante, though the aspiration, it must be emphasized, arises from profound differences in temperament and situation. The quotation is from *Inferno* XXVII, and the words are spoken by Guido da Montefeltro: "If I thought my answer were to one who ever could return to the world, this flame should shake no more; but since none ever did return alive from this depth, if what I hear be true, without fear of infamy I answer thee." By the time we reach the opening lines of the poem itself the implication is plain: this is hell and there is no possibility of escaping from it. Indeed, the first words "Let us go then, you and I" recall the many passages in which Virgil gently urges Dante on in their journey through the *Inferno* and *Purgatorio*. These opening lines are already some of the best known in English poetry. The way in which these, and so many other of his lines, etch themselves ineradicably into the memory is a sign of Eliot's genius as a poet (and this, it should be added, is something quite different from the mechanical memorability of mnemonics and jingles).

> Let us go then, you and I,
> When the evening is spread outside against the sky
> Like a patient etherised upon a table.

These lines have their own bizarre beauty and, as Eliot once claimed about poetry in general, can be appreciated before they are fully understood. Indeed, it is precisely in their efforts to understand these lines, and everything that follows, that so many readers of the poem go astray. There was a time when it was believed that because of Eliot's interest in the Metaphysical poets, such strange similes as this were really examples of the "metaphysical conceit"; yet this belief is a delusion. The conceit depended for its effect on the sudden sharp realization of an intellectually coherent resemblance between elements of experience that seem at first sight quite disconnected. In Eliot's poem it is not possible to see any way in which the evening is really like a patient etherized upon a table, or in which the fog resembles a domestic animal wandering outside a house. The similes remain powerful; but the appropriate question to ask is, What kind of consciousness is it that sees the world in such terms? Similarly, a great deal of energy has been misapplied in trying to extract a "story" from "Prufrock," and in working out who the characters are, and what time scheme is involved. It is as futile to do this as to try to trace elements of photographic likeness or "correct" perspective in, say, Picasso's *Demoiselles d'Avignon,* a work which has an innovative importance similar to that of Eliot's poem.

"Prufrock" offers not a verifiable account of the world, nor the unfolding revelation of a "real" character, but rather, as Hugh Kenner has said, "a zone of consciousness" which each reader has to pass through for himself and which may not present itself to the same reader in identical terms on successive readings. If Prufrock has an analogue in previous literature, it is to be found in Frédéric Moreau, the aloof and timorous hero of Flaubert's *L'Education Sentimentale,* a novel for which Eliot had an intense admiration. In his essay on Ben Jonson he writes of Frédéric:

He is constructed partly by negative definition, built up by a great number of observations. We cannot isolate him from the environment in which we find him; it may be an environment which is or can be much universalized; nevertheless it, and the figure in it, consist of very many observed particular facts, the actual world. Without this world the figure dissolves.

For all the vividness with which the poem presents notations of an urban scene and a trivial social world, it is impossible to say which of these elements are externally "there" and which are the *disjecta membra* of a disordered consciousness. The reader has to make, provisionally perhaps, many decisions for himself; as a major work in the symbolist manner, "Prufrock" forces the reader into a collaboratively creative role. Yet within its enveloping "zone of consciousness" certain elements are unmistakable. We are involved, whether we like it or not, in a dual sense of boredom at the inauthenticities of a predictable social round ("I have measured out my life with coffee spoons") and of terror at the sexual undercurrents in such a life. And in "Prufrock" the hints of dehumanization in "Portrait of a Lady" are made explicit.

In the following lines we see a convergence of the poem's main themes, or obsessions. "Eyes" were to become a dominant motif in

Eliot's poetry, and in this passage we notice his inclination toward the French fashion of using impersonally the definite article with parts of the body, thereby fragmenting any sense of personal identity:

> And I have known the eyes already, known them all—
> The eyes that fix you in a formulated phrase,
> And when I am formulated, sprawling on a pin,
> When I am pinned and wriggling on the wall,
> Then how should I begin
> To spit out all the butt-ends of my days and ways?

"Prufrock," as Hugh Kenner has said, offers not a character but "a name plus a Voice." The name is unforgettable and the Voice, as it meditates calmly on tedium and terror and further possibilities of disintegration—"I should have been a pair of ragged claws / Scuttling across the floors of silent seas"—nevertheless impresses us as a strong and finely articulate voice. In this respect, "Prufrock" offers a remarkable anticipation of Samuel Beckett's late fiction. Whatever chaos of feelings gives rise to Eliot's early poetry —and what may begin as an adolescent nervousness about sex is soon transformed into metaphysical dread—the power of language never fails to offer order and consolation, even though, in "Prufrock," the order is constantly on the verge of disintegration.

Many years later Eliot wrote "In my end is my beginning," and, as I have suggested, there is no coherent time sequence in "The Love Song of J. Alfred Prufrock." The voice goes on calmly recording or anticipating decisions and indecisions, disasters and recoveries, and by the time we reach the end of the poem it is impossible to say whether we have made any progress at all in time and action from the opening lines. The process could in fact continue almost indefinitely, or so it seems, at least until we reach the celebrated line, so Tennysonian in its plangency, "I shall wear the bottoms of my trousers rolled," which seems to point to a fresh variation on a theme rather than any sense of finality. Yet Eliot must end the poem at some point, and he does so with lines that for all their beauty might have come from a different and more conventional poem: the nervous sexuality of a small world

of novels and teacups and skirts that trail along the floor is exchanged for the pure but remote eroticism of the "sea-girls
wreathed with seaweed red and brown." The last line, with its
ambivalent suggestions both of waking and drowning, offers an
eventual possibility of escaping—despite the message of the epigraph—from one of the most intense, yet controlled, immersions
in extreme experience in modern literature.

Regarded as a whole, "Prufrock" shows both the characteristic
limitations of Eliot's imagination and his equally characteristic
power of overcoming them. It is a matter of record that the final
version of the poem was assembled in 1911 from a number of
sections written over the past year; in a letter written to Harriet
Monroe in 1915, Ezra Pound remarked of "Prufrock": "I dislike
the paragraph about Hamlet, but it is an early and cherished bit
and T. E. won't give it up . . ." And what is true of "Prufrock" is
also true of most of Eliot's other major poems: *The Waste Land,*
"The Hollow Men," *Ash-Wednesday,* and "Burnt Norton" were
all put together out of fragments, in some cases written over a
period of years and known to have previously existed in other
combinations. In 1956 Eliot remarked that "poetic originality is
largely an original way of assembling the most disparate and
unlikely material to make a new whole." A traditionally minded
reader might well regard "Prufrock" as "formless," whereas a
sympathetic reader would rightly say that its form was musical
rather than that of a preexisting literary mode. It is less often
remarked, though I think it is true, that the forms of T. S. Eliot's
major poems do not inevitably exclude other possible arrange-
ments of their constituent fragments.

For Eliot, I suggest, experience presented itself in an intensely
realized but disparate series of elements. And there was no possibility of organizing them into larger structures by the power of
the rational intellect or by relying on familiar literary forms. Nevertheless, Eliot did possess an extraordinary ability, that seems
to have existed below the level of conscious experience, of synthe-
sizing his fragmentary perceptions. One senses it in the strong yet
immensely subtle sense of rhythm that gives his poems their particular power; and it is a rhythm that seems to go deeper than

mere aural values. The late Anton Ehrenzweig, in his fascinating book *The Hidden Order of Art,* refers to "an ego rhythm that underlies all creative work" and some such quality seems obscurely to have fused the constituent elements in Eliot's poetry, just as it does in the juxtaposed heterogeneous forms, or *collage* compositions, of many modern painters. Such an "ego rhythm" is by definition wholly personal and represents a form of calligraphy, where a man's signature is unmistakably his own, but never "inevitably" so, since no two signatures will be absolutely identical. This kind of form, though real enough, is far less tangible than the classical precepts absorbed from Irving Babbitt and other conservative masters, and may help to explain why Eliot regarded the act of creation as a surrender to obscure and possibly dangerous forces. In *The Sacred Wood* he praised Dante for "the most comprehensive, and the most *ordered* presentation of emotions that has ever been made." Such an order, which in the *Divine Comedy* is simultaneously moral, intellectual, and aesthetic, was not within Eliot's compass as an artist, however much he may have valued it as a critic. It is this, I think, which explains the peculiar intensity of Eliot's attachment to Dante, the poet who dominated his *oeuvre,* from the words of Guido da Montefeltro at the beginning of "Prufrock" to the superb Dantesque re-creation in "Little Gidding."

The four "Preludes," written in 1910 and 1911, dwell on the same low aspects of urban life that we see depicted in "Prufrock." The first two present a purely "objective" rendering of the city at evening and morning—small-scale equivalents, as E. D. H. Greene has suggested, of Baudelaire's "Crépuscule du Soir" and "Crépuscule du Matin"—and are in effect perfect Imagist poems, written before Ezra Pound sponsored an Imagist movement in London in 1912. Hugh Kenner has denied the Imagist element in the "Preludes," saying that they are haunted by the need for an absent significance, whereas the Imagists relied simply on the self-sufficient presentation of an object. Whatever their precepts may have been, it seems to me that in practice the best Imagist poems, like Pound's "Dans le Metro" or "Fan piece for her imperial lord," do reach after human significance. "Preludes" I and

II are examples of a kind of urban poetry that had existed fitfully in England since the middle of the nineteenth century. One
can recall Tennyson's superb stanza from "In Memoriam":

> He is not here; but far away
>   The noise of life begins again,
>   And ghastly thro' the drizzling rain
> On the bald street breaks the blank day.

And there are some interesting examples written in the nineties,
under the direct influence of Baudelaire. The first line of "Preludes" II, "The morning comes to consciousness," shows Eliot's
conviction, so fully expressed in "Portrait of a Lady" and "Prufrock," that the objects of perception, for all our attempts at ob-
jectivity, can never be wholly separated from the mind that per-
ceives. In "Preludes" III and IV he makes explicit the mind's
yearning for significance beyond the random contents of consciousness, presented in cubist disjunctiveness:

> And short square fingers stuffing pipes,
> And evening newspapers, and eyes
> Assured of certain certainties.

Hence the wistful aspiration for "such a vision of the street / As
the street hardly understands" or "The notion of some infinitely
gentle / Infinitely suffering thing."

"Preludes" contain some of the most memorable epiphanies of
urban experience in English, and the city is shown as essentially
anonymous. Yet it is interesting to note that the early drafts of
these poems, contained in a leather-bound notebook in the Berg
Collection at the New York Public Library (which also includes
drafts of several other poems written at this time, so far unpublished), referred specifically to parts of Boston in their titles; it
was a happy decision of Eliot's to delete them before publishing
the poems, thereby leaving them a wide range of potential reference.

"Rhapsody on a Windy Night," a product of Eliot's stay in
Paris, also explores a gloomy urban environment, though a more
definably French one. Phrases drawn from Laforgue are combined with others from Baudelaire and Charles-Louis Philippe;

and some commentators have seen in the phrase "Dissolve the floors of memory" evidence of Bergsonian influence. The "Rhapsody" is a unique poem in Eliot's work: a record, as it seems, of a noctambulistic movement through city streets, which presents the contents of memory in bizarre images with many dream-like juxtapositions. The flux of time is divided by the chiming of the hours, a precarious and arbitrary imposition of order. The poem is intensely and characteristically visual; there are several instances of Eliot's obsessive image of eyes and an imagistic concentration on objects that dwells, as a painter might, on their quiddity while hinting at their larger implications. The "Rhapsody" is visual in its detail and musical in its organization, a pure example of the "music of images," to use a somewhat overworked phrase. It is, I think, a superb poem in a vein that Eliot did not follow up: possibly it involved a degree of symbolist remoteness from the discursive that Eliot, for all his preference for music over statement, was disinclined to accept.

There remains, from the first phase of Eliot's poetry, "La Figlia che Piange," which was written after his return to Harvard. This poem was an early favorite of conventionally minded readers and anthologists, for whom its fairly straightforward lyricism was in agreeable contrast to the radical imagery and associations of Eliot's other poems. As a result, it assumed for a time the kind of place in Eliot's career that "The Lake Isle of Innisfree" did in Yeats's, or "The Goodly Fere" in Pound's, to his understandable dissatisfaction. It has worn less well than "Prufrock" and the others, though it is technically adroit in the way it blends Pre-Raphaelite imagery and plangency of sound with Eliot's characteristically nervous subtlety of rhythm. F. R. Leavis has lately argued that the excellence of this poem lies in "love unequivocally presented, love that calls for lyrical expression—the poem is unique in the Eliot volume." It is, however, scarcely unequivocal; the poem is, in fact, an essay in Laforguian evasiveness, where the relation between the narrator and the male lover is extremely ambiguous, and one is no more sure than in "Prufrock" of the objective pattern of events. To my mind, there is a certain suggestion of a scene being set up for voyeuristic contemplation: the thematic affinity with "Prufrock" is closer than one might imagine. And while acknowledging the direct though rather formal lyricism of the first part of the poem, one also has to notice the carefully distancing diction in the final lines, where the ironic mode reasserts itself. Nevertheless, it is worth remarking that Eliot did not use the recurring "staircase" image in such an elevated way again until *Ash-Wednesday*.

The poems of 1910–1912 were the first and unmistakable signs of Eliot's genius; some aspects of them were to develop throughout his poetic career while others remained undeveloped. They also contain characteristics that have frequently troubled critics. One of them concerns Eliot's use of literary sources, for which he is still sometimes accused of plagiarism. One can say briefly that Eliot was not, in principle, doing anything different from Chaucer or Spenser or even Shakespeare, all of whom made free use of foreign sources for their own good ends, though Eliot admittedly drew on a more eclectic and obscure range of writers than they did. Eliot's use of French Symbolist poetry was essential for him in the formation of a language: in general he used foreign poets to help him understand and express his own experience, rather than in any jackdaw-like search for exotic beauties. Eliot's use of other literature was more existential and less purely aesthetic than Pound's, despite the similarity of their approaches.

Again, Eliot's early poems clearly manifest an intense sense of erotic failure and bewilderment; there is no point in denying that much of the motivating force of his poetry arises from an unhappy sexual obsession. He was not, if one wants to use such a phrase, "on the side of Life," and for this he has been regularly called to account, perhaps more in sorrow than in anger, by many critics in whom an orthodoxy of sexual fulfillment proves just as tyrannical as religious orthodoxies were for earlier generations. If Eliot expressed such failures in his poetry and tried to come to terms with them, then he was in fact expressing a perennial aspect of the human condition, however unfashionable it may be to recognize the fact.

3

Eliot returned to Harvard in the autumn of 1911, "perceptibly Europeanized," in Conrad Aiken's words, carrying a cane in a very un-American way and gravely concerned about its "nice conduct." More significantly he brought back with him a painting by Gauguin, and sharply denied a suggestion that it was an example of "sophisticated primitivism." Eliot may have been right: but an interest in the primitive was to be an important element in his literary makeup, as was made apparent by his later absorption in Frazer's *Golden Bough* and Stravinsky's *Rite of Spring.* In 1918 he remarked, "The artist, I believe, is more *primitive,* as well as more civilized, than his contemporaries. . . ." Eliot became involved in a more personal form of primitivism by taking boxing lessons at a gymnasium in Boston's South End from an Irishman who may have been the original of Sweeney; he also, in his own words, learned "how to swarm with passion up a rope."

Although his work for the M.A. had been mostly in English literature, Eliot's studies for the Ph.D. on which he now embarked were in philosophy, and in Oriental studies, of which there was a well-established tradition at Harvard. In later years he came to feel that this choice was a mistake: "Two years spent in the study of Sanskrit under Charles Lanman, and a year in the mazes of Patanjali's metaphysics under the guidance of James Woods, left me in a state of enlightened mystification." To come to terms with the extreme subtleties of the Indian philosophers would mean forgetting everything he had ever learned about Western philosophy: indeed, as Eliot put it, "my only hope of really penetrating to the heart of that mystery would lie in forgetting how to think and feel as an American or European: which, for practical as well as sentimental reasons, I did not wish to do." Nevertheless, he seems to have appreciated the Sanskrit poetry that he read, and once guardedly said "my own poetry shows the influence of Indian thought and sensibility." There are, of course, to look no further, the Sanskrit tags at the end of *The Waste Land* (Stephen Spender once heard Eliot say that at the time of writing that poem he seriously thought of becoming a Buddhist) and references to the *Bhagavad-Gita* in "The Dry Salvages." Beyond this, to search for specifically Indian elements in Eliot's poetry would be a matter for specialized and possibly fruitless inquiry. Yet he seems to have preserved a certain legendary reputation as a Sanskrit specialist. David Garnett describes a dinner party given by Lady Rothermere in about 1921, at which Eliot and the Russian mystagogue P. D. Ouspensky were among the guests. The hostess remarked that both Eliot and Ouspensky knew Sanskrit and unsuccessfully tried to make them converse in it.

For his doctoral dissertation Eliot turned away from Eastern philosophy and embarked on the study of a distinguished English contemporary, F. H. Bradley. After remaining in typescript at Harvard for many years, the dissertation was published in 1964 under the title of *Knowledge and Experience in the Philosophy of F. H. Bradley,* with an introduction in which Eliot referred to it as a philosophical curiosity and claimed that he was no longer able to understand what he had written. Richard Wollheim, a professional philosopher and an expert on Bradley, has described it as "a painfully obscure work," a judgment which the nonphilosophical reader will find reassuring. Professor Wollheim's essay on Eliot and Bradley is a definitive study to which anyone interested in their relationship can be directed.

Some critics have tried to see Bradley's influence on Eliot as crucial, though in the light of what Wollheim has to say this seems doubtful. It is more realistic to regard Eliot's study of the philosopher as an intense but somewhat self-contained phase in his career, during which he used his interest in Bradley to develop some of his own basic attitudes. Even Hugh Kenner, who has written more penetratingly about Eliot's early poems than any other critic, seems inclined to exaggerate the effect of Bradley, whom Eliot may well not have read as early as 1910. Undoubtedly Bradley gives reasons for dissolving the solidity of the ego, but the disintegration of the substantial self has been a fundamental motive in modern literature, at least from Dostoyevsky and Rimbaud onward. Eliot would have found an immediate literary source for skepticism about the persistence of the ego in Laforgue:

> Bref, j'allais me donner d'un "Je vous aime"
> Quand, je m'avisai non sans peine
> Que d'abord je me possédais pas bien moi-même.

> (Mon Moi, c'est Galathée aveuglant Pygmalion!
> Impossible de modifier cette situation.)

Ainsi donc, pâle et piètre individu
Qui ne croit à son Moi qu'à ses moments perdus. . . .

In short, I was going to give myself with an "I love you," when I realized not without anguish that, in the first place, I did not really possess
myself. (Myself is Galatea blinding Pygmalion! It is impossible to
change this situation.) So then, a poor, pale and wretched creature,
only believing in his self at forgotten moments. . . .

Nevertheless, it is possible to find, in Eliot's infinitely subtle
philosophical probing at the relations between the mind and
reality in his study of Bradley, passages which recall the characteristic dilemmas and strategies of "Prufrock," "Gerontion," and
The Waste Land—as when he writes, "Everything, from one point
of view, is subjective; and everything, from another point of view
is objective; and there is no *absolute* point of view from which a
decision may be pronounced." Here Eliot is not so much drawing
a doctrine from Bradley as using Bradley to formulate his own
deep-rooted skepticism. Doubts about the ego are expressed in
this way:

We have no right, except in the most provisional way, to speak of *my*
experience, since the I is a construction out of experience, an abstrac-
tion from it; and the *thats*, the browns and hards and flats are equally
ideal constructions from experience, as ideal as atoms.

Again, such words as these could well be used as a gloss on the
poems: "An hallucination, we are constantly tempted to forget,
is not an object but a sphere of reality; its existence is internal
as well as external."

After he abandoned the study of philosophy Eliot continued
to admire Bradley—in 1928 he used a review of Bradley's *Ethical
Studies* as a stick for Matthew Arnold's back—but primarily as a
stylist. In 1919 he wrote to Lytton Strachey, "Anything *I* have
picked up about writing is due to having spent (as I once thought,
wasted) a year absorbing the style of F. H. Bradley—the finest
philosopher in English," adding that Bradley's *Appearance and
Reality* was *L'Education Sentimentale* of abstract thought. A
valuable essay by Adrian Cunningham has suggested unexpected
ways in which Bradley's mode of thinking may have influenced
Eliot's prose style:

This theory of partial truth, the fluidity of object and subject in their definition by context and relationship, indicates a pervasive characteristic of Eliot's processes of thought, the fairly consistent and deliberate evasion of precise definition, every point seeming to overlap with the next until imperceptibly the two emphases of a single conception stand in apparent opposition. Eliot's writing is often at the most crucial points simultaneously dense, allusive, elliptical, the meaning suggested only in the organization of a particular context.[5]

This is undoubtedly an accurate account of much of Eliot's prose, which can convey an effect of extreme evasiveness despite its polemical sharpness of tone. This process is particularly evident in the editorial commentaries in *The Criterion* during the nineteen-thirties, where the anfractuosities of Eliot's thought make it impossible to say, in clear terms, just what his attitude is to the public issues he is discussing. This degree of subtlety manifested itself more acceptably in the poetry of the *Four Quartets,* which can be regarded as an attempt to capture the extreme refinements of fleeting experience. Though Bradley must certainly have influenced the development of Eliot's thought, he was hardly responsible for its basic characteristics.

As a graduate student Eliot was an active member of the philosophy department at Harvard: he was a teaching assistant for two years, taking a weekly tutorial, and was president of the university philosophical club during 1913–1914. He also participated in the seminars of the distinguished philosopher Josiah Royce, and a record has been preserved of some of these discussions. At one meeting Eliot read a paper on the role of interpretation in the social sciences, which indicated his early interest in questions of primitive religion and ritual; he spoke mostly on Durkheim and Levy-Bruhl, but also showed himself acquainted with Frazer and Jane Harrison. In the spring of 1914 Bertrand Russell was a visiting professor at Harvard and Eliot attended his classes. Russell gave his initial impression of him in a letter written to Lady Ottoline Morrell on March 27: "This morning two of my pupils came together to ask me a question about work —one named Eliot is very well dressed and polished with manners

[5] Graham Martin, ed., *Eliot in Perspective* (London: Macmillan & Co., 1970), p. 215.

of the finest Etonian type." Russell at first thought that Eliot and his friend—an unshaven Greek called Demos—were lacking in a thorough intellectual grounding, but within a few weeks he had formed a high opinion of Eliot. In May he wrote of a weekend party:

My pupil Eliot was there—the only one who is civilized, and he is ultra-civilized, knows his classics very well, is familiar with all French literature from Villon to Vildrach, and is altogether impeccable in his taste but has no vigour or life—or enthusiasm. He is going to Oxford where I expect he will be very happy.[6]

Eliot's own impression of Russell at that time is preserved in the poem called "Mr. Apollinax."

Eliot had been awarded a Sheldon Traveling Fellowship and spent part of the summer of 1914 in Germany at the University of Marburg. On August 4 the First World War broke out, and soon afterward he arrived in London.

[6] Robert Gathorne-Hardy, ed., *Ottoline* (London: Faber & Faber, 1963), p. 257.

II

London Reputation

1915–1920

E ZRA POUND, who had lived in London since 1908, was, in
 Richard Aldington's words, "a small but persistent volcano
in the dim levels of London literary society," and in the summer
of 1914 he was more than usually active. As well as a productive
poet and critic, Pound was by nature an entrepreneur and impres-
sario who regarded it as his mission to improve the quality of
English culture. In 1912 he had launched the Imagist movement,
consisting at first of himself and two young protégés, Richard Aldington and Hilda Doolittle (who wrote over the initials H. D.
and became Aldington's wife). Early in 1914 there appeared an
anthology called *Des Imagistes*, anonymously edited by Pound,
which contained liberal contributions from these three poets, together with a number of others who had been rather arbitrarily
ushered into the Imagist fold (though not T. E. Hulme, who had
written proto-Imagist poems before Pound launched the movement and then abandoned poetry for metaphysics and aesthetics).
By the time *Des Imagistes* came out the restless Pound had already
moved on to other interests, sponsoring the prose of James Joyce
and the paintings and sculpture of Henri Gaudier-Brzeska. He became increasingly interested in the visual arts, and was associated
with Wyndham Lewis and Gaudier in the Vorticist movement,
whose iconoclastic magazine *Blast*—"the puce coloured monster"
—was published in July. It contained a good deal of literary ma-

terial by Pound, who had decided that Vorticism was the equivalent in painting of Imagism in poetry, though Lewis and the other painters in the movement were skeptical of Pound's pretensions and regarded him mainly as a useful publicity agent. In the meantime the wealthy American poetess Amy Lowell had arrived in London and was making a take-over bid for Imagism which was largely successful. In the next few years three more Imagist anthologies came out, from which Pound was absent and in which Amy Lowell was copiously represented; Imagism, Pound sourly remarked, had become "Amygism," and he was correspondingly estranged from his former associates. But his main interest was still, for a time, in Vorticism, a movement of genuine significance in the visual arts, which was a real attempt to foster a native English version of cubism and futurism, and the first English art-movement of much interest since the Pre-Raphaelites, though its promise was quickly destroyed by the war. For a few weeks after the outbreak of war, however, artistic life went on as before, despite the prevailing waves of patriotic excitement. It seemed, in any case, that the war might be over by Christmas. Plans were under way for the second number of *Blast* and Pound was involved in an abortive scheme for a Vorticist college of arts, to be staffed by himself, Lewis, Gaudier-Brzeska, Edward Wadsworth, and Arnold Dolmetsch, among others.

It was against this literary and cultural background that Eliot arrived in London. He had been preceded by his old friend, Conrad Aiken, who had spent the summer in London and had devotedly tried to find a publisher for Eliot's poems. He showed two of them—"Prufrock" and "La Figlia che Piange"—to Harold Monro, the owner of the Poetry Bookshop and editor of *Poetry and Drama,* and a man of cautiously progressive tastes. *Poetry and Drama* had provided the first English publication of Marinetti's futurist manifesto, and *Des Imagistes* had appeared under the Poetry Bookshop's imprint. But Monro was unable to make anything of Eliot's poems and brusquely rejected them, a decision which he later came to regret. By the time Eliot arrived in London Aiken had returned to America; but he had left Eliot an introduction to Pound, who noted on September 22, "An American called Eliot called this P.M. I think he has some sense tho he has not yet sent me any verse." Pound was London correspondent of the magazine *Poetry* of Chicago, and two years before he had introduced Aldington and H. D. to its readers; now he was ready to find new talent. On September 30 Pound wrote jubilantly to Harriet Monroe, the editor of *Poetry*: "I was jolly well right about Eliot. He has sent me in the best poem I have yet had or seen from an American." Eliot, he acutely remarked, had "actually trained himself *and* modernized himself *on his own*. The rest of the *promising young* have done one or the other but never both . . ." Here, evidently, was someone of far superior talent to Pound's Imagist protégés. The poem Eliot had shown him was "Prufrock," and Pound at once sent it to Miss Monroe with the injunction to "get it *in* soon," though she seems not to have been much more enthusiastic about it than Harold Monro had been. Throughout the winter of 1914–1915 Pound was urging her to publish "Prufrock" quickly and brushing aside her attempted criticisms; in the end "Prufrock" did appear in *Poetry*, but not until the June 1915 issue. Eliot's initial response to Pound was cool: he wrote to Conrad Aiken, "Pound is rather intelligent as a talker; his verse is touchingly incompetent." The note of asperity is characteristic, but Eliot soon formed a far more favorable opinion: in the years to come he was to publish anonymously a short introduction to Pound's poetry, and then dedicate *The Waste Land* to him.

In October Eliot went to Oxford to embark on his last year as a student of philosophy. He became a member of Merton College, which was Bradley's college, but the philosopher was in very bad health and Eliot never met him. He was, however, supervised by Professor Harold Joachim, whom he described as "the disciple of Bradley who was closest to the Master," and devoted himself to the close study of Aristotle in Greek. Although Eliot was to live in England for the rest of his life his early impressions were not favorable. He disliked London and told Aiken, "a people which is satisfied with such disgusting food *is not* civilized." Oxford was no better: "Oxford is very pretty, but I don't like to be dead . . . O conversation, the staff of life, shall I get any at Oxford?" During 1914–1915 Eliot was energetically cultivated by Pound, and was noticed as an enigmatic new arrival among the visitors to the celebrated triangular sitting-room of Pound's small flat in Kensington. For all his longing for conversation, Eliot was chiefly remarkable for his immense taciturnity—Douglas Goldring was struck by his ability to sit for a whole afternoon in complete silence—as well as for his exotic good looks. Wyndham Lewis described him as "a kind of Harvardian Rupert Brooke," recalling "a sleek, tall, attractive apparition—with a sort of Gioconda smile."

Lewis was still collecting material for the long-delayed second issue of *Blast* and early in 1915 he wrote to Pound: "Eliot has sent me Bullshit and the Ballad for Big Louise. They are excellent bits of scholarly ribaldry. I am trying to print them in *Blast,* but stick to my naive determination to have no 'words ending in -Uck, -Unt, and -Ugger.'" This "scholarly ribaldry" may have been part of the unpublished saga about a figure called King Bolo that Eliot started at Harvard and worked at intermittently for several years; as late as 1935 Pound referred to Eliot's "Bolo" "which I am afraid his religion won't now let him print." There is a remark in Eliot's *After Strange Gods* which may be relevant: "the indecent that is funny may be the legitimate source of innocent merriment, while the absence of humour reveals it as purely disgusting." Eliot's talent for light verse was later directed into more universally acceptable channels with *Old Possum's Book of Practical Cats.*

When the second number of *Blast* finally appeared in July 1915 its contribution from Eliot was not "scholarly ribaldry" but some of the finest poetry of his Harvard and Paris days, "Preludes" and "Rhapsody on a Windy Night"—the first British publication of any of his work. Eliot, so far as is known, had written no poetry since "La Figlia che Piange" but, perhaps inspired by Pound's encouragement, he began writing again, and one of the first of these new poems was "Morning at the Window," a slighter version of the urban impressionism of "Preludes." During 1915 and 1916 some of his recent poems, together with others from the earlier period, were published in America in *Others* and *Poetry.* In November 1915 Richard Aldington in a note on *Poetry* in *The Egoist* said that "in her choice of poets Miss Monroe has the able assistance of Mrs. Henderson and Mr. Ezra Pound. One of their latest discoveries is Mr. T. S. Eliot, also printed in *Blast,* whose poetry has an individual flavour." Eliot was also the recipient of less favorable attention. Late in 1915 Elkin Matthews published the *Catholic Anthology*, edited by Pound. (The name was not meant to have any religious implications, but some Roman Catholics appear to have found it provocative, and Pound accused the Jesuits of preventing the book from being reviewed.) Eliot was well represented in the anthology, which included "Prufrock" and "Portrait of a Lady" as well as slighter pieces. Arthur Waugh, an established critic of conservative tastes, in the course of reviewing some recent anthologies of poetry in the *Quarterly Review* unfavorably compared the contributors to the *Catholic Anthology* with the Georgians. He quoted lines by Pound and another, now forgotten contributor called Orrick Johns, and, without naming the author, six lines from "Prufrock" beginning "I grow old . . . I grow old . . ." Waugh denounced the "unmetrical, incoherent banalities of these literary 'Cubists' " but concluded that they might serve as an awful warning to other young poets:

It was a classic custom in the family hall, when the feast was at its height, to display a drunken slave among the sons of the household, to the end that they, being ashamed at the ignominious folly of his gesticulations, might determine never to be tempted into such a pitiable condition themselves.

This passing reference by Arthur Waugh was subsequently simplified by Pound into the charge that Waugh had described Eliot and himself, *tout court*, as "drunken helots," and in this inaccurate form the allegation has been widely circulated.

In June 1915 Eliot married Vivien (or Vivienne) Haigh Haigh-Wood, who was the daughter of a painter. This marriage was a crucial event in Eliot's life. It was to cause him much unhappiness and appears to have reinforced rather than assuaged the sexual anxieties expressed in his early poetry. Little is known about the course of Eliot's marriage, save for a few hints dropped by his friends and contemporaries about the intensity of his private suffering. From the beginning the Eliots struck those who knew them as sharply contrasted temperaments: if T. S. Eliot was reticent and complex and found personal relations difficult, Vivien Eliot was, in Stephen Spender's words, "gay, talkative, a chatterbox."

Herbert Read has written, "Posterity will probably judge Vivienne Eliot harshly, but I remember her in moments when she was sweet and vivacious; later her hysteria became embarrassing." Bertrand Russell, with whom Eliot had resumed contact, remarked in a letter of July 1915:

I dined with my Harvard pupil, Eliot and his bride. I expected her to be terrible, from his mysteriousness; but she was not so bad. She is light, a little vulgar, adventurous, full of life—an artist I think he said, but I should have thought her an actress. He is exquisite and listless; she says she married him to stimulate him, but finds she can't do it. Obviously he married in order to be stimulated. I think she will soon be tired of him. She refuses to go to America to see his people, for fear of submarines. He is ashamed of his marriage, and very grateful if one is kind to her.[1]

In the late summer of 1915 Eliot made a brief visit to America by himself; this was the last time he saw his father, who died in 1919, and Eliot did not revisit the United States until 1932. Bertrand Russell, showing a rather paternal concern for his former pupil, wrote in November 1915:

It is quite funny how I have come to love him, as if he were my son. He is becoming much more of a man. He has a profound and quite unselfish devotion to his wife, and she is really very fond of him, but has impulses of cruelty from time to time.

Russell helped the Eliots, who were hard up, in highly practical ways: he lent them a room in his flat and gave Eliot £3,000 worth of engineering debentures, which Russell, as a convinced pacifist, wished to dispose of since the firm was making munitions. (After the war, when Eliot was better off, he returned them to Russell.) In the summer of 1918 when Vivien Eliot wanted to get out of London he lent them a house at Marlow in Buckinghamshire. Russell wrote in his *Autobiography* that he "endeavoured to help them in their troubles until I discovered that their troubles were what they enjoyed." Aldous Huxley, then a master at nearby Eton, visited the Eliots at Marlow and rather took to Vivien:

[1] *The Autobiography of Bertrand Russell* (Boston: Little, Brown & Co.; London: George Allen & Unwin, 1968), vol. II, p. 54.

"she is such a genuine person, vulgar, but with no attempt to conceal her vulgarity, with no snobbery of the kind that makes people say they like things, such as Bach or Cézanne, when they don't."

Brigit Patmore has left an attractive description of Vivien Eliot: "slim and rather small, but by no means insignificant. Light brown hair and shining grey eyes. The shape of her face was narrowed to a pointed oval chin and her mouth was good." Brigit Patmore and the Eliots found a common enjoyment in dancing and the three of them went to "discreet Sunday afternoon dances at a hall in Queensway," a practice initiated by Vivien Eliot in the hope that "Tom might come and not be bored." He seems, in fact, to have enjoyed dancing, having dutifully learned at Harvard, and once even announced at a dinner party that the only two things he cared for were dancing and brandy. Brigit Patmore recalls a charming incident that took place after one of these dances, which suggests that a very real degree of tenderness existed between the Eliots in the early years of their marriage. They went into a chemist's shop to buy aspirin and Vivien, who had been trained as a ballet dancer, said:

"I think I can do what Karsavina does at that moment." And she held on to the counter with one hand, rose on her toes and held out the other hand which Tom took in his right hand, watching Vivien's feet with ardent interest whilst he supported her with real tenderness. From him it was unexpected. Most husbands would have said, "Not here, for Heaven's sake!" But he looked as if he did indeed want to help Vivien in her chosen work.[2]

But on other occasions Vivien Eliot was near hysteria and complaining of "the frightful time I have with Tom." Her physical health deteriorated and in later years she became mentally ill.

Marriage meant that Eliot, who had been a student for nearly ten years, had to take a job. He became a schoolmaster, and was engaged by High Wycombe Grammar School to teach French, mathematics, history, geography, drawing, and swimming for the sum of £140 per year, plus a daily meal. After one term he

[2] Brigit Patmore, *My Friends When Young* (London: William Heinemann, Ltd., 1968), pp. 85–86.

moved to Highgate Junior School, where he was paid £160 and provided with dinner and tea. One of his pupils at Highgate was John Betjeman, who remembers "a tall, quiet usher there whom we called 'The American Master.'" He was rumored to be a poet and Betjeman, then aged about ten, presented him with a manuscript called "The Best Poems of Betjeman," which Eliot remembered when he met Betjeman again in the thirties. Eliot did not enjoy teaching but he stayed at Highgate for over a year. He had expected to be able to write during the vacations but found that teaching took too much out of him; he could not effectively hold his classes' attention by projecting his personality at them. At the same time he was supplementing his income by evening lectures to adult education classes; between 1916 and 1918 he gave courses on modern French literature, modern English literature, Victorian literature, and Elizabethan literature.

In 1917 Eliot gave up schoolteaching and took a post in the foreign department at Lloyds Bank in the City of London, where he remained for eight years. At first he was paid less than he had been as a teacher and there were no meals provided, but his salary rose steadily until in 1922 he was earning £600 a year, a substantial amount at that time. His period at the bank was often regarded—and still is—as an unqualified martyrdom, though for a man of Eliot's temperament it was probably far preferable to schoolteaching and, however tiring, would have entailed less nervous strain. There is, in fact, quite a lot to be said for a poet supporting himself in some regular nonliterary employment, rather than by the nervous strain of teaching or the distractions of literary journalism. There have been, for instance, the distinguished examples of Wallace Stevens, who was the vice president of an insurance company, and of Roy Fuller, who was a lawyer for most of his working life. In 1932 Eliot wrote:

I prefer . . . a condition of affairs in which I have a daily routine of work or business, the greater part of which I find boring . . . a certain amount of routine, of dullness and of necessity seems inseparable from work; and for myself, I am too sceptical of my own abilities to be able to make a whole-time job of writing poetry, even if I had the means.[3]

[3] *The Criterion,* January 1932.

During his eight years at Lloyds Bank Eliot wrote some of his finest poetry and most of his important literary criticism, as well as acting as literary editor of *The Egoist* between 1917 and 1919, and launching *The Criterion* in 1922. Eliot was, in fact, intensively productive throughout the whole period, particularly of prose; it is astonishing that he managed to write so much after his full days at the bank, where his work was becoming increasingly responsible and exacting, in addition to the frequent illnesses of Vivien Eliot and the other difficulties of his married life. All this was not accomplished without tangible signs of strain and fatigue; nearly everyone who knew Eliot at that time has remarked on his customary appearance of near-exhaustion, though it never affected his extreme personal elegance.

In 1916 Eliot rounded off his career as a philosopher. He completed his doctoral dissertation and sent a copy to Harvard; he felt that he owed it to his university to make this gesture toward completing his graduate work, in return for the Sheldon Fellowship which had brought him to Europe. His former teacher, James Haughton Woods, was enthusiastic about the dissertation and reported that the department of philosophy had accepted it without any hesitation and that Josiah Royce had called it "the work of an expert." Woods added, as though he had some doubts about the extent of Eliot's present commitment to the subject, "Please let us be reassured that your interest in Philosophy is as strong as ever." It would have been necessary for Eliot to return to Harvard to take his oral examinations before he could be awarded the doctorate, and he made plans to sail in April 1916, accompanied by a trunk-load of Vorticist paintings that Pound wanted him to transport for a forthcoming exhibition in New York. But in the end Eliot did not go, whether through lack of funds or fear of German submarines, and he never received the degree. Professor Woods was not alone in wanting assurance that Eliot would continue to be a philosopher. In May his mother, Mrs. Charlotte Eliot, wrote to Bertrand Russell, "I am sure your influence will in every way confirm my son in his choice of Philosophy as a life work." She hoped that he would shortly take a university post in philosophy, adding, "I have absolute faith in his Philosophy but not in the vers libres." In 1916 Eliot published two highly technical articles on Leibniz and Bradley in *The Monist,* a Chicago philosophical magazine to which Russell had introduced him, and he continued to contribute book reviews to the *International Journal of Ethics* until 1918. But after 1916 there was no longer any serious possibility that Eliot would make philosophy his life's work: we do not know to what extent Russell may have tried to persuade him to persist in his original course, but Ezra Pound would certainly have exerted energetic pressure in the direction of literature.

Steadily and unobtrusively Eliot's literary reputation was growing. Early in 1917 Pound recommended him to Margaret Anderson, editor of the American *Little Review,* of which he was foreign editor: "I should count on Eliot a good deal for such current criticism and appreciation. He is in touch with various papers here and sees what is going on." Eliot had started contributing occasional reviews to the *Manchester Guardian* and the *New Statesman* in 1916: his "Reflections on *Vers Libre*" appeared in the latter on March 3, 1917, and was reprinted in 1965 in *To Criticize the Critic.* This trenchant and lively essay shows Eliot's emerging mastery as a critic and points directly to his later work. There is a passing reference to tradition—"one might imagine the good New growing naturally out of the good Old, without the need for polemic and theory; this would be a society with a living tradition"—and illustrations from Hulme and Pound and John Webster. After some intelligent discussion of meter and rhyme, which engages directly with his own poetic practice, Eliot concludes that "the division between Conservative Verse and *vers libre* does not exist, for there is only good verse, bad verse, and chaos." A crisply legislative tone is already apparent. Eliot did not, as Pound had hoped, become a regular contributor to the *Little Review,* although it published his whimsical philosophical dialogue "Eeldrop and Appleplex" and two groups of poems.

In June 1917 Eliot became assistant editor of *The Egoist,* which Huxley called a "horrid little paper" and hoped Eliot would improve. *The Egoist* had been started in 1913 as *The New Freewoman,* an organ of philosophical feminism; the name was shortly changed and Pound took over the literary section, then passed the job on to Richard Aldington. *The Egoist* had a

curious dual identity: the front part of the paper was given
over to abstruse philosophical reflections, often by its "contributing editor" Dora Marsden, while the literary pages provided a
convenient platform for the Imagists and their friends. It published some important fiction, serializing first Joyce's *Portrait of
the Artist* and then Wyndham Lewis's *Tarr,* and printed some of
the early episodes of *Ulysses.* In 1916 Aldington went into the
army; his wife, H. D., edited the literary pages for a while and
then Eliot took over. From a fortnightly *The Egoist* had been
reduced to a monthly, and finally a bi-monthly, with a tiny circulation and a strong coterie flavor. Yet it provided Eliot with a
valuable opportunity of developing his critical ideas in a series
of reviews of modern English, American, and French poetry.

In his contributions to *The Egoist* he combined intellectual
acuteness with an ironical and light-hearted tone. What he later
called "the braggadocio of the mild-mannered man safely en-
trenched behind his type writer" is much in evidence, as, for instance, when a collection of poems by Alec Waugh receives the
comment, "Mr. Waugh is said to be very young, and to have
written a novel. That is a bad beginning, but something might be
made of him." Even when launching into a highly serious discussion Eliot could open with a note of urbane mockery that struck
a new note in English literary journalism:

Each of us, even the most gifted, can find room in his brain for hardly
more than two or three new ideas, or ideas so perfectly assimilated as to
be original; for an idea is a speciality, and no-one has time for more
than a few. With these, or with one, say, hexagonal or octagonal idea,
each sets to work and industriously and obliviously begins building
cells; not rebelling against the square or the circle, but occasionally
coming into contact with some other Bee which has rectangular or circular ideas.[4]

Eliot's master in this kind of writing was Remy de Gourmont,
whom he had been reading under Pound's influence. Eliot shared
Pound's conviction that the establishment of new literary ideas
meant an unrelenting struggle against English cultural philistinism, but his feline tone was very different from Pound's embattled

[4] *The Egoist,* November 1917.

outbursts. Eliot brought to a fine point of development the art of deliberately provocative iconoclasm: "Who, for instance, has a first-hand opinion of Shakespeare? Yet I have no doubt that much could be learned by a serious study of that semi-mythical figure." But his provocative flights were never merely frivolous; they were part of his personal campaign to raise the level of critical intelligence and to rewrite the history of English poetry. Eliot was still enough of an outsider to look dispassionately at English *mores* and cherished idols:

The Englishman, completely untrained in critical judgment, looks complacently back over the nineteenth century as an accumulation of Great Writers. England puts her Great Writers away securely in a Safe Deposit Vault, and curls to sleep like Fafner. There they go rotten; for if our predecessors cannot teach us to write better than themselves, they will surely teach us to write worse; because we have never learned to criticize Keats, Shelley, and Wordsworth (poets of assured though modest merit), Keats, Shelley and Wordsworth punish us from their graves with the annual scourge of the Georgian Anthology.

Eliot's urbanity can rise to moments of striking eloquence:

I have seen the forces of death with Mr. Chesterton at their head upon a white horse. Mr. Pound, Mr. Joyce, and Mr. Lewis write living English; one does not realize the awfulness of death until one meets with the living language.

At this time Eliot regarded Chesterton as a typical representative of English literary flaccidity, though much later Chesterton became a respected contributor to *The Criterion*. Eliot's contributions to *The Egoist* contain much penetrating criticism, and show him at his wittiest and most sparkling. Unfortunately only one of his contributions is at all well known, and this is the most famous of all his critical essays, "Tradition and the Individual Talent," which appeared late in 1919 in the last two numbers of *The Egoist*. It provides a sustained development of ideas he had been throwing out in his reviews during the two previous years, but is more heavy-handed.

The Egoist also provided the imprint for Eliot's first collection of poems, the celebrated *Prufrock and Other Observations*, which came out in June 1917 in an edition of five hundred copies, price

one shilling. It contained only twelve poems, six written between
1909 and 1912, the rest in 1915–1916. The Egoist Ltd. had already published Joyce's *Portrait* in book form, and they published Eliot's poems at Pound's direct instigation; unknown to
Eliot he had borrowed the cost of printing. Although such a fugitive publication could hardly arouse widespread interest, it was
certainly not ignored. If the *Times Literary Supplement* published
a dismissive review, other periodicals were kinder and more per-
ceptive. The *Westminster Gazette* saw Eliot as "a poet who finds
even poetry laughable, who views life with a dry derision and
comments on it with the true disengagement of wit. He is not like
any other poet, not even the Imagists, whom he seems at first
sight to follow. . . ." The *New Statesman* commented, "Mr. Eliot
may possibly give us the quintessence of twenty-first century
poetry."

The reception of *Prufrock* was an early example of Eliot's happy
knack of finding not necessarily a large audience, but a receptive
and influential one. E. M. Forster, then living in Cairo, somehow got hold of a copy, which he read with immense satisfaction
while recovering from a sprained ankle; he found in Eliot's gestures of ironic diffidence a welcome contrast to the violent rhetoric
of a world at war. Clive Bell recalls taking several copies of *Prufrock* to a weekend party at Lady Ottoline Morrell's country
house at Garsington, and distributing them to the assembled
guests, who included prominent representatives of the Bloomsbury world. Katherine Mansfield read some of Eliot's poems
aloud, and one admiring listener was John Middleton Murry,
who later employed Eliot as a frequent reviewer for the *Athenaeum*. The Bloomsbury connection was undoubtedly useful to
Eliot, though, as Herbert Read has written, "whatever the pos-
sessive attitude of Bloomsburyites such as Clive Bell may have
been, the truth is that Eliot carefully kept his distance." Given
his temperament he could scarcely have done otherwise, and he
seems to have been at some pains elaborately to rebuff Lytton
Strachey's rather uneasy attempts at friendship. Nevertheless,
he was an occasional guest at Garsington, and became a close
friend of Leonard and Virginia Woolf, who in 1919 printed
Poems—his second book of verse which was even more exiguous

than *Prufrock,* containing only seven poems, three of them in French—in a limited edition on their hand press at Hogarth House, Richmond.

Soon after the publication of *Prufrock* Eliot was able to do something to repay Pound for his support. The recently established American firm of Alfred A. Knopf was bringing out a collection of Pound's poems, together with his translations from the Noh drama, and John Quinn, the New York lawyer and patron of the arts, suggested that an accompanying brochure on Pound should be issued to introduce him to a larger American public. Quinn agreed to pay for this publication and Eliot was commissioned to write it, though Pound insisted that the essay be anonymous, remarking, ". . . I want to boom Eliot, and one cant have too obvious a ping-pong match at that sort of thing (Not unless one is Amy Lowell and J. G. Fletcher)." *Ezra Pound: His Metric and Poetry* was issued anonymously by Knopf in January 1918, and was not reprinted in Eliot's lifetime, though it is now available in *To Criticize the Critic.* Eliot's essay is a straightforward study of the evolution of Pound's poetry and his developing reputation, from *A Lume Spento* to the first three *Cantos.* He quotes liberally from Pound's verse and prose and from reviews of his work, and is particularly concerned with Pound's metrical finesse. But there are occasional asides which show that Eliot was writing in the spirit of his *Egoist* reviews, with a propagandist edge: "Such a relation between poetry and music is very different from what is called the 'music' of Shelley or Swinburne, a music often nearer to rhetoric (or the art of the orator) than to the instrument."

In London Eliot continued to enlarge his circle of literary and social acquaintances. In December 1917 he was one of a group of poets who took part in a poetry reading given for charity at the house of Mrs. Sybil Colefax, a well-known society hostess. Aldous Huxley, who also read, made the occasion sound singularly grim:

Gosse in the chair—the bloodiest little old man I have ever seen—dear Robbie Ross stage-managing, Bob Nichols thrusting himself to the fore as the leader of us young bards (*bards* was the sort of thing Gosse called us)—then myself, Viola Tree, a girl called McLeod and troops of Shufflcbottoms, alias Sitwells bringing up the rear: last and best, Eliot. But oh—what a performance: Eliot and I were the only people who had any dignity: Bob Nichols raved and screamed and hooted and moaned his filthy war poems like a Lyceum Villain who hasn't learnt how to act.[5]

Lady Cynthia Asquith, who was in the audience, noted that "the author of 'Prufrock' read quite a funny poem comparing the Church to a Hippopotamus." Another of the readers was Sir Osbert Sitwell; he recalls that Eliot was publicly rebuked by Sir Edmund Gosse for arriving a few minutes late, though he had come straight from the bank; Eliot, with his customary good manners, showed no sign of annoyance. Another member of the audience at Mrs. Colefax's was Arnold Bennett, who appreciated the reading of "The Hippopotamus"; some months later he remarked of Eliot, in a letter to a friend, "I was so struck by his work that I made his acquaintance. He came to see me, and I was well content."

In 1918 the war caught up with Eliot. Aldous Huxley wrote that Eliot had been called up for the American army and wondered what could be done to protect him. In fact an old hernia condition made him unfit for ordinary military service, and he had been trying for some time to get a post in the U.S. intelligence service. After long delay he was sent for by Navy Intelligence and offered an appointment as chief yeoman with the promise of an early commission. He had actually resigned from Lloyds Bank when matters were delayed again by Washington. By now the war was coming to an end; the armistice intervened, and Eliot went back to the bank, his civilian status unimpaired.

Eliot's reputation as poet and critic, although growing, was essentially of a coterie kind. But in 1919 Middleton Murry took over the editorship of the *Athenaeum*, which had once been a distinguished organ of Victorian opinion but had fallen on bad days during the war. He invited Eliot to contribute to the literary pages as part of a brilliant circle that included Leonard and Virginia Woolf, Lytton Strachey, Clive Bell, and Roger Fry. Aldous Huxley was assistant editor, and Murry tried unsuccessfully to get

[5] Grover Smith, ed., *Letters of Aldous Huxley* (New York: Harper & Row, 1970), p. 141.

the paper's owner to put up enough money to provide a similar post for Eliot. (Huxley's experiences in the job gave him the opportunity of caricaturing Murry, as Burlap, in *Point Counter Point.*) The *Athenaeum* commanded a larger and more important audience than *The Egoist,* and in 1919–1920 Eliot contributed a series of review articles that contain some of his finest criticism, where he brings off time and again the difficult task of making an intelligent appraisal of the book he is discussing, while at the same time advancing his own literary ideas.

With his contributions to the *Athenaeum,* and subsequently to the *Times Literary Supplement,* Eliot moved closer to the center of the English literary establishment than Pound had ever been. Richard Aldington has given a lucid account of the process:

Tom Eliot's career in England has been exactly the reverse of Ezra's. Ezra Pound started out in a time of peace and prosperity with everything in his favour and muffed his chances of becoming literary dictator of London—to which he undoubtedly aspired—by his own conceit, folly, and bad manners. Eliot started in the enormous confusion of war and post-war England, handicapped in every way. Yet by merit, tact, prudence, and pertinacity he succeeded in doing what no other American had ever done—imposing his personality, taste, and even many of his opinions on literary England.[6]

Although Pound and Eliot remained on terms of close friendship, Pound, in the midst of his own endless troubles with editors, looked with some asperity at Eliot's connection with the *Athenaeum.* In October 1919 Eliot reviewed a book of Pound's poems favorably enough, but Pound commented in a letter to John Quinn:

Eliot has done a dull but, I think, valuable puff in the *Athenaeum;* granite wreaths, leaden laurels, no sign of exhilaration; but I daresay it is what is best in that quarter.

He has shown in earlier articles the "English Department" universitaire attitude: literature not something enjoyable, but something which your blasted New England conscience makes you feel you *ought* to enjoy.

---

[6] *Life for Life's Sake* (New York: Viking Press, 1941; London: Cassell & Co., 1968), p. 199.

Despite the shared literary aims, the temperamental differences between Eliot and Pound were becoming apparent. The latter had grown increasingly disillusioned with English intellectual life and at the end of 1920 left London for Paris.

In 1919 the twelve poems of *Prufrock* were followed by the seven poems of the Hogarth Press *Poems*—the printing history of which is interestingly described by Leonard Woolf in *Beginning Again*—and this minute *oeuvre* was already beginning to make an impact, in Eliot's characteristic fashion of achieving a maximum effect with minimum means. As early as December 1918 Pound wrote to Marianne Moore, apropos of the *Little Review*, "I am rejecting imitators of T. S. E. . . . ." In December 1919 Robert Nichols contributed a crude imitation of Eliot's quatrain poems to *Coterie* (Eliot's "A Cooking Egg" had appeared in the first number, a few months before):

> Sinclair's looks can never lie,
>   He is well shaved, has curved lips,
> His nose is straight, so is his eye,
>   Also he boasts substantial hips.
>
> Sinclair would make his muslin choice—
>   Spring and his father say he must:
> Corah has ankles and a voice,
>   Nancy has French and a neat bust.

And similar imitations by other poets appeared in later issues. In 1919 Eliot wrote little verse, though "Gerontion" was composed in that year; on November 5 he wrote to John Quinn, "I hope to get started on a poem that I have in mind." This, presumably, was *The Waste Land*.

He was, however, writing an immense amount of criticism, while his work at Lloyds Bank became increasingly demanding. In June 1919 he wrote to Lytton Strachey about a "tour of the provinces" on which he was being sent by the bank:

You are very—ingenuous—if you can conceive me conversing with rural deans in the cathedral close. I do not go to cathedral towns but to centres of industry. My thoughts are absorbed in questions more important than ever enters the heads of deans—as *why* it is cheaper to buy steel bars from America than Middlesborough, and the probable effects—the exchange difficulties with Poland—and the appreciation of the rupee.[7]

Eliot's characteristic note of urbane lifemanship is apparent here, although it was true that he had become expert in the intricacies of foreign trade. (In his entry in the *Harvard College Class of 1910 Quindecennial Report* for 1925, there is a reference to a book called *Literature and Export Trade*, about which Eliot later expressed bafflement, saying that it might have been "a small leg-pull of my own.") I. A. Richards, who got to know Eliot in about 1920, has described visiting him in his office:

What they showed me was a figure stooping, very like a dark bird in a feeder, over a big table covered with all sorts and sizes of foreign correspondence. The big table almost entirely filled a little room under the street. Within a foot of our heads when we stood were the thick, green glass squares of the pavement on which hammered all but incessantly the heels of the passers-by. There was just room for two perches beside the table . . .

What was he doing there under the pavement? Setting in order the affairs of the late Houston Stewart Chamberlain, one of the philosophic fathers of Fascism. A multi-lingual correspondence of the utmost complication, I gathered. Not the adding up of figures but a big, long headache of sorting out a highly tangled story.[8]

Richards also mentions meeting a senior official of Lloyds Bank while on vacation in the Alps. This man, having discovered that Richards knew Eliot in a literary connection, questioned him about the value of Eliot's poetry and expressed relief and even pleasure on hearing that Richards considered him a good poet. He said that Eliot was well regarded at the bank, and might one day get to be a branch manager.

Ezra Pound, in the meantime, was already trying to find ways of rescuing Eliot from the bank. On June 4, 1920 he wrote to John Quinn:

[7] Michael Holroyd, *Lytton Strachey* (New York: Henry Holt & Co.; London: William Heinemann, 1968), vol. II, p. 365.

[8] Allen Tate, ed., *T. S. Eliot: The Man and His Work* (New York: Delacorte Press, 1966; London: Chatto & Windus, 1967), p. 436.

No use blinking the fact that it is a crime against literature to let him
waste eight hours vitality per diem in that bank. Nor on the other hand
that it will take £400 per year, with 3 or 5 years guarantee to get him
out of it.

(His wife hasn't a cent and is an invalid always cracking up, & needing
doctors, & incapable of earning anything—though she has tried—poor
little brute).[9]

Nothing came of the plan at that time, though two years later
Pound revived it in a more ambitious way as the *Bel Esprit*
scheme.

Eliot spent the summer vacation of 1920 in Brittany with Wyndham Lewis; on the way they stopped off in Paris to see Joyce,
whom Eliot had never met, though he had warmly admired
him ever since the publication of *Portrait of the Artist*. Before
leaving London, Eliot was given a heavy parcel by Pound with
instructions to deliver it personally to Joyce. Wyndham Lewis's
account of the meeting, in his superbly energetic prose, makes it
seem an occasion of high farce:

Joyce lay back in the stiff chair he had taken from behind him, crossed
his leg, the lifted leg laid out horizontally upon the one in support like
an artificial limb, an arm flung back over the summit of the sumptuous
chair. He dangled negligently his straw hat, a regulation "boater." We
were on either side of the table, upon which stood the enigmatical
parcel.

Eliot now rose to his feet. He approached the table, and with one
eyebrow drawn up, and a finger pointing, announced to James Joyce
that *this* was the parcel, to which he had referred in his wire, and which
had been given into his care, and he formally delivered it, thus acquit-
ting himself of his commission.

"Ah! Is this the parcel you mentioned in your note?" enquired Joyce,
overcoming the elegant reluctance of a certain undisguised fatigue in
his person. And Eliot admitted that it was, and resumed his seat . . .

James Joyce was by now attempting to untie the crafty housewifely
knots of the cunning old Ezra. After a little he asked his son crossly for
a penknife. Still more crossly his son informed him that he had no penknife. But Eliot got up, saying "You want a knife? I have not got a

    [9] B. L. Reid, *The Man From New York: John Quinn and His Friends* (New
York: Oxford University Press, 1968), p. 436.

knife, I think!" We were able, ultimately, to provide a pair of nail scissors.

At last the strings were cut. A little gingerly Joyce unrolled the slovenly swaddlings of damp British brown paper in which the good-hearted American had packed up what he put inside. Thereupon, along with some nondescript garments for the trunk—there were no trousers I believe—a fairly presentable pair of *old brown shoes* stood revealed, in the centre of the bourgeois French table.

After this Joyce took Eliot and Lewis out to dinner and insisted on paying for everything, as he did every time they met during the rest of their stay in Paris; as Lewis commented, "our stay there was one long fete." Eliot, as reported by Lewis, was distinctly disconcerted by Joyce:

"Oh yes. He is polite, he is polite enough. But he is exceedingly arrogant. Underneath. That is why he is so polite. I should be better pleased if he were less polite." Eliot was very grim.

Eliot expressed himself more circumspectly in a letter to John Quinn:

I found him charming, and liked him; though I can see that he is certainly a handful. With the true fanatic's conviction that everyone ought to forward the interests of his work. It is, however, the conviction of the fanatic, and not the artfulness or pertinacity of ordinary push; and the latter part of "Ulysses," which I have been reading in manuscript, is truly magnificent.

Despite the growth of his reputation, Eliot was concerned that although he had stayed in England in order to devote himself to literature, against the wishes of his family, he had not so far produced much tangible evidence of literary success. As he wrote to John Quinn in 1919, a proper book would help "toward satisfying them that I have not made a mess of my life, as they are inclined to believe." But his poetic output remained sparse, and in criticism his energy went into scattered essays rather than a sustained book. In February 1920 a collection of poems by Eliot called *Ara Vos Prec* appeared under the imprint of the Ovid Press, which had just been set up by the poet and novelist, John Rodker. This book showed once again Eliot's inclination for small presses and limited editions, and there was little that was new in it. *Ara Vos*

Prec reprinted *Prufrock* and the Hogarth Press *Poems,* together with a few uncollected poems. The Provençal words of the title mean "Now I pray you" and they come from the lines spoken by Arnaut Daniel in *Purgatorio* XXVI, a passage which deeply affected Eliot's imagination, and which he alludes to in *The Waste Land* and throughout *Ash-Wednesday.* Richard Aldington complained that Eliot had picked up from Pound the affectation of giving his book a foreign title, and it is true that Pound's first book of verse, *A Lume Spento,* had also been titled with a tag from the *Purgatorio.* In this case, however, Eliot can reasonably be accused of having been too clever by half, since the words were wrongly printed on the title page as *Ara Vus Prec;* the mistake was not discovered until all the sheets were printed and was only corrected on the wrapper. As Eliot cheerfully admitted to Donald Gallup, "It only happened to be *Vus* on the title page because I don't know Provençal, and I was quoting from an Italian edition of Dante the editor of which apparently did not know Provençal either." At the same time that *Ara Vos Prec* appeared in London, Eliot's *Poems* was published by Knopf in New York—the first collection of his poetry to appear in America and the first to be published by a commercial publisher. With one exception, the contents of the two books were identical. In 1920, too, Eliot published *The Sacred Wood,* a selection of his critical essays. It was a short work of only a hundred and fifty pages, but it was to prove immensely influential; an American edition followed soon afterward from Knopf. With these books Eliot emerged from the coterie world of the little review and the fugitive publication, to which Pound still essentially belonged, and became an established man of letters with a reputation on both sides of the Atlantic.

2

The first results of Eliot's fresh start as a poet in 1915 were slight enough: the vague, uneasy urban impressionism of "Morning at the Window," with its unfortunate phrase about "the damp souls of housemaids"; and "The *Boston Evening Transcript,*" "Aunt Helen," and "Cousin Nancy," which have Eliot's characteristic crispness of movement and some good lines, but do not suggest any very striking possibility of poetic renewal. These three poems are essays in a Harvard manner of the 1900s, when it was fashionable to direct brief satiric shafts at Boston society. Together with "Mr. Apollinax" they have something in common with Pound's ironic commentaries on the contemporary scene in *Lustra* and may, indeed, even have been influenced by them. (Eliot wrote other poems at this time which remain unpublished; there are manuscript drafts in the Berg Collection at the New York Public Library.) For a time Eliot was considerably influenced by Pound; or, more precisely, he accepted Pound's judgment about appropriate poetic models. In Pound's own words:

That is to say, at a particular date in a particular room, two authors, neither engaged in picking the other's pocket, decided that the dilution of *vers libre,* Amygism, Lee Masterism, general floppiness had gone too far and that some counter-current must be set going. Parallel situation centuries ago in China. Remedy prescribed "Emaux et Camées" (or the Bay State Hymn Book). Rhyme and regular strophes.

Results: Poems in Mr. Eliot's *second* volume not contained in his first (Prufrock, *Egoist,* 1917), also "H. S. Mauberley."[10]

Seven poems by Eliot in the 1920 volume reflect his reading of Gautier's "Emaux et Camées" and the conviction that *vers libre* must be replaced by regular forms. These "quatrain" poems, first published between 1917 and 1919, are "The Hippopotamus," "Sweeney Among the Nightingales," "Whispers of Immortality," "Mr. Eliot's Sunday Morning Service," "A Cooking Egg," "Burbank with a Baedeker: Bleistein with a Cigar," and "Sweeney Erect." More than any other poems by Eliot, they have been the objects of controversy: if, as Eliot complained to Virginia Woolf in 1921, he was regarded as "learned and cold," then these poems were largely responsible for that reputation. At the same time they were witty, fantastic, and highly memorable. And, as I have already pointed out, they were quickly imitated. Yeats, who was generally cool about Eliot's poetry, included three of these poems in the *Oxford Book of Modern Verse,* and claimed that the only place where Eliot approached the "grand manner" in

[10] *The Criterion,* July 1932.

his early work was in the final lines of "Sweeney Among the Night-ingales." Grover Smith, a devoted expositor of Eliot's poetry, has condemned these poems for their preciosity and bad taste: "His verse in quatrains is largely an exhibition of functional plagiarism, a triumph of mystification." But John Fuller has made a vigorous defense of them, and the argument still continues.

Their bold images and sharp distortions and catchy rhythms have a flavor of jazz and *art deco,* and form part of the same climate as Aldous Huxley's early fiction and Walton's *Façade.* The same thing might, indeed, be said of *The Waste Land,* but that poem, like "Prufrock" before it, has a great capacity to transcend its initial cultural context. The quatrain poems are far less substantial compositions. In places, undoubtedly, they sink beneath their own unassimilated erudition: Bertrand Russell, on first meeting Eliot in 1914 had thought his learning faintly suspect, and remarked, "window-dressing seems inevitable to Americans." In his conquest of the English literary establishment, Eliot had found his learning—and still more his reputation for learning—a useful weapon, though it was not always tactfully or relevantly employed. The epigraph to "Burbank with a Baedeker" is a flagrant example: in a piece of composite prose of just over six lines Eliot constructs a mosaic of Venetian allusions, drawn from Gautier, a Latin inscription on a painting by Mantegna in a Venetian church, Henry James (as paraphrased by Ford Madox Ford), Browning, Byron, and Shakespeare, and, finally, a non-Venetian reference from John Marston. As Grover Smith puts it, "Eliot's epigraph was perhaps intended mainly to bowl the reader over," and the poem itself is scarcely less allusive. Such a density of exhibited learning, deployed in such an atomistic fashion, indicates, I think, something more than a simple desire to impress. At this period in his life Eliot appears to have had a deep need both to exploit and to lean on his wide and varied reading, and a line from *The Waste Land,* "These fragments I have shored against my ruins," reflects the state of mind that produced not only *The Waste Land* but the other poems where his learning is most notoriously on view.

A further point to be made about the quatrain poems is that although Eliot uses the stanzaic form with immense skill, showing fine subtleties of rhythm and satisfying variations in verbal texture, this form was not, basically, one which suited him. Pound used Gautier impressively in "Mauberley," but though Eliot let himself be persuaded that Gautier's formal regularity would benefit him too, his need was not at all the same as Pound's. Such strictness of form tended to unite Eliot's fragmentary perceptions of experience in a superficial and factitious way, as opposed to the musical organization and deeper rhythmic unity of his major poems. A characteristic air of sexual unease pervades these poems, but the emotion lacks focus, notably in such poems as "Burbank with a Baedeker" and "Sweeney Among the Nightingales," where a pressing disarray of feelings is marshaled by the smartness of the allusions and tightness of the stanzaic form, but it remains unresolved. Another poem, "A Cooking Egg," seems to me frankly trivial, though its ambiguities and lacunae have made it the object of a rather absurd weight of critical argument.

The most accomplished and satisfying of the quatrain poems are, in my view, "The Hippopotamus," "Whispers of Immortality," and "Mr. Eliot's Sunday Morning Service." The first of these, a brilliant expansion of Gautier's "L'Hippopotame," develops, in an immaculately impassive manner, a calculated pseudo-conceit: the poem seems constantly about to show just how the Hippopotamus and the Church are related, but never does, and at the end of the poem they are further apart than ever—one in heaven, the other "Wrapt in the old miasmal mist." "Whispers of Immortality" presents an absolute opposition between death and sexuality, and shows a recognition of the power and terror of the latter— summed up, as elsewhere in Eliot, by "female smells in shuttered rooms." Such a recoil may be reprehensibly anti-life, but it arises from a sense of deeply disturbing experience, in comparison with which, death, though equally terrible, is at least a familiar literary idea. "Whispers of Immortality" suggests that Eliot found more in the Jacobeans than a stylistic model: the poem, which specifically names Webster and Donne, recalls the tension beneath sex and death that we find in Tourneur or Middleton, and so has covert affinities with "Gerontion."

"Mr. Eliot's Sunday Morning Service," which can be interest-

ingly compared with Wallace Stevens's far finer "Sunday Morning," has been described, and suitably analyzed, by John Fuller
as "rather cool juggling with religious history." Certainly the poet
who wrote it had a long way to go before he could produce *Ash-
Wednesday* or *The Rock*, as he glances in an uncommitted way
from the Word of the Fathers to some minor Italian master's
representation of the Baptism of Christ, and ends with a nice
balance between Sweeney, as *l'homme moyen sensuel*, taking his
bath on Sunday morning, and the endlessly refined discussion of
professional theologians. F. W. Bateson has recently questioned
the correctness of Eliot's Greek phrase and the appropriateness
of the word "mensual," but adds, "Eliot's enjoyment in this poem
communicates itself to the sympathetic reader, whether or not
he is aware of the errors of scholarship." It is certainly true that,
compared with the other quatrain poems, "Mr. Eliot's Sunday
Morning Service" takes a positive delight in its playing with words
and generally arcane references. However precious and remote
the language may be, it is deployed with a profoundly human
relish.

In 1917 and 1918 Eliot published the four poems in French
that form part of his *Collected Poems*. They are very skillful exercises that reflect the influence of Tristan Corbière, who had
somewhat replaced Laforgue in Eliot's interest in French poets,
and in whom he found a fusion of thought and feeling akin to
that apparent in Donne. These poems, and their French sources,
have been expertly discussed by E. D. H. Greene in *T. S. Eliot
et La France*, to which the interested reader can be referred.
They arose from a period when Eliot's immersion in French
poetry was at its greatest, sufficiently so to induce him to write in
that language. In "Mélange Adultère de Tout" Eliot sardonically
presents a drifting figure, whose various roles recall Eliot's own
and it ends with a Rimbaudian apotheosis in Africa. Another of
these poems, "Dans le Restaurant," contains the lines that Eliot
later extracted and translated into English to form part IV of *The
Waste Land*. In "Lune de Miel" he contrasts human banality with
the cultural glories of the past. A wretched, flea-bitten honey-
moon couple travel from Padua to Milan to find the Last Supper
and a cheap restaurant. Meanwhile at Ravenna, where they have

passed an uncomfortable night, the great church of Saint Apolli-
naire preserves the forms of Byzantium. The superiority of the
hard lines of Byzantine art over humanistic fluidity was an important tenet of modernist aesthetics, particularly as expounded
by T. E. Hulme, though Eliot was not familiar with his writings
when he wrote the poem.

Eliot had visited northern Italy in 1911, and been married in
1915, and these two experiences may or may not have been fused
in "Lune de Miel." Another poem, "Ode," which was printed
only in *Ara Vos Prec* and thereafter suppressed, unmistakably
refers, through a mass of heterogeneous literary allusions, to a
sexual disaster and a disconcerted bridegroom. This poem is certainly the worst that Eliot ever allowed to be printed, and its
suppression was a prudent act. (Years later a line from "Ode"
embodying one of Eliot's perennial motifs turned up, slightly
altered, in "New Hampshire" as "Children's voices in the or-
chard.")

Eliot's most considerable poem of the period between 1915 and
1919 is "Gerontion," which he placed at the beginning of *Ara Vos
Prec*. Here Eliot returned to the *vers libre* in which he was most
at home, and to a musical rather than a stanzaic mode of composition. Like "Prufrock" "Gerontion" is a dramatic monologue, and
as in "Prufrock" we move through a zone of consciousness, where
the ostensible narrator is, in Hugh Kenner's words, no more than
a name and voice. In this poem, though, the protagonist has not
even a proper name, since *gerontion* is Greek for "a little old
man." Technically the poem reflects Eliot's absorption in the
Jacobean dramatists, who combined a strong yet flexible blank
verse with the accents of the speaking voice. These lines from
Thomas Middleton's *The Changeling* offer a good example of the
kind of verse that Eliot admired:

> I that am of your blood was taken from you
> For your better health; look no more upon't,
> But cast it to the ground regardlessly.

"Gerontion" is, like the quatrain poems, highly allusive, and commentators have noted phrases taken from A. C. Benson's *Edward
FitzGerald*, a Nativity sermon preached by Bishop Lancelot An-

drewes in 1618, and *The Education of Henry Adams.* But Eliot's use of these sources is not obtrusive, and the reader who is unaware of them will not lose anything; it is, however, important to recognize the presence in the poem of some of Eliot's dominating themes. The old man vainly trying to find meaning in past experience is tormented by some elusive memory of erotic failure, as we see in these lines (which echo those from Middleton quoted above):

> I that was near your heart was removed therefrom
> To lose beauty in terror, terror in inquisition.
> I have lost my passion: why should I need to keep it
> Since what is kept must be adulterated?
> I have lost my sight, smell, hearing, taste and touch:
> How should I use them for your closer contact?

At the same time the poem develops the interest in Christianity first apparent in "Mr. Eliot's Sunday Morning Service." Christ came once, in the spring of the year, but now the power and even the meaning of his arrival have been lost. Essentially, "Gerontion" is about the loss of significance in living, and to this extent it can serve as a prelude to *The Waste Land*, as, indeed, Eliot wished to use it, until dissuaded by Pound. The old man, like the consciousness of the longer poem, is "waiting for rain." Both poems superimpose the remote past and the present: in "Gerontion" "the hot gates" is a literal translation of Thermopylae, while at the same time there are apparent references to the Polish Corridor ("contrived corridors"), a result of the Treaty of Versailles recently signed in the Hall of Mirrors ("a wilderness of mirrors"), and even, in "fractured atoms," to the first splitting of the atom in 1919. And in both poems we have the fleeting apparition of vague cosmopolitan figures, known only for a moment by their strangely evocative names: Mr. Silvero, Hakagawa, Madame de Tornquist, Fräulein von Kulp, de Bailhache, Fresca, Mrs. Cammel, soon to be joined by Madame Sosostris, Stetson, and Mr. Eugenides. (These apparitions, it seems to me, have something in common with those of the *Inferno* and *Purgatorio*, with the crucial difference that for Dante the people he met had histories and identities as well as names, and were part, both in life and in death, of an ordered, hierarchical world.) Yet despite the resemblances, I am sure that Pound was right in wanting to keep the two poems separate.

Although I do not wish to minimize the difficulties of *The Waste Land*, "Gerontion" is certainly much more obscure. Comparing it with any one section of the longer poem, one sees at once that the latter, for all its problems of allusion and transition, is lucid and coherent. "Gerontion" is, in fact, Eliot's one poem where the language itself forms a barrier or smoke screen between the reader and the essential experience of the poem; as other critics have remarked, Eliot's words in his contemporary essay on *Hamlet* can well be applied to this poem: "full of some stuff that the writer could not drag to light, contemplate, or manipulate into art." In its linguistic procedure "Gerontion" is quite unlike *The Waste Land* and, indeed, represents something unique in Eliot's *oeuvre*. It is, in aspiration, his most Shakespearean poem; that is to say, it aims at a maximum exploitation of the connotative resources of the language, allowing implications and suggestions to proliferate almost without limit. There is a relevant passage in another essay by Eliot, written just after "Gerontion," whose significance was pointed out by C. K. Stead. In "Ben Jonson" Eliot refers to Jonson's great contemporaries, "Shakespeare, and also Donne and Webster and Tourneur (and sometimes Middleton)," whose words "have often a network of tentacular roots reaching down to the deepest terrors and desires." As Professor Stead has shown, Eliot took this "reaching down" process with great seriousness, but he did not again try to achieve it in the manner of "Gerontion." The poem hints brokenly at the "deepest terrors and desires" but is unable to find an adequate objective correlative for them, to use another celebrated phrase from the *Hamlet* essay. It contains, without doubt, some brilliant passages: the command of rhythm and syntax in the first half-dozen lines alone is a clear sign of Eliot's genius. But taken as a whole it fails because of the slipperiness of its language: the desire to preserve a maximum openness to verbal suggestiveness makes "Gerontion" an echo chamber where there is much interesting noise but

nothing can be clearly distinguished. Thereafter, Eliot used
verbal implication more subtly, with a Dantean concern for precision, both in speech and visual definition.

3

T. S. Eliot's first book of criticism, *The Sacred Wood,* appeared
under the Methuen imprint in December 1920, and an American
edition followed soon afterward from Knopf. Although it has
been kept in print by the original publisher, most of the essays in
The Sacred Wood were reprinted in Eliot's *Selected Essays,*
where the majority of his readers are likely to encounter them.
Yet it is worth considering in its original form, for this short
book, of less than 50,000 words, firmly established Eliot as a critic.
Amy Lowell, in her *A Critical Fable* (1921), wrote of Eliot:

> Since the poet's not the half of him, we must include
> The critical anchorite of his *Sacred Wood.*
> "This slim duodecimo you must have your eye on
> If you'd be up to date," say his friends. He's a sly one
> To have chosen this format—the book's heavy as iron.
> I'm acutely aware that its grave erudition
> Is quite in the line of a certain tradition,
> That one which is commonly known as tuition.
> To read it is much like a lengthy sojourning
> In at least two or three institutions of learning.

F. W. Bateson, who was an Oxford undergraduate at the time,
was a more responsive reader: "Until the publication of *The
Waste Land* in *The Criterion* (October 1922) we were hardly
aware of Eliot the poet, whereas we were very much aware of
Eliot the critic. *The Sacred Wood* was almost our sacred book."
The somewhat precious brevity of *The Sacred Wood* may recall
that of Eliot's first small collections of verse, *Prufrock* of 1917,
and the Hogarth Press *Poems* of 1919, but it had a different cause;
he was far more productive as a critic than as a poet. Between
1917 and 1920 he wrote a great many reviews and critical articles,
but in *The Sacred Wood* he reprinted only a selection of these
pieces, and the book is carefully arranged with certain strategic
ends in view. In his later years Eliot more than once remarked

that his early criticism was a by-product of his creative work as a poet, and had essentially the interest of "workshop criticism." This is broadly true, insofar as in *The Sacred Wood* Eliot was both trying to bring into existence a receptive audience for the kind of poetry he wanted to write, and to show how certain poets had provided valuable models in writing it. Yet there are other essays, still buried in the files of *The Egoist* and the *Athenaeum*, which, though less germane to Eliot's development as a poet, are still extremely relevant to his struggle to achieve a distinctive literary identity—I am thinking particularly of his essays on Henry James, Henry Adams, and other American writers.

Like all Eliot's subsequent books of criticism, *The Sacred Wood* is a collection of occasional pieces, mostly review articles written during his critical *annus mirabilis* of 1919–1920. Despite his subsequent eminence as a literary critic, Eliot never found the time or inclination to produce a sustained critical work. As he wrote in *To Criticize the Critic*, "these early essays were all written for money, which I needed, and the occasion was always a new book about an author, a new edition of his works, or an anniversary." His later criticism customarily took the form of lectures or addresses, with an accompanying formality of manner. Yet *The Sacred Wood* seems a sufficiently unified book; partly because the questions that were preoccupying Eliot recur from one essay to another, and partly because the book, like many of his poems, illustrates his skill in assembling a collection of fragments to form a coherent whole. The essays fall into three groups: first, those on criticism, culminating in "Tradition and the Individual Talent"; second, those on poetic drama, providing Eliot's initial probing at a topic that was to interest him all his life, but to which he never gave wholly adequate creative expression; and, finally, three essays on particular poets who were significant for him at that time.

There is no hint in *The Sacred Wood* that the author is a poet with propagandist aims, apart from the crucial one concealed in the Latin epigraph from Petronius: " 'I am a poet,' he said, 'and one, I hope, of no mean imagination, if one can reckon at all by crowns of honour, which gratitude can set even on unworthy heads.' " The manner and range of *The Sacred Wood* are, in fact,

not those of the practicing artist but of the disengaged critic, and
may be considered a disguise assumed by the "invisible poet," as
Hugh Kenner called him, an appellation which Eliot himself
found acceptable. The introduction begins in an overtly Arnoldian manner, with the observation that it is time for the author to
make amends to Matthew Arnold, whose work he has known for
the past twelve years; although Arnold's "faults and foibles" are
still evident to him, he is better able to recognize the force of
Arnold's position. Arnold may have called, in *Essays in Criticism*,
for more intellectual rigor in English cultural life, for more of the
critical spirit that provides a proper climate for great art, and, in
particular, for a certain emulation of the French "conscience in
intellectual matters." But in 1920, Eliot remarks, Arnold would
find that his work would all need to be done again, and Eliot, by
implication, has reluctantly to take up the task. There are several
references to Arnold in the first part of *The Sacred Wood* and the
supercilious urbanity of Eliot's manner seems equally derived
from Arnold and from Remy de Gourmont. In particular, Eliot
draws from Arnold his central conviction that the critical spirit is
a concomitant of the creative spirit, rather than something essentially opposed to it, as in the conventional post-Romantic assumption. Nevertheless, Eliot is concerned with strictly literary
matters, whereas Arnold used "criticism" in a very broad sense to
mean a general concern with the whole cultural health of a society; and "criticism," as used in *Essays in Criticism*, is easily
transformed into "culture" in *Culture and Anarchy*. In *The
Sacred Wood* Eliot initiates a lifelong uneasy relationship with
Matthew Arnold, who seems to have been a writer he could neither live with nor without; throughout his critical writings, Eliot
sometimes mentioned Arnold with respect for his insight and
understanding, and at other times scolded and sneered at him for
not seeing and understanding much more than he did. After
Eliot's conversion to Christianity, the insufficiencies of Arnold's
religious attitudes gave him firmer grounds for attack. Yet the
extent of Eliot's critical indebtedness to Arnold can hardly be
denied.

Eliot also follows Arnold in his orientation toward France,
though he gives more concrete instances of his admiration than

ever Arnold did, for *The Sacred Wood* arose from that period in Eliot's career as poet and critic when he was most profoundly absorbed in French literature. One sees the extent of that interest in the scattered approving references to Villon and Stendhal, and the historical insight of such a remark as "The French of Montaigne is a mature language, and the English of Florio's living translation is not." Above all there is the pervasive influence of Remy de Gourmont, "the perfect critic" of the opening essay, which is prefaced with a quotation from Gourmont, *Eriger en lois ses impressions personnelles, c'est le grand effort d'un homme s'il est sincère.* Eliot takes it for granted that criticism must begin in *impressions personnelles,* but cannot remain there, as it does in impressionistic critics like Pater and Arthur Symons; it must conclude in something objective and intellectually apprehensible. This is what Gourmont meant by saying *eriger en lois,* though the phrase is misleading since the *lois* cannot be legislative or prescriptive. Toward the end of the essay, Eliot provides his own gloss on Gourmont's phrase, and gives an acute description of the critical process:

. . . the true generalization is not something superposed upon an accumulation of perceptions; the perceptions do not, in a really appreciative mind, accumulate as a mass, but form themselves as a structure; and criticism is the statement in language of this structure; it is a development of sensibility.

For a while Gourmont had the same effect on Eliot's criticism that Laforgue had once had on his poetry. It was from Gourmont that Eliot acquired the ideas of impersonality, and, in part at least, of the dissociation of sensibility, though Eliot, having a more powerful mind, was able to do more with these ideas than Gourmont ever could. Eliot's reliance on Gourmont does not diminish his importance as an English critic, any more than Coleridge's critical stature is reduced by his well-known debt to German aesthetics. Stylistically Eliot picked up from Gourmont the politely ironic manner which does not quite conceal a patent unwillingness to suffer fools gladly. Rather extravagantly, perhaps, he regarded Gourmont as the modern critic who had most of "the general intelligence of Aristotle." And of Aristotle—whose

philosophy he had once spent a year in studying—Eliot wrote, in a
striking paragraph:

One must be firmly distrustful of accepting Aristotle in a canonical
spirit; this is to lose the whole living force of him. The ordinary intelligence is good only for certain classes of objects; a brilliant man of science, if he is interested in poetry at all, may conceive grotesque judgments: like one poet because he reminds him of himself, or another because he expresses emotions which he admires; he may use art, in fact,
as the outlet for the egotism which is suppressed in his own speciality.
But Aristotle had none of these impure desires to satisfy; in whatever
sphere of interest, he looked solely and steadfastly at the object; in his
short and broken treatise he provides an eternal example—not of laws,
or even of method, for there is no method except to be very intelligent,
but of intelligence itself swiftly operating the analysis of sensation to the
point of principle and definition.

Here we have, in embryonic form, the essential approach of the
New Criticism, as it was systematically developed in England and
America during the 1930s. Eliot himself did not practice the
methods of close analysis that derived from Richards and Emp-
son; but his concern for the poem in itself, as an objective entity
rather than an outlet for the reader's fantasy or egotism, was of
crucial importance. For Eliot's own early criticism the significant
words are, "there is no method except to be very intelligent."
Beyond a certain reliance on "comparison and analysis," he employs no systematic method, however much later academic commentators have tried to find one.

Eliot did possess in abundance the gift, surely essential for a
critic, of finding the right passages to quote and there are many
memorable quotations in *The Sacred Wood*; to this extent he is
inheriting the spirit of the Arnoldian "touchstone." Indeed, it is a
paradox, and perhaps a contradiction, in Eliot's writings on poetic drama that whereas in principle he is insistent that such
drama must be an indissoluble unity of words and action, and
deplores the habit, as exemplified by Lamb and Swinburne, of
ransacking Elizabethan drama for passages of isolated poetic
beauty, in practice he himself has adopted a not dissimilar approach. At least, it is thanks to Eliot that one is firmly possessed
of such isolated felicities as Tourneur's

> Does the silkworm expend her yellow labours
> For thee? For thee does she undo herself?
> Are lordships sold to maintain ladyships
> For the poor benefit of a bewildering minute,

or the mysterious and enchanting lines of John Ford,

> Remember
> When we last gathered roses in the garden,
> I found my wits; but truly you lost yours.

But what, above all, distinguishes Eliot's early criticism is the intensity of intelligence that he brings to it, in the way that he himself had admired in Gourmont and Aristotle. In England in the early twentieth century it was not usual for literary criticism to show the degree of intellectual application that might be taken for granted in scientific or philosophical discourse; it was this that made Eliot's criticism so striking, combined with his unusual breadth of reading, and the outsider's view of English literature that his American origins and French affiliations gave him.

The best-known essay in *The Sacred Wood,* and indeed the most famous of all Eliot's essays, is "Tradition and the Individual Talent." In later years Eliot was inclined to regret its celebrity, since he regarded it as an immature expression of his views. Nevertheless, the ideas in this essay have become critical commonplaces wherever English literature is studied, and after fifty years it retains its contentious vitality. If F. R. Leavis has condemned it for "its ambiguities, its logical inconsequences, its pseudo-precisions, its fallaciousness, and the aplomb of its specious cogency," F. W. Bateson regards the essay as "a classic of our criticism, one comparable to chapter XIV of the *Biographia Literaria* or to Arnold's 'The Function of Criticism at the Present Time.'" Bateson is surely right to point out that the essay must be seen in its initial situation: just as the inhuman angularity of cubism or futurism in painting was a necessary reaction against the sentimentality and fluidity of so much late-nineteenth-century art, whether academic or impressionist, so Eliot's stress on "impersonality," which so much scandalizes Leavis (inevitably setting Eliot up against D. H. Lawrence and finding him wanting), was an inevitable response to the pervasive literary climate of subjectivism, inspiration, and self-expression. Eliot was writing in the minority tradition of modernist aesthetics already exemplified by Gourmont, Hulme, Pound, and Lewis, and he certainly could not have foreseen in 1919, when his essay appeared in the little-read pages of *The Egoist*, that its doctrines were going to become an academic orthodoxy.

Insofar as "Tradition and the Individual Talent" has a propagandist purpose, its aim is to persuade the reader that there is more to the production of literature than the desire and even the talent to do so. To write a poem we must first know what a poem is, and learn from other poets how poems may be written. In the cultural milieu in which Eliot was writing, originality was everything and there was no general sense that writing a poem added to and altered an existing corpus of literature. Against this individualistic stance he asserted the importance of tradition: "Whereas if we approach a poet without this prejudice we shall often find that not only the best, but the most individual parts of his work may be those in which the dead poets, his ancestors, assert their individuality most vigorously." Tradition is, however, no inert academic canon; it involves the poet acquiring, with great difficulty, an historical sense which

compels a man to write not merely with his own generation in his bones, but with a feeling that the whole of the literature of Europe from Homer and within it the whole of the literature of his own country has a simultaneous existence and composes a simultaneous order.

Eliot here is simply prescribing the impossible, however necessary "tradition" may be as a notion. As he later acknowledges, no one can be expected to have read so much before he writes a poem, and he modifies his prescription into the far more modest claim that the poet should have a developing consciousness of the past throughout his career which need not imply prodigious erudition: "Shakespeare acquired more essential history from Plutarch than most men could from the whole British Museum." Eliot's problem in exploiting the notion of "tradition" is that he wanted it to mean more than one thing at a time. It seems to have had a number of sources in his own thought. One of them, as E. D. H. Greene points out, is in Gourmont, who wrote:

Il n'est pas, dans la littérature, pas plus que dans la nature, de génération spontanée. L'originalité absolue n'est qu'une conception d'ignorant: elle serait d'ailleurs contraire aux lois, absurde et incompréhensible.

Spontaneous generation does not occur in literature any more than in nature. Absolute originality is a notion of the uninformed; furthermore, it would be against all principle, absurd and incomprehensible.

In Eliot's *Knowledge and Experience in the Philosophy of F. H. Bradley* there is a passage which anticipates the notion of the whole of literature existing in a simultaneous ideal order:

These ideas do not qualify a real past and future, for there is no real past or future for them to qualify; past and future are as such themselves ideal constructions. Ideas of the past are true, not by correspondence with a real past, but by their coherence with each other and ultimately with the present moment: an idea of the past is true, we have found, by virtue of relations among ideas.

A more literary source for the idea of the "simultaneous order" can be found in Dante. As I have previously suggested, Dante represented for Eliot much that he admired and could never attain; Dante was an embodiment of what he called, in "Tradition and the Individual Talent," the "Mind of Europe." In Dante, whose art was rooted in the life of the city of Florence and who yet embraced the whole known civilization of his time, there was harmony between two opposed aspirations that Eliot could never resolve: the need for locality and rootedness, and the need for cultural universality. In a very concrete way, the *Divine Comedy* offers illustrations of the simultaneous ideal order among poets, shown first in the companionship of Dante and Virgil, and then expanded in *Inferno* IV, where they encounter the great poets of antiquity:

> Lo buon maestro cominciò a dire:
>   "Mira colui con quella spada in mano,
>   che vien dinanzi a' tre sì come sire:
>
> quegli è Omero poeta sovrano
>   l'altro è Orazio satiro, che viene;
>   Ovido è il terzo, e l'ultimo Lucano.

(The good master began to speak: "Mark him with that sword in hand, who comes before these three as their lord: that is Homer, the sovereign Poet; the next who comes is Horace the satirist; Ovid is the third, and the last is Lucan.")

Elsewhere Eliot uses lines from Dante to reinforce the notion of an ideal order existing among poets, living and dead. Thus, after the dedication of *Prufrock and Other Observations* to Jean Verdenal, we have as epigraph the beautiful lines from *Purgatorio* XXI which describe the meeting of Virgil and Statius:

> Or puoi la quantitate
> comprender dell'amor ch'a te mi scalda,
> quando dismento nostra vanitate,
> trattando l'ombre come cosa salda.

(Now canst thou comprehend the measure of the love which warms me toward thee, when I forget our nothingness, and treat shades as solid things.)

Again, the phrase which accompanied the dedication of *The Waste Land* to Ezra Pound, *il miglior fabbro*—"the better craftsman"—comes from *Purgatorio* XXVI, where Dante uses it about Arnaut Daniel. The process culminates triumphantly in the superimpositions of section II of "Little Gidding," where Brunetto Latini and, again, Arnaut Daniel from Dante coexist with Mallarmé and Yeats.

The idea of tradition, first adumbrated in Eliot's essay, was to remain crucial to his thought; in 1919 "tradition" was wholly a matter of literature, and particularly poetry; but in the later development of Eliot's thought it was to acquire a wider reference, and to embrace religious and political meanings. "Tradition and the Individual Talent" advances some incontrovertible ideas; namely, that no poet writes in isolation from his fellows and ancestors; and that it is possible to regard the literature of the past, or some part of it, as a synchronic entity, coexisting with the present. What is not at all clear from Eliot's essay is how much of the tradition the poet must be directly possessed of, or what laborious means he must use to possess it. There is a basic division in Eliot's mind between the idea of a culturally comprehensive tradition—in fact, the "mind of Europe"—that his American antecedents, and in particular his Harvard education, would have given him, and which would be broadly equivalent to Arnold's "the best that has been thought and said"; and his requirements as a practicing poet, devising his own idiosyncratic and highly partial tradition of usable authors. In later years Eliot slyly acknowledged the force of this dilemma when he wrote in *After Strange Gods*, "Mr. Yeats was in search of tradition a little too consciously perhaps—like all of us."

It is, however, not so much the idea of tradition that has caused "Tradition and the Individual Talent" to be attacked, as the doctrine of "impersonality." Some of Eliot's phrases have given offense for suggesting that the creative process was a passive, quasi-automatic affair, particularly the notorious simile that ends part one of the essay:

I shall, therefore, invite you to consider, as a suggestive analogy, the action which takes place when a bit of finely filiated platinum is introduced into a chamber containing oxygen and sulphur dioxide.

The invitation comes with superb aplomb from one who had failed the entrance examination to Smith Academy in physics, but it scarcely sheds much light on how the mind of the poet operates; and its scientific inaccuracy was tartly exposed by an anonymous reviewer of Eliot's *Selected Essays* in *The Criterion* in 1932. F. W. Bateson acknowledges that the analogy is objectionable, and ingeniously suggests that Eliot inserted it at the end of the first installment, as printed in *The Egoist*, in order to arouse the reader's expectations for the rest of the essay. Eliot goes on to say:

The poet's mind is in fact a receptacle for seizing and storing up numberless feelings, phrases, images, which remain there until all the particles which can unite to form a new compound are present together.

The mechanical implications of "receptacle" have been objected to, and Eliot was probably being deliberately provocative here, in the face of a public opinion that held to a rhapsodic notion of poetic inspiration. Richard Wollheim has suggested that in this essay Eliot was influenced by his Bradleyan studies, which gave him "a peculiarly empty or hollow way of conceiving the mind." In rejecting the notion of poetry as the direct expression of personality, Eliot cautiously observed that "the point of view which I am struggling to attack is perhaps related to the metaphysical theory of the substantial unity of the soul."

Nevertheless, toward the end of the essay, having asserted that "poetry is not a turning loose of emotion, but an escape from emotion; it is not the expression of personality, but an escape from personality," Eliot adds to these often-quoted words a crucial qualification: "But, of course, only those who have personality and emotions know what it means to want to escape from these things." And only a substantial self can have personality and emotions. Eliot's basic objection to the idea of self-expression was, I think, its superficiality. As C. K. Stead has shown, for Eliot, writing poetry means a surrender of the quotidian self in order to move to a deeper level. The disparate elements in the "receptacle" of the poet's mind will not be fused into a new unity without the unbiddable intervention of some mysterious force not subject to consciousness or will; Eliot here relies quite markedly on the section on "subconscious creation" in Gourmont's *La Culture des idées.* What is essential is the ultimate transformation of "personality into a personal work of art," as he remarks elsewhere in *The Sacred Wood,* in the essay on Massinger. This phrase is followed by a relevant quotation from Gourmont, which stresses that this transformation can be a painful discipline, as it was for Flaubert; all traces of the superficial and inauthentic elements in the ordinary personality must be stripped off:

La vie est un dépouillement. Le but de l'activité propre de l'homme est de nettoyer sa personalité, de la laver de toutes les souillures qu'y déposa l'éducation, de la dégager de toutes les empreintes qu'y laissèrant nos admirations adolescentes.

Life is a process of sloughing off. The proper end of man's activities is to scour his personality, to cleanse it of all the stains deposited by education, to free it of all the imprints left by adolescent admirations.

Eliot, as I remarked earlier, regarded poetic creation as inherently painful, involving a descent and a surrender to possibly terrifying forces. As he wrote in a letter to the *Athenaeum,* published on June 25, 1920, "the creation of a work of art is like some other forms of creation, a painful and unpleasant business; it is a sacrifice of the man to the work, it is a kind of death." (The notion of artistic creation as an inherently sacrificial activity was interestingly developed by Anton Ehrenzweig in *The Hidden Order of Art*.) It is in this context that Eliot's doctrine of "impersonality" must be understood. To some extent he can be blamed for not making his ideas clearer in "Tradition and the Individual Talent," which is indeed an ambiguous document, both in its failure to be clear about the nature of tradition and to relate coherently the two items of its title, and in its description of "impersonality" in highly misleading language. Yet this essay, for all its conscious formality of manner, is an extremely personal and tentative working out of a position by Eliot, in which the deeper meanings he wants to convey remain elusive; and, as I have remarked, he could not have foreseen its subsequent canonical status.

In the rest of *The Sacred Wood* Eliot works in more direct and less ambitious terms, turning his attention as a critic to a variety of works and authors. The essays on Elizabethan drama have, of course, become academic properties and have provided tips and formulae for innumerable students and teachers, even if in the *Hamlet* essay Eliot was covertly using Shakespeare to raise some of his own creative problems. The book concludes strategically with an essay on Dante, which is Eliot's first public attempt to *Onorate l'altissimo poeta*, though it is less satisfactory than either the long essay on Dante first published as a book in 1929 and then included in *Selected Essays*, or "What Dante Means to Me" in *To Criticize the Critic*. More interesting are the essays on Swinburne and Blake which precede it. In the first of them Eliot takes the measure of Swinburne as a brilliant practitioner of the kind of poetry that he was most in revolt against, though without exactly attacking Swinburne. He sees Swinburne as writing a singular poetry where all the vitality is in the language, which has no relation at all to the world of actual events, and he remarks that "only a man of genius could dwell so exclusively and consistently among words as Swinburne." Eliot, whose own poetic language was so calculatedly intense, might well have regarded Swinburne as a warning not to allow language to become quite autonomous, whatever the temptations. The essay on Blake is an illuminating example of Eliot using a poet seemingly remote from him as a means of examining his own problems, while at the same time saying quite relevant things in the way of criticism. In the first part of the essay Blake is praised for having made himself as a poet entirely on his own, without reference to conventional influences, just as Eliot had at Harvard and Paris between 1909 and 1912. He had successfully undergone the *dépouillement* described by Gourmont in the previously quoted passage, and Eliot virtually paraphrases Gourmont in what he says about Blake:

It is important that the artist should be highly educated in his own art; but his education is one that is hindered rather than helped by the ordinary processes of society which constitute education for the ordinary man. For these processes consist largely in the acquisition of impersonal ideas which obscure what we really are and feel, what we really want, and what really excites our interest. It is of course not the actual information acquired, but the conformity which the accumulation of knowledge is apt to impose, that is harmful. Tennyson is a very fair example of a poet almost wholly encrusted with parasitic opinion, almost wholly merged into his environment. Blake, on the other hand, knew what interested him, and he therefore presents only the essential, only, in fact, what can be presented, and need not be explained. And because he was not distracted, or frightened, or occupied in anything but exact statement, he understood. He was naked, and saw man naked, and from the centre of his own crystal. . . . There was nothing of the superior person about him. This makes him terrifying.

The essay was, in fact, called "The Naked Man" when it first appeared in the *Athenaeum*. In the second part of the essay Eliot writes not as a fellow poet, but as a culture-critic concerned with "tradition" in the embracing, orthodox sense, and he finds fault with Blake in Arnoldian terms for not knowing enough: "And about Blake's supernatural territories, as about the supposed ideas that dwell there, we cannot help commenting on a certain meanness of culture." Eliot's criticism of Blake's poetry seems to me cogent; but the essay is most remarkable for the way it shifts ground, concretely illustrating the dichotomy that underlies "Tradition and the Individual Talent."

It is hardly an exaggeration to say that *The Sacred Wood*, for all its brevity and unostentatious manner, changed the literary taste of a generation, though one must add that the book appeared at precisely the right moment to effect such a change. Eliot argued in "The Perfect Critic" that "in matters of great importance the critic must not coerce, and he must not make judgments of worse and better. He must simply elucidate: the reader will form the correct judgment for himself." This was a precept that Eliot often failed to follow, for *The Sacred Wood* is full of small-scale hierarchies of better and worse, some of them very cryptic, as when Eliot complains that if Arnold had done a better job he would have "shown his contemporaries exactly why the author of *Amos Barton* is a more *serious* writer than Dickens, and why the author of *La Chartreuse de Parme* is more serious than either." (Eliot had a curious attachment at this time to "Amos Barton," the first of George Eliot's *Scenes of Clerical Life*.) Nevertheless, the valuations which *The Sacred Wood*, taken as a whole, leaves with the reader are not those established by direct prescription, but rather those which emerge from Eliot's casual asides, from the way in which some names are tacitly assumed to be considerable, and others of little account. We pick up in passing, for instance, the point that Marlowe's Mephistopheles renders Milton's Satan superfluous; that Keats and Shelley "were too young to be judged"; that Villon is immeasurably superior to Ronsard; that it is a matter of grave suspicion if a critic admires George Meredith; and though "there may be a good deal to be said for Romanticism in life, there is no place for it in letters." By such a quiet but highly persuasive rhetoric Eliot succeeded, probably without intending to, in institutionalizing his own tastes, so that simplified and often misunderstood versions of them became commonplace in the literary discussions of the twenties. And in 1924 the example of *The Sacred Wood* was reinforced by the short but incalculably influential essays on Marvell and the Metaphysical poets in *Homage to John Dryden*. A few years later Eliot himself became institutionalized as a literary critic; he continued to say valuable things, but the peculiar tone of *The Sacred Wood*, the cool outsider's gaze and the poised intellectual gaiety, had disappeared.

III

Poet and Editor

1921–1927

IN SEPTEMBER 1920 Eliot stayed with Leonard and Virginia Woolf at Monk's House, Rodmell, Sussex; Mrs. Woolf noted in her diary:

The odd thing about Eliot is that his eyes are lively and youthful when the cast of his face and the shape of his sentences are formal and even heavy. Rather like a sculpted face—no upper lip, formidable, powerful, pale. Then those hazel eyes, seeming to escape from the rest of him.

The distinction between an inner *esprit,* and the severity and formality with which he faced the world, was basic to Eliot's personality. Leonard Woolf claims that he and Virginia had "something to do with changing Tom, with loosening up the pomposity and priggishness which constricted him, with thawing out the essential warmth of his nature . . ." He records a curious incident during one of Eliot's early visits to the Woolfs. When the three of them were walking across the fields, Woolf fell behind to micturate. On catching up with his companions again, he noticed that Eliot seemed uncomfortable and even shocked. Woolf then engaged him in what he described as a "perfectly frank conversation about conventions and formality," in which he elicited from Eliot the admission that not only could he not have done the same thing himself, but that he would never dream of shaving in the presence of anyone else, even his wife. Early in

1921 Eliot dined with the Woolfs in a London restaurant, and Virginia's note on the occasion catches something of the vulnerability that lay beneath his habitual manner:

Pale, marmoreal Eliot was there last week, like a chapped office boy on a high stool, with a cold in his head, until he warms a little, which he did. We walked back along the Strand. "The critics say I am learned and cold," he said. "The truth is I am neither." As he said this, I think coldness at least must be a sore point with him.

The impressions formed by Virginia Woolf, and Eliot's other acquaintances at that time, all suggest a sensibility that needed a protective armature of extreme formality in dress, speech, and manners, which became, in fact, an essential part of Eliot's public personality. And the extension of this personality into the cultural realm involved the large concepts of tradition, orthodoxy, and the "mind of Europe" which he employed as a critic. In this respect Eliot's Americanism was crucial. He wrote in *The Egoist* in 1918 in an essay called "In Memory of Henry James," "It is the final perfection, the consummation of an American to become, not an Englishman, but a European—something which no born European, no person of any European nationality, can become." The phrasing suggests that no matter how privileged such a position may be, there is something factitious about it. The corollary is that only an American could have written "Tradition and the Individual Talent," which projects a comprehensive notion of the European tradition that must inevitably seem somewhat remote to practicing writers in particular European countries. In any case, "Europe" was too narrow a concept to define the range of models available to poets in 1919, as Eliot, who had studied Indian poetry and knew Pound's versions from the Chinese, might have realized.

Nevertheless, Eliot's stress on the importance of the past was salutary in the immediate postwar period. It was a time when young writers were iconoclastically rejecting established cultural idols, and since they admired Eliot's seemingly revolutionary poetry they were also inclined to adopt his literary allegiances. As a result there was much talk in the nineteen-twenties about Dante and Donne and Baudelaire, and though this was often snobbish and uninformed, it was preferable to a blanket rejection of the past.

There was, however, a more existential sense in which Eliot needed the idea of tradition. As I have said, he regarded poetic creation as a possibly dangerous and even sacrificial surrender to unknown forces. Thus described, Eliot's poetic seems unexpectedly romantic; yet it is to be sharply distinguished from what he would have regarded as the egoism and delinquent romanticism of Rousseau or Lawrence. If their main concern was with self-expression, with rendering as faithfully as possible the pulsations of the ego, Eliot was dedicated to "the transformation of a personality into a personal work of art" and it was in the act of transformation that the sense of tradition was important. If one lacks this sense, as Blake did, for all his integrity, then one will not be adequately safeguarded against subjective idiosyncrasy. The sense of tradition is a life line that keeps the poet in touch with order and reality while he is submerged in the dark waters of the creative imagination. As C. K. Stead puts it, "the saturation of the poet's sensibility in the vats of tradition and orthodoxy ensures a healthy 'embryo' and a healthy poem—something which no effort of the will can achieve." Originally the idea of "tradition" was a personal myth that had two functions for Eliot: to contain the irrationality that he knew lay at the heart of his own creative methods as a poet, and to offer him a sustaining frame of reference in his penetration of English literary culture. In practice, the dichotomy between the poet and the culture-critic is sometimes apparent in his early criticism. By degrees the idea of "tradition" ceased to have purely literary implications for Eliot; it became enlarged into "orthodoxy" and by the late twenties it had acquired very specific social and ideological overtones. The process culminates in *After Strange Gods* where Eliot separates the creative gifts of several eminent modern writers from the orthodoxy of their sensibility, and devotes himself to testing the latter and, for the most part, finding it wanting.

If Eliot's ultimate allegiance was to what he regarded as the European tradition, his particular attachment to the English tradition, both in life and in art, became by degrees more noticeable, in ways which inevitably reflected his American origins. For his first few years in England Eliot had looked at English life and letters with cool detachment, and a constant readiness to deflate absurdity. This is the tone of his contributions to *The Egoist*, and one can invoke his own words about Byron's *Don Juan:* "what Byron understands and dislikes about English society is very much what an intelligent foreigner in the same position would understand and dislike." Yet there were elements of vulnerability in Eliot's makeup that increasingly undercut his poised, ironic manner. Like other American expatriates before him, he had a somewhat excessive regard for the aristocracy, and a keen feeling for the niceties of English social gradation. He thoroughly assimilated a particular concept of the English tradition: his dress, speech, and manners were all impeccably English, though, if anything, excessive in their perfection. And before long, under the influence of such men as Charles Whibley, Eliot began to manifest a self-conscious toryism and a slightly absurd attachment to external aspects of English life. Richard Aldington recalls dining with Eliot and Whibley, who was a cranky Cambridge don and literary journalist, just after the death of the famous Liberal statesman and man of letters, Lord Morley, in 1923. Eliot and Whibley spent much of the meal scarifying Morley and denouncing the horrors of Whigs and Whiggism. Then Eliot, forgetting that he was still an alien, said something that went too far even for Whibley who, after a suitable pause, turned on Eliot with the words "There was one good thing about Morley—he always hated Americans." Later in the conversation Eliot said that in the next war he intended to join the British army and, in Aldington's words, "worked himself up almost to blood-heat in a fine frenzy of patriotism." After the meal Aldington was astonished to see Eliot raise his hat to the sentry outside Marlborough House, one of the royal residences in London.

There was, however, a quite different aspect of Eliot's literary personality, which was at least as important as his attachment to tradition. I am referring to his interest in primitive cultural forms, which gave his critical and poetic activity an anthropological as well as a literary dimension, and was directly related to his sense of the irrational and intuitive nature of the creative process. As I remarked earlier, Eliot, in his review of Wyndham Lewis's

Tarr in *The Egoist* in 1918, wrote, "The artist, I believe, is more *primitive*, as well as more civilized, than his contemporaries, his experience is deeper than civilization, and he only uses the phenomena of civilization in expressing it." And the following year, reviewing a book called *The Path of the Rainbow: An Anthology of Songs and Chants from the Indians of North America*, he wrote:

And as it is certain that some study of primitive man furthers our understanding of civilized man, so it is certain that primitive art and poetry help our understanding of civilized art and poetry. Primitive art and poetry can even, through the studies and experiments of the artist or poet revivify the contemporary activities.[1]

The truth of this had been demonstrated by Picasso and Stravinsky, and was to be shown by Eliot himself in the use he made in *The Waste Land* of the anthropological discoveries made by J. G. Frazer and Jessie L. Weston. All of this would, no doubt, have been unintelligible to a conventional defender of literary tradition like Irving Babbitt. So, too, one imagines, would Eliot's interest in other ways of escaping from too literary an understanding of culture. There is, for instance, his remark in "The Possibility of a Poetic Drama" that "our problem should be to take a form of entertainment, and subject it to the process which would leave it a form of art"; and his expressed desire for an uneducated audience. There was, too, his devotion to the music hall and the ballet, and his admiration for great entertainers like Mistinguette and Marie Lloyd. Although Eliot was to become, like Arnold, a public upholder of the ideal of minority culture, this did not affect his interest—intermittent and never consistently expressed though it may have been—in quite other kinds of cultural activity. In his later life he attempted to reconcile these interests in *Notes Towards the Definition of Culture*.

Eliot's love of the music hall is apparent in the "London Letters" that he contributed to *The Dial* in 1921 and 1922. Under the editorship of Scofield Thayer, whom Eliot had known at Milton and Harvard, this long-established monthly had become a brilliant vehicle for the postwar *avant-garde*, and it regularly

[1] *Athenaeum,* October 17, 1919.

included work by most of the distinguished writers of the modern movement, whether American, British, or European. In the April 1921 number Eliot deplores "English stupidity" and attacks an anthology of Georgian poetry in Arnoldian terms: "Culture is traditional and loves novelty; the General Reading Public knows no tradition, and loves staleness." But he found consolation in the excellent variety bill at the London Palladium, which featured Marie Lloyd, Little Tich, George Mozart, and Ernie Lotinga. Two months later he returns to the subject and praises the comic genius of performers like Nellie Wallace, Little Tich, and George Robey. Most interestingly he describes a revue comedienne called Ethel Levey in terms which directly recall such vital moments in the development of modernist aesthetics as Pater's description of the Mona Lisa, and Stephen Dedalus's reflections on the aloofness and impersonality of the artist:

She is the most aloof and impersonal of personalities: indifferent, rather than contemptuous, towards the audience; her appearance and movement are of an extremely modern type of beauty . . . she plays for herself rather than for the audience.

In 1913 Ethel Levey had been praised by another poet, Rupert Brooke. Eliot is writing in a tradition which had previously been exemplified by the poets of the nineties, who had also seen pure aesthetic significance in music-hall artists and ballet girls. Eliot wanted to capture for "serious" drama the stylized forms, the theatrical energy, and the large, unselfconscious audiences of the music hall; here, too, he had been anticipated by an earlier generation. In 1892 the poet John Gray had found the perfection of modern acting in the music-hall artist, and expressed the hope that "the Variety Stage of today is the embryo of a great theatre." In *The Use of Poetry and the Use of Criticism* Eliot remarked "From one point of view the poet aspires to the condition of the music-hall comedian."

At about this time, Eliot's thoughts turned again to the long poem that had been in his mind since 1919. In May 1921 he wrote to John Quinn about pressure of work at Lloyds Bank; it was his responsibility, he said, to deal with all debts and claims of the bank arising out of the peace treaties. Nevertheless, he added that he had "a long poem in mind and partly on paper which I am wishful to finish." The chance to finish it came later in the year, in a somewhat unexpected fashion. Meantime he continued to frequent theaters, with his own dramatic aspirations consciously in mind; in August he wrote of Diaghilev: "the ballet will probably be one of the influences forming a new drama, if a new drama ever comes . . . what is needed of art is a simplification of current life into something rich and strange." For Eliot, the music hall, the modern ballet, and the comedy of Ben Jonson all offered possible modes of such simplification, and an escape from the stultifying conventions of the contemporary realistic theater. In the October issue of *The Dial* he gave his impressions of Stravinsky's *Sacre du Printemps.* He approved of the music, but found the underlying myth too simple, no more than "a pageant of primitive culture":

It was interesting to anyone who had read *The Golden Bough,* but hardly more than interesting. In art there should be interpenetration and metamorphosis. Even *The Golden Bough* can be read in two ways: as a collection of entertaining myths, or as a revelation of that vanished mind of which our mind is a continuation.

Eliot's connection with *The Dial* had given him the conviction that some comparable periodical was needed in England, and there was even a suggestion that *The Dial* would publish a British edition, of which Eliot would be editor. Lady Rothermere, the wife of a newspaper magnate, was known to be a possible backer, and Eliot was introduced to her by Sidney Schiff, an active middleman of the arts, who earlier in the same year had arranged an embarrassingly unproductive meeting between Joyce and Proust. (As Stephen Hudson, Schiff wrote a number of admirable though now neglected novels.) But before the scheme could get under way, Eliot's health, under strain during so many years of overwork, gave way. On October 13, 1921, Vivien Eliot told Scofield Thayer, "Tom had to stop all work and go away for three months."

2

After three weeks at the Albemarle Hotel in Margate, Eliot went to a sanatorium at Lausanne, and this enforced rest gave him the opportunity to finish the poem that he had been attempting to write for so long. There are hints of his sojourn in these resorts in the completed work—"By the waters of Leman I sat down and wept" and "On Margate Sands / I can connect / Nothing with nothing"—and Eliot may have been alluding to its composition when he wrote in *The Use of Poetry and the Use of Criticism:*

I know, for instance, that some forms of ill-health, debility or anaemia, may (if other circumstances are favourable) produce an efflux of poetry in a way approaching the condition of automatic writing—though, in contrast to the claims sometimes made for the latter, the material has obviously been incubating within the poet, and cannot be suspected of being a present from a friendly or impertinent demon.

In December 1921 Eliot visited Paris and presented Ezra Pound with the manuscript draft of *The Waste Land,* which Eliot regarded then, and for some time afterward, as a series of poems rather than a single unified work. Pound at once recognized it as a work of genius, but decided it needed editing and suggested to Eliot a number of cuts and revisions, most of which were gratefully accepted: he later remarked that Pound's editing turned *The Waste Land* "from a jumble of good and bad passages into a poem." The extent of Pound's emendations was a matter for critical speculation for many years; however, the original manuscript of *The Waste Land* turned up in 1968 and is now available in a facsimile edition. Soon after his return to London in January 1922 Eliot wrote to Scofield Thayer, offering him the poem for *The Dial,* where it appeared in the November issue; it was published simultaneously in the first number of *The Criterion,* the literary magazine edited by Eliot and financed by Lady Rothermere, which had been projected in 1921, and finally launched in the autumn of 1922. Eliot also received *The Dial's* annual award of $2,000, which he accepted gratefully though with some reluctance, as he felt Pound was a more deserving recipient; Pound did get an award in the end, but not for another five years.

On December 15, 1922 *The Waste Land* was published in book form by Boni & Liveright of New York, and for this edition the celebrated notes were added at the end of the poem. Here is Eliot's account of them:

I had at first intended only to put down all the references for my quotations, with a view to spiking the guns of critics of my earlier poems who had accused me of plagiarism. Then, when it came to print *The Waste Land* as a little book—for the poem on its first appearance in *The Dial* and in *The Criterion* had no notes whatever—it was discovered that the poem was inconveniently short, so I set to work to expand the notes, in order to provide a few more pages of printed matter, with the result that they became the remarkable exposition of bogus scholarship that is still on view today.[2]

The first British edition of the poem came out in September 1923; it was printed by the Woolfs at the Hogarth Press, not without a quantity of misprints. Some reviewers of *The Waste Land* regarded it as a hoax, but there were others who responded positively, like Edmund Wilson, Conrad Aiken, and Gilbert Seldes. The anonymous reviewer in the *Times Literary Supplement* was sympathetically responsive to some aspects of the poem, though his final judgment was unfavorable; he perceptively noticed the importance of the line "These fragments I have shored against my ruins" in shedding light on what has gone before. But as Edmund Wilson wrote in *Axel's Castle*, "where some of even the finest intelligences of the elder generation read *The Waste Land* with blankness or laughter, the young had recognised a poet." In 1928 E. M. Forster echoed this judgment, remarking on Eliot's influence on readers aged between eighteen and thirty: "Mr. Eliot's work, particularly *The Waste Land*, has made a profound impression on them, and given them precisely the food they needed ... He is the most important author of their day."

One thinks of Evelyn Waugh's Anthony Blanche, as an exquisitely aesthetic undergraduate at Oxford, standing on a balcony and reciting passages from *The Waste Land* "to the sweatered and muffled throng that was on its way to the river." The poet James Reeves, who attended Cambridge in the late twenties, recalls being handed Eliot's *Poems 1909–1925* and *The Sacred Wood*, rather as a stranger entering an Anglican service is handed *Hymns Ancient and Modern* and *The Book of Common Prayer:* "those who played the part of sidesmen were not, it should per-

[2] *On Poetry and Poets* (New York: Farrar, Straus & Giroux, 1957; London: Faber & Faber, 1957), p. 109.

haps be said, my tutors but my fellow-undergraduates." At Cambridge some members of the recently founded English faculty were devoted admirers of Eliot's poetry, particularly I. A. Richards, who had been enraptured by *Ara Vos Prec* and on the strength of it had tried unsuccessfully to get Eliot to come to Cambridge as a teacher. Richards made enthusiastic references to Eliot in his *Science and Poetry* and in the second edition of *Principles of Literary Criticism,* and a more extended Cambridge tribute to Eliot came in the early thirties in Leavis's *New Bearings in English Poetry.* Eliot delivered the Clark lectures at Cambridge in 1926. This Cambridge connection provided a new and potent means of extending Eliot's reputation and influence, supplementing his existing associations with the Anglo-American *avant-garde* and the Bloomsbury group.

In January 1922 Eliot went back to work at Lloyds Bank, though by no means fully restored to health, and Pound tried to revive the scheme, outlined to John Quinn two years before, of establishing a fund that would enable Eliot to be liberated from his work at the bank. Plans were drawn up for the fund which was known as *Bel Esprit,* and a circular printed by John Rodker which opened:

In order that T. S. Eliot may leave his work at Lloyd's Bank and devote his whole time to literature, we are raising a fund, to be £300 annually; this being in our opinion the minimum possible for this purpose. Method, £10, Fifty dollars . . . payable yearly by 300 subscribers.

The sponsors of the fund were Pound, Richard Aldington, and May Sinclair; a public advertisement appeared in the *New Age* on March 30, though it was couched in general terms and did not mention Eliot as the intended beneficiary. Pound's scheme showed all his characteristic loyalty and generosity, and it attracted a fair measure of support: John Quinn, a firm admirer of Eliot's, pledged himself to contribute $300. Nevertheless, *Bel Esprit* also showed Pound's impracticality, for Eliot had not been consulted and when he heard about the scheme he was not at all enthusiastic; he regarded Pound's plan, however nobly intended, as "bordering on the precarious and slightly undignified charity." His job at the bank brought him, by that time, £600 per annum and offered complete security and this, in view of his wife's worsening health and his own indifferent physical condition, was not something he could lightly abandon. Pound persisted with *Bel Esprit* for several more months, but in the end came to realize that although some funds were available, the pledges for the future were insufficient and that in the face of Eliot's opposition the scheme would have to be dropped. A committee had been set up in England to launch an appeal for the fund there, formed by Richard Aldington and some of the Bloomsbury circle; Lytton Strachey promised to contribute £100, and went on to parody their circular in a letter to Leonard and Virginia Woolf:

It has been known for some time to Mr. Lytton Strachey's friends that his income is in excess of his expenditure, and that he has a large balance at the bank. It is impossible, if his royalties continue to accumulate at the present rate, that he should be in a position to spend them entirely upon himself, without serious injury to his reputation among his more impecunious acquaintances.[3]

Meanwhile Eliot was engaged in preparing the first issue of *The Criterion,* which he intended to be a living embodiment of the "mind of Europe," and a fitting rival to *The Dial* and the *Nouvelle Revue Française. The Criterion* lasted for seventeen years, for most of that time as a quarterly, though briefly as a monthly, and at the end of its life Eliot could take pride in the range and quality of its contributors. During the twenties *The Criterion* provided the first English publication of such distinguished European figures as Marcel Proust, Paul Valéry, Jacques Rivière, Jean Cocteau, Ramon Fernandez, Jacques Maritain, Charles Maurras, Henri Massis, Wilhelm Worringer, Max Scheler, and E. R. Curtius. At the same time it published work by many celebrated British authors: Lawrence, Joyce, Huxley, Forster, Virginia Woolf, Wyndham Lewis, and Eliot himself, to which names were added, in the thirties, those of Auden and Spender.

Despite Eliot's dedication to the idea of a great European review, the assiduousness with which he kept the magazine in

---

[3] Michael Holroyd, *Lytton Strachey* (New York: Henry Holt & Co.; London: William Heinemann, 1968), vol. II, p. 365.

being for so many years, and the distinguished galaxy of its contributors, *The Criterion* was always something less than a living cultural force. One problem may have been that Eliot—so conscious of the nature of the audience in his writings about drama —seems to have had little sense of the potential readership of *The Criterion;* its price was high and its circulation low, even for an avowedly minority publication. Eliot seems never wholly to have freed himself of the coterie spirit that he had picked up as assistant editor of *The Egoist.* F. R. Leavis has commented harshly but with some accuracy:

It seems to me that there was nothing more adequate behind *The Criterion* than the general idea of a great European review; the idea as it might have been formed in (say) Irving Babbitt's lecture room. What Eliot learnt from Ezra Pound or Wyndham Lewis or the social-literary world in which he formed his notion of England didn't help him to anything better.[4]

Undeniably *The Criterion,* despite the excellence of so many of its contributions, conveyed an attitude to high culture that, no matter how reverential, was also external and compilatory. There is an inevitable contrast to be made with Leavis's own review, *Scrutiny.* (Leavis shared the editorial responsibilities with a number of like-minded colleagues, but there can be no doubt that he was the moving spirit behind the magazine during its twenty-one years of life.) *Scrutiny* was founded at Cambridge in 1932, partly in a spirit of dissatisfaction with the way in which *The Criterion* had developed. From the beginning it was directed at a wide but identifiable audience, namely, those who were engaged in the study and teaching of English in universities, colleges of education, and schools. And it was occupied with a recognizable set of issues: the way in which the academic study of English literature and the practice of criticism interpenetrated with the realities of mass culture and industrial civilization. Its conviction of the humane relevance of English was at the heart of the *Scrutiny* approach, and, in the earlier days of the review's life, provided a center from which to engage with other literatures and

[4] *Anna Karenina and Other Essays* (London: Chatto & Windus, 1967; New York: Pantheon, 1968), p. 194.

other disciplines. The narrowness and dogmatism of *Scrutiny* in its later years are, of course, notorious, and its influence was sometimes pernicious; nevertheless, it did have an influence throughout the English-speaking world and one which is still evident, nearly twenty years after the magazine ceased publication. To this extent it succeeded while *The Criterion* remained infertile.

In the thirties *The Criterion* had increasing difficulty in remaining true to its own ideals: the European community of letters, which had seemed a reality in the twenties, was disintegrating in the face of rival totalitarianisms and the growing threat of war. And as John Peter has shown, the review was curiously divided between Eliot's own religious preoccupations, which invited a growing list of clerical contributors, and his sponsoring of the admired young writers of the left. He tended to regard communism as a very respectable opponent, a worthy rival religion to Christianity: such an attitude may have been intellectually valid, but in terms of the political debates and passions of the thirties it must have seemed unreal, and the resulting bifurcation was very damaging to *The Criterion*.

On the whole, I suggest, Eliot's long association with the review did him personally more harm than good, despite its real achievement in introducing new forms of literature and thought to a select English public. After he became editor of *The Criterion*, Eliot ceased to be the clear-sighted, iconoclastic outsider who had contributed to *The Egoist* and the *Athenaeum* and had published *The Sacred Wood*. In this new role he became institutionalized, and a part of the English literary establishment that he had previously spent much time in attacking. And because of the conscious importance of the journal, Eliot seems to have felt an increasing sense of personal responsibility for the "mind of Europe." In his theater chronicle in the third issue of *The Criterion* (April 1923) Eliot could still reveal his customary *esprit:*

If there must be telephoning on the stage, Lucien and Sacha Guitry know how to do it better than anybody, and they are only in London for a short season now and then; but the spectacle of Sir Seymour Hicks telephoning for months on end is enough to discredit the use of that instrument altogether.

And later in the same piece he reveals the same deeply personal aesthetic interests that had marked his earlier writings about the modern theater; he remarks that the dancer Leonide Massine "seems to me the greatest actor we have in London . . . Massine, the most completely unhuman, impersonal, abstract, belongs to the future stage." Whether or not Eliot was right about Massine, in such remarks he is speaking from his own central interests as an artist. But his role with *The Criterion* gave increasing encouragement to the culture-critic and public commentator, who felt impelled to adopt a heavily judicious manner, and the quality of his writing suffered accordingly. The process culminated in the deeply uneasy and obscure commentaries of the thirties, which contain some of the worst prose that Eliot ever committed to print.

By the mid-twenties Eliot's literary attachment to tradition was becoming modified by his need to see it in more extensively ideological terms. The influence of Charles Maurras—first encountered during his stay in Paris in 1910–1911—and other intellectuals of the French right, was thrusting him toward a cultural and political stance akin to theirs, and led him to adopt for a while the absurd intellectual red herring of "classicism," which did him no good as poet or critic, and merely brought him into bad company. In *The Criterion* for October 1923 Eliot was arguing, in Maurrasian terms, for the supreme importance of Mediterranean civilization, and even claimed that "England is a 'Latin' country." The posthumous publication of T. E. Hulme's *Speculations* in 1924 seems to have given Eliot a further thrust toward "classicism," though he recognized that compared with Charles Maurras, Albert Sorel, and Pierre Lasserre, "Hulme is immature and unsubstantial." Nevertheless, "Hulme is classical, reactionary and revolutionary; he is the antipodes of the eclectic, tolerant, and democratic mind of the end of the last century." In his essay, "The Idea of a Literary Review" (*The Criterion*, January 1926) Eliot disowns a purely "literary" approach to literature: "Even the purest literature is alimented from non-literary sources, and has non-literary consequences." A Marxist would readily agree with such a formulation, and it marks Eliot's growing divergence from Pound, who represented a modernist continuation of the pure aestheticism of the nineties. Nevertheless, for Eliot the ex-traliterary context was not to be found in social or economic factors, but in the ideology of a reactionary classicism. *The Criterion* would not adopt anything so specific as a program or plat-form, but it would manifest a "tendency," and what this tendency was might be discovered in such works as Georges Sorel's *Réflexions sur la violence;* Maurras's *L'Avenir de l'intelligence;* Julien Benda's *Belphégor;* Hulme's *Speculations;* Jacques Mari-tain's *Réflexions sur l'intelligence;* and Irving Babbitt's *Democracy and Leadership.* Significantly enough, this "tendency" did not prevent *The Criterion* from publishing work by committed Marxists a few years later. When he made this formulation, Eliot's perennial search for a sense of cultural identity, and his growing desire to see the mind of Europe as something more than a mere literary community, was forcing him into a quagmire of exotic and potentially sinister intellectual influences, from which he was happy to escape before long into the more temperate embraces of the Anglican church.

In 1924 and 1925 Eliot's public life, as represented by the edit-ing of *The Criterion,* and his private life, in the person of Vivien Eliot, became for a time curiously intertwined. Her health had been bad for several years, and in October 1923 Eliot told Ber-trand Russell, "Vivien has had a frightful illness, and nearly died, in the spring," adding that she had been living in the country ever since. But in April 1925 another letter to Russell hints at an es-trangement due to more than mere physical causes: "everything has turned out as you predicted 10 years ago. You are a great psychologist." And a third letter, written a few weeks later, says that Vivien's health was worse than before, and "the fact that liv-ing with me has done her so much damage does not help me to come to any decision." Vivien, he said, was perpetually baffling and deceptive; she seemed like a child of six with an immensely clever and precocious mind. And, "She writes *extremely* well (stories, etc.) and great originality." From the tone of this letter it seems that Eliot was contemplating a separation from his wife, though he did not in fact take this step for several more years. Whatever the deeper implications of the turn Eliot's marriage had taken, he printed a considerable number of Vivien's literary compositions in *The Criterion.* These were short stories or brief prose sketches, and one poem, and they appeared under a variety of pseudonyms: Fanny Marlow, Feiron Morris, Felix Morrison, and the initials F. M. One story, "On the Eve" (January 1925), though composed by Vivien was actually signed by Eliot. Another piece, "Letters of the Moment II" (February 1924), includes twenty lines of verse in couplets which were part of the original opening of section III of *The Waste Land,* removed at Pound's suggestion. Vivien Eliot's stories are lightly written little accounts of random encounters, on the Left Bank in Paris, or in a nightclub or *thé dansant* in London, and several of them feature two girls called Felice and Sibylla. They do not indicate, as Eliot fondly told Russell, that "she writes *extremely* well," though they do show a degree of imitative literary competence, of the kind that might well produce acceptable commercial fiction. Yet, for whatever reason, Eliot was publishing these extremely slight pieces in his great European review, placing two or even three in each issue, in a way that one can only regard as both touching and disconcerting. But after July 1925 no more appeared.

Given Eliot's own constant state of overwork and his generally poor health, not to mention his marital difficulties, taking on *The Criterion* was, in commonsense terms, foolhardy: he was not paid for the work, which had to be carried on in his limited spare time after his work at Lloyds Bank. And indeed, in 1923 he wrote to John Quinn bitterly regretting that he had ever accepted the editorship:

In order to carry on the Criterion I have had to neglect not only the writing I ought to be doing but my private affairs of every description which for some time past I have not had a moment to deal with. I have not even time to go to a dentist or to have my hair cut . . . I am worn out. I cannot go on.[5]

As I have suggested, it might have been all to the good if Eliot could have given up *The Criterion,* but in fact he came to feel an increasingly deep commitment to the review. After the collapse of the *Bel Esprit* project Eliot was suggested as a possible literary editor for the *Nation and Athenaeum,* and on February

[5] *Atlantic Monthly,* January 1970.

23, 1923, Virginia Woolf wrote to Lytton Strachey asking for his assistance:

In fact, the poor man is becoming (in his highly American way, which is tedious and longwinded to a degree) desperate. I think he will be forced to leave the Bank anyhow. So if you would write me a line giving some sort of promise that you would write, or at least be more inclined to write for him than another we should all be very grateful.[6]

Nothing came of this scheme either and Eliot stayed at the bank, although by now he was freely admitting his ultimate intention of moving when a suitable opportunity arose; as he told John Quinn the main problem was, as always, providing security for his wife. In September 1924, after a meeting with Eliot at the Reform Club, Arnold Bennett noted in his journal: "He works at Lloyds Bank, in a department of his own, 'digesting' foreign financial and economic journals. Interesting work, he said, but he would prefer to be doing something else." At length, however, Eliot found a suitable alternative. In 1925 he finally left the bank and joined the newly formed publishing house of Faber and Gwyer (later to become Faber and Faber), where he remained for the rest of his life. One of his colleagues at Faber, F. V. Morley, has suggested that Eliot was taken on less for his literary eminence than for his banking experience:

He was a gentleman; he was literate; he was patient; he got on well with difficult people; he had charm; and, he had been in the City. He had good qualifications for a man of business, and it was as a man of business, I suggest, that he was taken on.[7]

In 1926 Faber took over the financial responsibility for *The Criterion* in place of Lady Rothermere, who had given up her support, and remained its publishers until 1939.

In October 1924 the Hogarth Press published as part of the Hogarth Essays series a predictably slim volume by Eliot called *Homage to John Dryden*, with the subtitle "Three Essays on Poetry of the Seventeenth Century": the essays in question, "John

[6] Holroyd, *Lytton Strachey*, vol. II, p. 369.
[7] Richard March and Tambimuttu, eds., *T. S. Eliot: A Symposium* (London: Poetry London, 1948; Chicago: Henry Regnery Co., 1949), p. 20.

Dryden," "The Metaphysical Poets," and "Andrew Marvell," had first appeared in the *Times Literary Supplement* in 1921. This unpretentious booklet was to continue, and perhaps complete, the revolution in critical taste that Eliot had begun with *The Sacred Wood*. In Leavis's words:

It was the impact of this slender new collection that sent one back to *The Sacred Wood* and confirmed with decisive practical effect one's sense of the stimulus to be got from that rare thing, a fine intelligence in literary criticism—the fine intelligence so certainly present in the earlier and larger collection.[8]

The critical intelligence is still impressive, after half a century, and these three essays are not in any fundamental sense dated. Although there is a good deal more to be said about seventeenth-century poetry than Eliot contrived to say, what he did say remains central, however much it needs to be supplemented and qualified. Certainly, Rosamund Tuve and other scholars have undermined his assumption that the conceits of the Metaphysical poets are an anticipation of the juxtapositions and discontinuities of the Symbolists. And Frank Kermode has been sharply dismissive of the famous central argument of "The Metaphysical Poets": "In the seventeenth century a dissociation of sensibility set in from which we have never recovered . . ." In this form it was, of course, a vulnerable dictum, and Eliot could not have foreseen in 1921 what large critical edifices were to be erected on it, any more than he anticipated, two years before, the ramifying consequences of "Tradition and the Individual Talent." The phrase "dissociation of sensibility" is itself adapted from Gourmont's essay on Laforgue; and although it has outlived its usefulness in that form, Eliot's remarks did, I think, direct attention toward the remarkable transformation in cultural attitudes that took place in the middle of the seventeenth century; as shown, for instance, by the rapid change in English prose style (earlier discussed by Arnold in "The Study of Poetry"). For one reader at least, thought and feeling *are* combined in seventeenth-century poetry in a way that is not the case in nineteenth-century poetry, though to say this much does not necessarily entail the evaluations that

[8] *Anna Karenina and Other Essays*, p. 178.

Eliot puts forward, and which were systematized by F. R. Leavis in *Revaluation,* a book which is largely an expansion of hints offered in Eliot's essays on Marvell and the Metaphysical poets. The Dryden essay contains some excellent criticism, particularly in its account of Dryden's "poetry of statement," but accords a little oddly with the other two, for in "The Metaphysical Poets" Dryden is referred to as one of the two powerful poets—the other is Milton—who had "aggravated" the dissociation of sensibility. And at the end of the essay on Dryden, which is full of the highest praise, Eliot abruptly changes gear and announces that Dryden nevertheless had "a commonplace mind" and that "he lacked insight, he lacked profundity." As in Eliot's earlier essay on Ben Jonson, whom he calls Dryden's master, there is a palpable division between his admiration for a poetry of the surface and of strong, lucid statement, and his conviction that the real business of poetry involves an awareness of the depths of feeling, and of the associative and tentacular resources of language. And these qualities are to be found in the Metaphysical poets rather than in Dryden. If by 1924 Eliot felt the need to emphasize his admiration for Dryden, even to the extent of calling his book *Homage to John Dryden,* it may have been in the first flush of his conversion to "classicism."

These three essays are still of the highest interest to readers of seventeenth-century poetry; as I have said, they were astonishingly influential, considering their brevity, and their implications have been drawn out at length by the Scrutineers in England and the New Critics in America. Yet the essays on Marvell and the Metaphysicals, at least, are also very much what Eliot called "workshop criticism," and they directly relate to his own interests and aspirations as a poet. Significantly, "The Metaphysical Poets" was first published at the time of the breakdown in health that enabled Eliot to begin work seriously on *The Waste Land.* It is fruitless to look in Eliot's own poetry for direct traces of the influence of Donne or Marvell, as critics were once disposed to do; yet when he writes, in contradiction of Dr. Johnson's disparaging remarks about the Metaphysicals, that "a degree of heterogeneity of material compelled into unity by the operation of the poet's mind is omnipresent in poetry," he is clearly stating the basic assumption of *The Waste Land*. The poet's mind possesses a mysterious unifying force, just as, in the visual arts, a master of *collage* can fuse paint, canvas, and a variety of random objects into an aesthetic unity. Later in the essay Eliot expands the point in these famous sentences:

When a poet's mind is perfectly equipped for its work, it is constantly amalgamating disparate experience; the ordinary man's experience is chaotic, irregular, fragmentary. The latter falls in love, or reads Spinoza, and these two experiences have nothing to do with each other, or with the noise of the typewriter or the smell of cooking; in the mind of the poet these experiences are always forming new wholes.

And because of the immense variety and complexity of experience in the modern world, "it appears likely that poets in our civilization, as it exists at present, must be *difficult*."

In the years following the completion of *The Waste Land* Eliot had little time to write more poetry, but in 1924 and 1925 a number of separate poems appeared in *Commerce* (Paris), *The Chapbook, The Criterion,* and *The Dial,* which were finally assembled into "The Hollow Men," first published in that form in Eliot's *Poems 1909–1925.* And in 1926 and 1927 *The Criterion* printed "Fragment of a Prologue" and "Fragment of an Agon," Eliot's first recorded attempts at dramatic writing; they were eventually brought together as *Sweeney Agonistes* in 1932. Since "The Hollow Men" and the two "Fragments" directly relate to *The Waste Land* I shall discuss them together in the next section of this chapter.

3

It is a daunting thought that throughout the twenty-four hours of the day a lecture or seminar on *The Waste Land* is likely to be proceeding somewhere in the English-speaking world, and probably in other parts of the globe as well. Eliot was never enthusiastic about English literature as a university subject, and positively disapproved of the academic study of modern literature; despite his inclinations his poetry, and *The Waste Land* above all, has become an object of study and has generated a wealth of guides, commentaries, and other works destined to make the poetry more accessible to the student. The result has been that many academically trained readers can, in one sense, understand *The Waste Land* very well, and can talk persuasively about fertility myths and the sterility of the modern world, the roles of the Hyacinth Girl and the Fisher King, Mr. Eugenides and the young man carbuncular, and can efficiently unravel the allusions and quotations: Cleopatra, and Mrs. Porter and her daughter, and Arnaut Daniel, all falling neatly into place. And yet the same readers may, in another sense, have never grasped the poem at all, not even to the extent of reading it aloud. They have not been disturbed by it or surrendered with it to the deepest terrors and desires. In 1918 Eliot wrote in *The Egoist* of *Ulysses* and *Tarr*:

Both are terrifying. That is the test of a new work of art. When a work of art no longer terrifies us we may know that we were mistaken, or that our senses are dulled: we ought still to find *Othello* or *Lear* frightful.

This, of course, is not the classicizing Eliot of *The Criterion;* it is the voice of the practicing poet rather than the culture-critic, and Eliot's words are intensely relevant to *The Waste Land.* Speaking as a teacher, I prefer the honest response of the student who is genuinely baffled by the poem and yet senses it has something to say to him, to the skill of the cryptographer who can decode the poem while remaining quite unmoved by it.

What a truly personal response to *The Waste Land* might be like has been described by Ralph Ellison, who discovered the poem in the nineteen-thirties while a student at a Negro university:

The Waste Land seized my mind. I was intrigued by its power to move me while eluding my understanding. Somehow its rhythms were often closer to those of jazz than were those of the Negro poets, and even though I could not understand then, its range of allusion was as mixed and as varied as that of Louis Armstrong. Yet there were its discontinuities, its changes of pace and its hidden system of organization which escaped me.

There was nothing to do but look up the references in the footnotes to the poem, and thus began my conscious education in literature.[9]

[9] *Shadow and Act* (New York: Random House, 1964; London: Martin Secker & Warburg Ltd., 1967), pp. 159–60.

One imagines that Eliot, who said that poetry began with a savage beating a drum in a jungle, would have approved the comparison with jazz rhythms. In allowing the poem first to work upon him in this way, and only afterward looking up the allusions, Ellison showed a sure sense of the right way to read it.

The commentaries are, of course, useful in directing and informing the reading of the poem at a secondary stage, but it is doubtful whether we need many more of them. We need, rather, to encourage new readers to rest patiently for a while in their sense of confusion and bafflement, and to let the poem possess them gradually. In this process reading it aloud can be of immense value. One needs too, not more and more analysis and documentation of particular passages, but some approximate sense of what the poem as a whole is. I shall, therefore, offer a series of suggestions about ways of looking at it. In the first place, it is a *musical* poem in its organization, like "Portrait of a Lady," "Prufrock," and "Gerontion." That is to say, themes and motifs flow together and recur as they might in a work of late-romantic music, with a powerful emotional impact but with no regular or predictable structural elements. Intimately related to this aspect of *The Waste Land* is its quality as a *symbolist* poem, where there is much suggestion and implication, and many hints of possible burgeonings of meaning, but where nothing is stated with absolute finality, and where the reader finds himself as much involved in the poem as the poet. These two aspects of the poem taken together might make it seem excessively vague and invertebrate, and against this possibility one can set another aspect of *The Waste Land,* namely its quality as a *cubist* poem. Writing in *The Dial* in August 1921 Eliot remarked, "cubism is not licence, but an attempt to establish order." To achieve this order, Eliot breaks traditional poetic perspectives, juxtaposing elements from past and present, the mythic and the realistic, and making deliberate contrasts of language and poetic texture. The visual sharpness that results—certainly owing a good deal in its particular detail to the clear images of Dante—provides the necessary complement to the flowing and dissolving quality of its musical organization. (The combination of these two elements can also be called cinematic, and the point has been often made about the poem.) And finally, *The Waste Land* is, in its expression if not in its overall structure, a *dramatic* poem. Much of the speech echoes Eliot's interest in Elizabethan and Jacobean drama, and the words of the neurotic woman in part II—"My nerves are bad to-night. Yes, bad. Stay with me"—have a dramatic energy and flexibility that eluded Eliot when he began writing for the stage. But as we have seen, "the theater" was for Eliot in 1921 in large measure the music hall and the modern ballet. The Hyacinth Girl and Madame Sosostris and Mr. Eugenides have something of the sharpness of outline of figures in a modern ballet, while in my reading the typist and the small house agent's clerk enact a complete post-Diaghilev ballet. And the conversation of the Cockney women in part II is essentially in the spirit of a great music-hall artiste like Marie Lloyd. I shall enlarge on these points subsequently.

Eliot's lecture of 1953, "The Three Voices of Poetry," says much that is helpful in understanding the dramatic elements in *The Waste Land*. In his distinction, the three voices are: first, the poet speaking to himself, or to no one; the poet speaking to a particular audience; and the poet speaking through the voice of an invented, usually dramatic, character. Much of *The Waste Land*, I believe, consists of fragmentary dramatic monologues by a series of shifting, dissolving "voices," in a direct development from the manner of "Prufrock." (I find wholly misleading the assumption, based on Eliot's notes, that the whole poem is the first-person utterance of Tiresias.) And at the same time, through these voices can be heard Eliot himself speaking in the first voice, which utters lyric or meditative poetry arising directly from an obscure creative impulse:

In a poem which is neither didactic nor narrative, and not animated by any other social purpose, the poet may be concerned solely with expressing in verse—using all his resources of words, with their history, their connotations, their music—this obscure impulse. He does not know what he has to say until he has said it; and in the effort to say it he is not concerned with making other people understand anything.

More than one of the three voices can coexist in the same poem, and as Eliot shows, even in full-scale poetic drama there are times when an author seems to be speaking through his character's voice: *"Tomorrow and tomorrow and tomorrow . . .* Is not the perpetual shock and surprise of these hackneyed lines evidence that Shakespeare and Macbeth are uttering the words in unison, though perhaps with somewhat different meaning?" This, I think, is true of much of *The Waste Land;* in part V the themes converge, and the first voice speaks more directly.

For a long time *The Waste Land* was seen as expressing the decay of European civilization after the First World War, or, more immediately, something loosely known as the "disillusionment of the twenties," and it was this aspect that attracted young readers, as Edmund Wilson and E. M. Forster have recorded. But Eliot, although not in principle given to interpreting his own works, has denied that *The Waste Land* expressed "the disillusionment of a generation": "I may have expressed for them their own illusion of being disillusioned, but that did not form part of my intention." After fifty years, it has become increasingly clear that the historical and cultural dimension of the poem does not lie at its center, but exists as an objective correlative for the underlying feelings, which are deeply if obscurely personal:

The only way of expressing emotion in the form of art is by finding an "objective correlative"; in other words, a set of objects, a situation, a chain of events which shall be the formula of that *particular* emotion; such that when the external facts, which must terminate in sensory experience, are given, the emotion is immediately evoked.

Because of the poem's inherently symbolist method, the emotion can be felt but not at all accurately described. Prominent in the cultural dimension are the anthropological elements that Eliot derived from his reading of Sir James Frazer's *Golden Bough*—an allusion to Frazer's work having already been made in the title of *The Sacred Wood*—particularly the sections on Adonis, Attis, and Osiris, and Jessie L. Weston's recently published *From Ritual to Romance.* This aspect of *The Waste Land* has been considerably—perhaps sufficiently—emphasized by the commentators, and G. S. Fraser has given a lucid summary of its essence:

It is possible to read *The Waste Land* and feel its impact without grasping the underlying theme of the barren land which can only be re-

claimed to fertility by a ritual sacrifice. This theme underlies the legend
of the Grail and it is behind the myths of Adonis and Osiris, the young
men or young gods, slain in the springtime, and mourned by those who
slew them. The sacrificial victim was a sacred king and the representative of a god; the fertility of the land was magically involved in his own
youth and strength; and so he had to be regularly sacrificed in case,
with his own old age and decay, the land should wither too. But the
Grail legend is Christian, though with pagan undertones, and the sick
king cannot be slain; he can be cured through the instruments of the
passion of the greatest of the sacrificial kings, who is Christ, as God
incarnate; and the barren land which has to be reclaimed to fertility is
the human heart, full of selfishness and lust.[10]

It is not, I think, altogether true to describe the ritual regenera-
tion of the barren land as "the underlying theme" of the poem.
Important though it is, I would prefer to describe it as a guide
that Eliot used in composing the poem, just as Joyce employed
the *Odyssey* as a scaffolding in writing *Ulysses*. The real underlying themes lie deeper.

Set against the mythic references—to which must be added
those to Indian religion, like the fable of the Thunder from the
Upanishads—are those to recent history and contemporary life,
and particularly the images of London. In part I a crowd of City
workers flows over London Bridge in a line adapted from Dante,
and in part V the bridge is falling down in the words of the old
nursery rhyme. Several of these references are specifically to the
City of London, where Eliot spent his working day: Queen Vic-
toria Street, Lower Thames Street, Cannon Street, and Moorgate,
at which underground station he arrived each morning (no doubt
traveling on the Metropolitan line from his flat near Baker Street);
and churches like St. Mary Woolnoth and St. Magnus Martyr,
whose possible disappearance he had lamented in 1921:

the loss of these towers, to meet the eye down a grimy lane, and
of these empty naves, to receive the solitary visitor at noon from the
dust and tumult of Lombard Street, will be irreparable.[11]

        [10] *The Modern Writer and His World* (Harmondsworth: Penguin Books,
1964; New York: Praeger, 1965), pp. 269–70.
        [11] *The Dial,* June 1921.

As is often remarked, past and present coexist in *The Waste Land,*
whether in the City churches, or in the many historical and literary allusions. Yet for the most part Eliot refrains from facilely
setting a glorious past against a sordid present. The river Thames
of Elizabeth and Leicester, and of Spenser's "Prothalamion,"
bears much the same load of human suffering as the Thames of
Conrad's *Heart of Darkness* and the three modern Thames-
daughters. Cultures interpenetrate as in "Tradition and the Individual Talent," and time—as in the thought of F. H. Bradley—
has little objective reality.

All these cultural references, so bewildering in their diversity
and range and juxtapositions, point beyond themselves to the true
underlying themes of the poem. And these can be stated quite
simply: sexual disorder; and the lack, and need, of religious belief.
I. A. Richards wrote in 1926 of Eliot's "persistent concern with
sex, the problem of our generation, as religion was the problem
of the last." Both problems dominate *The Waste Land,* though
for predictable reasons the sexual motif is the more often remarked. In part I, after the love song from *Tristan and Isolde,* the
lines addressed to the Hyacinth Girl recall a shared experience,
whose intensity can be conveyed, but which can be neither described nor explained. To this extent we are encountering the
symbolist method of *The Waste Land;* yet the firmly expressive
movement of the words themselves exemplifies the poem's dramatic quality. In the rest of the poem, the sexual encounters are all
in some way sterile or empty or loveless: Tereus and Philomel,
Belladonna and the women in the pub, and, by implication, the
Duke and Bianca in Middleton's *Women Beware Women;* the
typist and the young man carbuncular; Elizabeth and Leicester;
and the Thames-daughters. The sterility of the barren land, seen
anthropologically, points to the inadequacy of the sexual relations.
This aspect of the poem, certainly, has caused much unease; what
looks like its wholly negative view of sex is often found disturbing.
Eliot once told an audience, "I wrote *The Waste Land* simply to
relieve my own feelings," and there can be no doubt that when
he wrote the poem the feelings of sexual unhappiness which are
evident in his earlier poetry had reached a new intensity. One
need not probe the autobiographical causes: it is sufficient to

acknowledge the difficulties of his married life. The theme of
sterility might well have had a painful significance to one who
had been haunted since his own childhood by "the hidden
laughter of children," and whose own marriage was childless.

When I. A. Richards remarked approvingly in 1926 that *The
Waste Land* represented a severance between poetry and all beliefs he was interpreting it in the spirit of the time. But if *The
Waste Land* does not express any positive beliefs, it is at the same
time very concerned with the lack of them. In "Gerontion" Christ
is "the tiger," and in *The Waste Land* he is the ultimate embodiment of the ritual victim; he is identified with the Hanged Man of
the Tarot cards, and the Hanged God of Frazer; and the opening
of part V ("What the Thunder said") specifically refers to the
passion and death of Christ. At this time Eliot was still seeing
Christ in anthropological terms: the influence of Frazer combined
with his own Unitarian background may have made Christianity
still inaccessible as a focus for active belief. In *The Waste Land*
belief is directed toward Indian religion, the influence of which
persisted from Eliot's Sanskrit studies at Harvard. However much
the poem moves through a condition of despair it certainly does
not end on that note: the thrice-repeated word *shantih* which
ends the poem is, as Eliot points out in his note, the formal ending
to an Upanishad, and for an English equivalent he alludes to St.
Paul: "And the peace of God, which passeth all understanding,
shall keep your hearts and minds through Christ Jesus."

This movement toward a concluding benediction suggests that
those critics are wrong who have argued that there is no progres-
sion in *The Waste Land*. As I have already remarked, such a claim
is wholly true of "Prufrock," which seems to take place outside
time altogether. In *The Waste Land* although time may be in a
Bradleyan sense "unreal," and is certainly not the time of clocks
and calendars, there is some sense of forward movement, corresponding, in the myth of the barren land and the Grail legend,
to the journey of the Quester to the Chapel Perilous. In part V
several themes converge: the nightmare eroticism of "A woman
drew her long black hair out tight" and the longing for belief of
"the empty chapel, only the wind's home." This part of the poem
contains some of Eliot's finest poetry; it is where he is writing

with most personal intensity, and where, in his own formulation, the poet's "first voice" is dominant. He told Bertrand Russell in 1923, "It gives me very great pleasure to know that you like the *Waste Land,* and especially Part V which in my opinion is not only the best part, but the only part that justifies the whole, at all." And in part V *The Waste Land,* as a major work in the symbolist manner, becomes explicit about its own aims and procedures.

> I sat upon the shore
> Fishing, with the arid plain behind me
> Shall I at least set my lands in order?

The fisher is now sitting by the shore and so is at the edge of the sea, no longer, as in part III, fishing "in the dull canal"; the "arid plain" is behind him, having been successfully traversed. When he asks "Shall I at least set my lands in order?" we are conscious of the poet turning to find whatever kinds of order he can ("cubism is not licence, but an attempt to establish order") by writing his poem: the movement is essentially the same as that followed by Joyce at the end of *Portrait of the Artist,* and by Proust in the final volume of his *Recherche.* The note of calm completion is continued in "These fragments I have shored against my ruins," where the balance between the cultural *disjecta membra* of "these fragments" and the personal intensity of "my ruins" encapsulates the essential method of the poem.

Several critics have noticed the significance of the line from Kyd's *Spanish Tragedy* which comes at the end of the set of polyglottal quotations in the final paragraph: "Why then Ile fit you. Hieronymo's mad againe." In Kyd's tragedy Hieronymo agrees to write a revenge play ("Why then Ile fit you") but goes on, in a vivid enactment of cultural fragmentation,

> Each one of us
> Must act his part in unknown languages,
> That it may breed the more variety:
> As you, my lord, in Latin, I in Greek,
> You in Italian, and for because I know
> That Bellimperia hath practised the French,
> In courtly French shall all her phrases be.

The objection,

> But this will be a mere confusion,
> And hardly shall we all be understood,

is answered by Hieronymo in words with which Eliot must have identified himself:

> It must be so: for the conclusion
> Shall prove the invention and all was good.

A little earlier in part V, in the paragraph that begins with the Sanskrit word *Datta* ("give"), Eliot suggests his own involvement in the poem. The "moment's surrender" seems to be, at an initial reading, sexual. Yet it also refers, I believe, to Eliot's conviction that "the creation of a work of art is like some other forms of creation, a painful and unpleasant business; it is a sacrifice of the man to the work, it is a kind of death." The moment of creation, the sudden fruition of an impulse, which Eliot described in several places in his criticism, was of supreme importance, and took precedence over any secondary concern—necessary in its own way—with culture and tradition. The mention of "obituaries," "memories draped by the beneficent spider," "seals broken by the lean solicitor," emphasizes the dichotomy already present in the essay on Blake.

In the foregoing paragraphs I have not attempted a consistent commentary on the poem, but have merely suggested approaches to it, and offered a perspective in which the more detailed readings of other critics may be seen. I also want to acknowledge the critical difficulties that have been often raised in the half-century since *The Waste Land* first appeared. There is, for instance, the celebrated crux of "keep the Dog far hence." Many conflicting versions have been offered about the meaning of "the Dog," and I have no idea which, if any, is "right": I think it is a fault in the writing that this kind of ambiguity should have been placed at such a conspicuous point in the poem. But it is a local fault, and can be left as such. There are, however, larger objections to the poem: the question of its formal unity, for example, and the widely felt dislike of its supposed snobbery and lack of moral health. Critics have often asked whether *The Waste Land* is really a single poem or a set of poems, and what effect Pound's editing had on the original concept. Certainly, in the correspondence between Pound and Eliot *The Waste Land* is referred to as though it were a series of poems. I suggest that this particular difficulty can be disposed of if we say that *The Waste Land* was a set of poems that *turned into* a single poem when readers learned to recognize the way in which the separate sections interrelated, on the basis of the poet's underlying "ego rhythm." The point may be surprising, but in the light of our knowledge of the psychology of perception it need not be so: in the visual arts, at least, it is a commonplace that perception is learned and to a large extent culturally conditioned, and that what seems random and chaotic when first encountered can, with familiarity, be seen to have a striking degree of unity. Anton Ehrenzweig's *The Hidden Order of Art,* though not concerned with literature, is very helpful in understanding this aspect of *The Waste Land.*

Pound's editing seems to have increased the potentiality for unity in *The Waste Land* by streamlining it, and cutting out a great deal of material which, from what he could sense of Eliot's implied intention, might be jettisoned. Pound seems to have been responsible for some of the more startling juxtapositions and transitions, imposing on Eliot's poem the "ideogrammatic" method of his own *Cantos,* already in progress. He was also unsympathetic to Eliot's interest in the popular theater; the original opening of "The Burial of the Dead" had a strong flavor of the music hall, and although *The Waste Land* is better off without it, the lack of this passage makes it harder to respond appropriately to the only other remaining section in this manner, the pub conversation in the second part of "A Game of Chess." The one case where Pound's editing has certainly diminished the poem is his insistence that Eliot cut out a long section describing a shipwreck at the beginning of part IV; these excellent lines are somewhat inspired by Dante's account of the voyage of Ulysses and in Eliot's original version they balanced the remaining lines about Phlebas. In Donald Gallup's words there was "a highly effective contrast between contemporary New Englander and Ancient Phoenician, each victim of the eternal Sea." Had this passage been kept, the lines in part V, "The boat responded / Gaily to the

hand expert with sail and oar," would have had greater resonance.
A few phrases from these deleted lines found their way into later
poems like "Marina" and "The Dry Salvages." The manuscript of
the poem shows that Eliot did not accept all Pound's suggested
emendations; significantly, though, he wanted to remove the lines
about Phlebas after the preceding account of the shipwreck was
cut, but kept them in at Pound's insistence. All in all, Pound's
treatment of *The Waste Land* showed his intense feeling for
what Eliot was trying to do, and his intuitive response to what
Eliot called the poet's "auditory imagination." Without Pound's
attentions *The Waste Land* would still have been impressive, but
it would have appeared, and remained, much more clearly a group
of separate poems.

There remains the problem of Eliot's social and moral attitudes.
It is certainly true that Eliot was, in a loose sense, a "snob"; as his
old friend Brigit Patmore records in her autobiography, he had
a considerable weakness for upper-class society, and his own
rootless and isolated position in English society meant that large
areas of national life were closed to him. Yet snobbery—if by that
one means an adopting of supposedly aristocratic values and a
corresponding disdain for the masses—is a common disease of
poets: one need only think of Spenser, Baudelaire, and Yeats.
Any reader who insists that literature must be inspired by progressive social attitudes had better ignore poetry—as Sartre does
in *What Is Literature?*—and concentrate on fiction and drama.
In fact, Eliot's social animus was largely directed against the
middle classes, whom he castigated in Arnoldian terms for their
philistinism and complacency. His attitude to the working class,
though certainly ignorant and possibly patronizing, was distinctly admiring, as we see in his essay on Marie Lloyd; no one
who despised working-class values could have been such an
enthusiastic devotee of the music hall as Eliot. A consistent failure to realize this has, I think, resulted in a general misreading of
the pub scene in "A Game of Chess," which is often quoted as an
example of Eliot's crippling ignorance of popular life and speech.
Without doubt, the language would seem impossibly stilted if it
were meant to be naturalistic, but I suggest that it is, in fact,
theatrical speech and presented with just the right degree of

stylization. The setting is not a real pub, but a music-hall adaptation of one, with a comedienne of the Marie Lloyd type delivering a spirited monologue just before closing time. She refers to the bitter realities of the life of the urban poor that her audience will be only too familiar with—the attempted abortion and the young mother old before her time—though she preserves a savage sense of humor, and a feeling for the minor compensations of existence, like a hot gammon dinner. At the end of the monologue the drinkers' companionable "goodnights" merge gently into Hamlet's "Good night, ladies," words which are used as an echo rather than a sharply ironic contrast, as is usually argued.

Elsewhere in the poem, it is alleged, Eliot's snobbery merges with his negative sexual attitudes, notably in the account of the typist and the clerk. This episode, too, is fundamentally theatrical; the figures are not presented with very much individuality and their language and movements are extremely stylized, despite the naturalistic decor. One recent critic, Ian Hamilton, pressing hard on the unsatisfactoriness of Eliot's attitudes to sex, has complained of "the arms-length vocabulary which Eliot employs here: " 'endeavours,' 'encounters,' 'requires,' 'assaults,' and so on—this is refrigerating language, prissily dignified, fastidiously embarrassed." Mr. Hamilton's comment is remarkable in the extent of its misreading; the language may be, in a sense, "arms-length," in that it imposes a deliberate distancing on the scene. But such adverbs as "prissily" and "fastidiously" convey nothing of the superbly confident movement of the lines; this is, in fact, one of the most assured and energetic passages in the poem. The latinate verbs that Mr. Hamilton disapproves of convey a fine sense of controlled, stylized movement, which develops with all the vigorous formality of a modern ballet; the scene is unlovely, granted, but the language gives it a peculiar austere beauty.

Mr. Hamilton is basically objecting not so much to the particularity of this passage but to the underlying preoccupation which it expresses. As he correctly remarks, in The Waste Land sex "is seen throughout as a kind of enervated reflex, a set of tired, distracting compulsions whose servants would as soon be free." This is very true, and it is, after all, a traditional way of seeing sex, which has many facets, all of them representing some permanent aspect of the human condition. If a modern critic refuses to recognize the validity of exploring *this* particular aspect of sexuality, then it is because the pressures of our culture permit only the positive, life-giving sides of sex to be acknowledged. If Eliot, courageously trying to make order out of the compulsions of his own temperament and situation, explored the negative aspects he was doing what Shakespeare—in the Sonnets and *Troilus and Cressida*—or Baudelaire had done before him. Mr. Hamilton, like Yvor Winters in an earlier essay, complains that Eliot does not effectively judge his experiences. The answer is that he is too deeply involved in them for that, though longing for liberation and for the peace which he invokes at the end of the poem. If the modern consciousness wants to conclude that Eliot was "sick," there is no point in arguing against the charge: it could apply equally to another great writer, who was also immersed in deep psychic waters, and not conventionally on the side of "life." I am referring to Dostoyevsky, whom Eliot greatly admired, and who appears peripherally in *The Waste Land*, in the passage quoted in the notes from Hermann Hesse's *Blick ins Chaos*, with its reference to the hymns of Dimitri Karamazov. Some uncollected observations on Dostoyevsky by Eliot seem to me to shed much light on the deeper meanings of *The Waste Land:*

Dostoeivesky's point of departure is always a human brain in a human environment, and the "aura" is simply the continuation of the quotidian experience into seldom experienced extremities of torture. Because most people are too unconscious of their own suffering to suffer much, this continuation appears fantastic.[12]

My own view is that Dostoeivesky had the gift, a sign of genius in itself, for utilizing his weaknesses: so that epilepsy and hysteria cease to be the defects of an individual and become—as a fundamental weakness can, given the ability to face and study it—the entrance to a genuine and personal universe.[13]

One of the difficulties about *The Waste Land* lies in its extremity and atypicality: it is extreme in its psychic explorations, and in the symbolist obliquity of its organization, which aban-

---

[12] *Athenaeum,* May 30, 1919.
[13] *The Dial,* September 1922.

dons so many of the devices usually thought necessary to the composition of extended poems, and which has never been successfully imitated by a poet of comparable gifts, so that the poem has established no tradition that would modify our reading of it. The *Waste Land* is as isolated in its singularity as when it first appeared in *The Criterion* and *The Dial* in 1922. Despite its extremity it has become thoroughly institutionalized as an object of academic study, and a major monument of the modern movement, in a clear example of the paradox discussed by Lionel Trilling in *Beyond Culture*. Hence, no doubt, the increasing unease that many readers feel, and the growing tendency to critical sniping. And yet for anyone who discovered the poem in his teens as Ralph Ellison did, it is ineradicably *there* and a part of one's lived experience; in Frank Kermode's words: "to have Eliot's great poem in one's life involves an irrevocable but repeated act of love." Even for a teacher of literature it is indestructible; the commentaries wear out and become unusable but not the poem. As is so often the case, Eliot's own words provide the best conclusion; in *The Use of Poetry and the Use of Criticism* he writes:

What I call the "auditory imagination" is the feeling for syllable and rhythm, penetrating far below the conscious levels of thought and feeling, invigorating every word; sinking to the most primitive and forgotten, returning to the origin and bringing something back, seeking the beginning and the end. It works through meanings, certainly, or not without meanings in the ordinary sense, and fuses the old and obliterated and the trite, the current, and the new and surprising, the most ancient, and the most civilized mentality.

4

"The Hollow Men" seems to have had its point of departure in fragments discarded from the earlier draft of *The Waste Land*. In its final version we return in spirit to the longer poem, and a characteristic landscape of disembodied eyes in a desert. If *The Waste Land* offered at least the possibility of escaping from despair "The Hollow Men" plunges us back into it, and excludes all large gestures of affirmation or renunciation. As its celebrated concluding lines quietly insist:

This is the way the world ends
Not with a bang but a whimper.

"The Hollow Men" appears at first glance to lack the obtrusive literary and cultural dimension of *The Waste Land*. But in fact, as Grover Smith and other commentators have shown, it is intensely allusive, full of references to the Gunpowder Plot and Guy Fawkes, Shakespeare's *Julius Caesar* (whence the phrase "hollow men"), Conrad's *Heart of Darkness,* and Dante. I will not dwell on these allusions here, apart from underlining the significance of two of them: the "hollow men," as they are presented in the first section of the poem, in a condition of "paralysed force, gesture without motion," are derived from those wretched souls in *Inferno* III who were neither positively for good nor for evil, and so were rejected both by God and his enemies. The predicament of those who live in that state of spiritual suspended animation deeply concerned Eliot, as we see in references in his critical and religious writings, particularly the essay on Baudelaire of 1930. He had already referred in *The Waste Land* to the plight of the "hollow men" of the *Inferno:* "I had not thought death had undone so many," adapted from canto III. The crowd flowing back and forth over London Bridge is seen in *The Waste Land* as "crowds of people, walking round in a ring," and this is ritualized in "The Hollow Men" to

Here we go round the prickly pear
At five o'clock in the morning.

The recurring "eyes" in the poem allude, among other things, to the eyes of Beatrice in the *Purgatorio,* and the "Multifoliate rose" of part IV momentarily points to the triumphant culmination of Dante's vision in *Paradiso* XXXII. Eliot here anticipates his later use of the rose symbol in *Ash-Wednesday,* and even suggests the resolution of "Little Gidding" when "the fire and the rose are one." Yet Eliot used these religious symbols before he could attach positive existential meanings to them—indeed, his religious development can be seen in his increasing capacity to do so—and "The Hollow Men" is a literally hopeless poem, though stylish in its despair.

The interest of unravelling the allusions in "The Hollow Men" has perhaps prevented sufficient attention from being paid to the singularity of the poem's form. It is unlike Eliot's previous poetry, in that he denies himself the extensive rhythmic and syntactical resources of which he was so much a master. We have, instead, a flickering imagistic concentration on the features of a *paysage intérieur,* which suggests the laconic notations of H. D.'s poetry. To use the terminology of recent art criticism, "The Hollow Men" is a "minimalist" poem, which scarcely wants to use words at all and which gropes for significance in a semiaudible hypnotic mumble. Or to change the metaphor, it has the teasing fascination of an almost-erased inscription. It is, nevertheless, a hauntingly beautiful poem in the symbolist mode. Although in this mode "a poem must not mean but be," there are indications that "The Hollow Men" wants to mean as well, and here the extent of its ambiguities is very inhibiting: as, for instance, in one's inability to tell what, if any, are the distinctions between "death's dream kingdom," "death's other kingdom," and "death's twilight kingdom." There are, however, lines that permit the poem's preoccupation to emerge with greater clarity than the objective correlatives drawn from Conrad and Dante permit, where we see the same concern with sexual incapacity, and the lack of religious belief, that ran through *The Waste Land:* "Lips that would kiss / Form prayers to broken stone." The final section of the poem reflects on the difficulty—or impossibility—of all forms of fulfilled action, and seems to dwell too, again in the symbolist manner, on the impossibility of writing a poem, even such a minimally articulate one as that which we have just read. "The Hollow Men" looks like a virtual surrender to the silence which has haunted so many modern writers, or at the very least a muted swan song. But knowing what was to follow, we can now see it as a *reculer pour mieux sauter.*

5

For several years Eliot had been interested in the drama, and had left many traces of his reflections in essays and reviews. Certain themes were often dwelt on: the necessity of poetry finding its highest expression in a revivified verse drama that would have a broad popular appeal as well as being high art, like the

Elizabethan theater; the dramatic implications of the ballet, the music hall, and Jonsonian comedy; the possibility that a new, stylized drama could embody the ritual themes uncovered by modern anthropology; and, above all, an emphasis on rhythm as the primary element in the theatrical experience, which can seize the audience below the level of consciousness. In such prescriptions Eliot showed his characteristic blend of sophistication and primitivism. It was easier to outline these principles than to enact them, but in 1924 Eliot made the attempt and tried to enlist the help of Arnold Bennett, who had been fairly successful as a dramatist. In September of that year Bennett noted in his journal that Eliot had given up writing poetry in the manner of *The Waste Land* and wanted to concentrate on dramatic writing (this was to be the first of several occasions on which Eliot claimed that he had given up "pure" poetry for the theater):

He wanted to write a drama of modern life (furnished flat sort of people) in a rhythmic prose "perhaps with certain things in it accentuated by drum-beats." And he wanted my advice. We arranged that he should do the scenario and some sample pages of dialogue.

Evidently Bennett heard no more about this project, and in a letter to Eliot three years later he remarked, "I have often wondered what happened to that Jazz play." What had happened, in short, was that Eliot had been unable to complete it, but had published two fragments in *The Criterion* in 1926 and 1927, under the heading, "Wanna Go Home, Baby?" In 1932 these pieces were published in book form with the new title of *Sweeney Agonistes: Fragments of an Aristophanic Melodrama:* the publication of literary "fragments" was, one might note in passing, very much in the manner of the Romantic poets, and is further evidence of how superficial was Eliot's adherence to "classicism."

Sweeney Agonistes can be regarded in a number of ways: as a set of exercises for the play he had discussed with Arnold Bennett; as an authentic piece of experimental theater; and as a quasidramatic poem, akin to "Prufrock" or "Gerontion," with a provisional completeness despite its fragmentary nature. For convenience I shall call the work a "play" even though this begs a number of questions. Although the setting may recall a smart revue sketch, the dialogue has some of the rapid but stylized exchanges of the music-hall turn, while the ragtime songs derive from an American form of popular theater, the minstrel show; there are traces of both these elements in *The Waste Land*. In *Sweeney* Eliot uses a superbly rhythmic language, which though seemingly naturalistic to the point of banality, wholly embodies his aspiration, recorded in his review of *The Duchess of Malfi* in 1919, for a verse drama that would "obtain, with verse, an effect as immediate and direct as that of the best ballet." This was entirely in keeping with his consistent interest in the ballet as a dramatic form; Massine, he had remarked, was the best actor in London. But the ballet is a silent form, which becomes dramatic by miming pure action; and Eliot, despite his professed reverence for Aristotle's *Poetics*, and his acknowledgment that "behind the drama of words is the drama of action, the timbre of voice and voice, the uplifting hand or tense muscle, and the particular emotion," was not able to project action in this nonverbal way. Nearly all of Eliot's critical discussion of the problems of poetic drama is concerned with the question of *language*. In *Sweeney* he developed a mode of dramatic speech that triumphantly met his demands, but he could not project an appropriate action to accompany it, which was, no doubt, why the play remained incomplete, for *Sweeney* is as essentially static as "Prufrock" or "Gerontion." This, at least, is the argument of Hugh Kenner, in his brilliant and indispensable account of the play in *The Invisible Poet*. Kenner sees *Sweeney* as the first draft of *The Family Reunion*:

Sweeney Agonistes is a drama about a man no-one else on the stage can understand; exactly as is *The Family Reunion*. And while *The Family Reunion* is written through to its conclusion, nothing is more difficult than to explain just what revelation frees Harry and allows him to take his departure. It is, as Eliot himself said, a good first act, followed by more of the same. The original conception, which we may trace back to *Sweeney*, was radically undramatic because inactive.

More recently, another critic, Katharine Worth, has disagreed with Kenner; she found the 1965 production of *Sweeney* in London, with jazz accompaniment by John Dankworth, a very vital theatrical experience, and she quotes the opinions of reviewers that the play was "in the same class as the Berlin classics of Brecht and Weill," and that it "uncannily" foreshadowed the British *avant-garde* drama of the fifties. As Mrs. Worth remarks, Eliot's early prescriptions about making serious theatrical use of the music hall and the minstrel show were fully developed by Beckett; having become familiar with *Waiting for Godot* we may be more inclined to appreciate *Sweeney Agonistes,* since Beckett offers striking examples of the dramatic possibilities of nothing happening. The "theatrical" is not necessarily the same as the "dramatic," and in an expert production with appropriate music, *Sweeney Agonistes* might still be effective as spectacle and verbal play even though deficient as drama. Eliot himself, writing about Seneca in 1927, said that in the Roman dramatist's work "the drama is all in the word, and the word has no further reality behind it . . . the characters in a play of Seneca behave more like members of a minstrel troupe sitting in a semicircle, rising in turn each to do his 'number,' or varying their recitations by a song or a little back-chat." The Senecan model, as well as the popular theater, lay behind *Sweeney.*

After he abandoned his "jazz play" Eliot did not attempt to write again for the stage for several more years, and when he finally returned to the drama he did not persist in the immensely original manner that he had opened up in *Sweeney.*

One must remark, finally, that *Sweeney* marked thematically an important stage in Eliot's movement toward Christian belief. The Sweeney in the second fragment of the play is a more serious and philosophical person than the *homme moyen sensuel* of "Sweeney Erect" or "Sweeney Among the Nightingales" who is also, presumably, the Sweeney who awaited Mrs. Porter in *The Waste Land.* This Sweeney is "much possessed by death" and has dwelt on the state of not knowing whether one is alive or dead; he is aware of the cyclical hopelessness of a life lived wholly in biological terms, without the possibility of transcendence:

> That's all the facts when you come to brass tacks:
> Birth, and copulation, and death.
> I've been born, and once is enough.

The others do not know what he is talking about: in Kenner's words, Sweeney is a "man no-one else on the stage can understand." The play has two significant epigraphs. One is from Aeschylus: "You don't see them, you don't—but *I* see them: they are hunting me down, I must move on." This was enlarged on in *The Family Reunion,* and indicates that Sweeney is a superior consciousness, haunted by powers that ordinary mortals cannot perceive. The second quotation is from St. John of the Cross: "Hence the soul cannot be possessed of the divine union, until it has divested itself of the love of created beings." Here we see Eliot, who had long been familiar with the *Bhagavad-Gita* and other major texts of Indian mysticism, publicly invoking for the first time one of the masters of Christian mysticism, who was to appear again in *Ash-Wednesday* and *Four Quartets.* St. John was writing of a high and rare stage in the ascent of the mystical ladder, and not uttering everyday spiritual counsel: nevertheless, a sense of disparity between divine and human love was to haunt Eliot's cruelly bleak mode of Christian belief. Only at the end of his life does a new and more affirmative mode enter.

IV

****

Religion, Politics, and Drama

1928–1939

T. S. ELIOT's conversion to Christianity was a cause of surprise and even scandal to many of his contemporaries, and can still appear inexplicable to readers impressed by the iconoclastic modernity of his early poetry. Yet that poetry was pervaded by a lament for the loss of faith, and sometimes hinted that it might be recovered. Eliot's interest in Christianity had so far seemed to be anthropological ("In the juvescence of the year / Came Christ the tiger"), and any positive orientation towards religious experience, as in *The Waste Land,* was to Eastern rather than Western forms. But a reader who remembered Eliot's note to *The Waste Land* that the collocation of St. Augustine and Buddha "as the culmination of this part of the poem, is not an accident" should not have been excessively surprised when Eliot turned toward Christianity. Insofar as there was general surprise it may be partly attributed to the influence of I. A. Richards. In a note published in *The Criterion* in 1925 and reprinted in his *Science and Poetry,* Richards used Eliot to illustrate his argument that poetry's power to console could and should exist in complete separation from any set of particular beliefs about the world. Eliot's great virtue, observed Richards, was that he "by effecting a complete separation between his poetry and *all* beliefs, and this without any weakening of the poetry, has realised what might otherwise have remained largely a speculative possibility." It was a view widely held in the twenties, when Eliot's poetry seemed most remarkable for its cynicism and even nihilism. This, however, was not Eliot's opinion; although, as always, he felt that he had no advantage in interpreting his own poetry over any other intelligent reader, he was impelled to reply to Richards. He did so in "A Note on Poetry and Belief," published in January 1927 in the first number of Wyndham Lewis's short-lived magazine, *The Enemy.*

Eliot's brief note clearly indicates the way in which his religious attitudes were developing, and how he related belief to his own poetry. He argues that modes of belief change immensely over the centuries, without necessarily progressing: Dante and Crashaw and Christina Rossetti were all sincere Christian poets but their ways of expressing what they believed could not be more different. He says of Richards's comments on *The Waste Land:*

As for the poem of my own in question, I cannot for the life of me see the "complete separation" from all belief—or it is something no more complete than the separation of Christina Rossetti from Dante. A "sense of desolation," etc. (if it is there) is not a separation from belief; it is nothing so pleasant. In fact, doubt, uncertainty, futility, etc., would seem to me to prove anything except this agreeable partition; for doubt and uncertainty are merely a variety of belief.

Eliot does not want to discuss his own work in detail, for he is more concerned with Richards's general position about the separation of poetry and belief, and he denies that any such separation can be made:

I cannot see that poetry can ever be separated from something which I should call belief, and to which I cannot see any reason for refusing the name of belief, unless we are to reshuffle names altogether. It should hardly be needful to say that it will not inevitably be orthodox Christian belief, although that possibility can be entertained, since Christianity will probably continue to modify itself, as in the past, into something that can be believed in (I do not mean *conscious* modifications like modernism, etc., which always have the opposite effect).

Soon afterward Eliot decided that orthodox Christianity had in fact modified itself "into something that can be believed in," or at least that his own views had developed sufficiently to permit him to accept Christianity; later in 1927 he was baptized and confirmed in the Church of England. This move was not, for a time, generally known, though Herbert Read who was spending a night in Eliot's house noticed with some surprise his friend going out before seven o'clock one morning to attend an early communion service. And on another occasion, Richards, entertaining Eliot in Cambridge, was struck by a "large, new, and to us awe-inspiring Prayer Book" that the author of "Mr. Eliot's Sunday Morning Service" had brought with him: "We were suddenly made aware of our total inability to advise on (or even discuss) the character of the various Services available on Sunday mornings."

Two poems written at this time reflect, in the form of dramatic monologues, something of Eliot's spiritual struggle: "Journey of the Magi" and "A Song for Simeon," published in the Faber Ariel Poets series in 1927 and 1928 respectively. In both poems the advent of Christ is seen as involving a painful rather than a joyful transformation of attitudes. Although Eliot went on to write, in *Ash-Wednesday* and *Four Quartets*, religious poetry of great beauty and authority, his prose reflections on religious subjects are rarely of more than secondary interest, and are nearly all concerned with the institutional and public aspects of religion. There is, however, one important exception; in his essay on Pascal, published in 1931, Eliot gives a generalized but vivid account of the process of conversion as he understood it:

The Christian thinker—and I mean the man who is trying consciously and conscientiously to explain to himself the sequence which culminates in faith, rather than the public apologist—proceeds by rejection and elimination. He finds the world to be so and so; he finds its character inexplicable by any non-religious theory: among religions he finds Christianity, and Catholic Christianity, to account most satisfactorily for the world and especially for the moral world within; and thus, by what Newman calls "powerful and concurrent" reasons, he finds himself inexorably committed to the dogma of the Incarnation.

This description helps one to understand Eliot's personal development during the twenties, and to see why his conversion was not a sudden transformation but the seemingly inexorable culmination of a process. In his essay on Pascal, Eliot pays a warm tribute to the religious thinker whom he found congenial above all others. As he says, it was part of Pascal's achievement to include and ultimately transcend the attractive and persuasive skepticism of Montaigne:

For every man who thinks and lives by thought must have his own scepticism, that which stops at the question, that which ends in denial, or that which leads to faith and which is somehow integrated into the faith which transcends it. And Pascal, as the type of one kind of religious believer, which is highly passionate and ardent, but passionate only through a powerful and regulated intellect, is in the first sections of his unfinished Apology for Christianity facing unflinchingly the demon of doubt which is inseparable from the spirit of belief.

Such wrestling with the "demon of doubt" is, of course, part of the experience of many twentieth-century Christians, though it would have been alien to the serene spirituality of Newman, whom Eliot much admired, and still more to the saints of earlier times. But in manifesting it Pascal showed, as Eliot perceived, a quality that the modern world could recognize: "I know of no religious writer more pertinent to our time." Hugh Sykes Davies has provided an apt biographical illustration of these remarks. He entertained Eliot at dinner at his Cambridge college in the thirties, and after the meal Eliot became engrossed in conversation with another guest, an Italian Marxist of great cultivation. Eventually, walking back in the small hours of the morning, Eliot remarked to Davies on the difference between the Marxists and himself, which was a question not merely of the content of their beliefs but of the way in which they were held: "They seem so certain of what they believe. My own beliefs are held with a scepticism which I never even hope to be quite rid of." In his essay Eliot notes the quality of Pascal's despair, and adds, almost in passing, "it was also a despair which was a necessary prelude to, and element in, the joy of faith." The "joy of faith" would no doubt have been recognized by Eliot, intellectually at least, as at the heart of Christianity, but it appears only fitfully in his poetry and not at all in his prose. Here we must acknowedge one of Eliot's temperamental limitations, which set him apart from Pascal, who wept tears of joy at his conversion. Such a limitation

would be crippling in a spiritual teacher, but Eliot never claimed
to be one, however much zealous disciples may have tried to
turn him into one in the forties and fifties. He was something
quite different, an artist; and as an artist he could use the peculi-
arities of his temperament in the service of his poetry.

Although the fact of Eliot's personal conversion to Christianity
might have been surprising to his friends, the way in which he
chose, ultimately, to make public his new allegiance was calculated to be disconcerting and even provocative to a wider audience. Thereafter Eliot's religious position was to be inevitably
allied with the cultural and even political concomitants with
which he unwisely chose to associate it. Soon after Eliot's reception into the church he was visited in London by his old friend
and teacher, Irving Babbitt. The news of Eliot's conversion was
not particularly well received by Babbitt, who was attached to
his own ethical system, humanism, but his only comment was,
"I think you should come out into the open." Eliot already had
a small collection of essays in preparation, which appeared in
1928 as *For Lancelot Andrewes*, with the monitory subtitle,
"Essays on Style and Order." In the preface he wrote, "The general point of view may be described as classicist in literature,
royalist in politics, and anglo-catholic in religion." It would be
further elaborated, he added, in "three small books in preparation
which will not be ready for a considerable time," to be called
The School of Donne, The Outline of Royalism, and *The Principles
of Modern Heresy.* (Of these three, only the last has seen the
light, as *After Strange Gods: A Primer of Modern Heresy,* in
1934.) Eliot soon came to regret this neat tripartite formulation;
as he remarked in 1961

the quotable sentence turned up in the preface to the book of essays I
had in preparation, swung into orbit and has been circling my little
world ever since. Well, my religious beliefs are unchanged, and I am
strongly in favour of the maintenance of the monarchy in all countries
which have a monarchy; as for Classicism and Romanticism, I find that
the terms have no longer the importance to me that they once had.[1]

[1] *To Criticize the Critic* (New York: Farrar, Straus & Giroux; London:
Faber & Faber, 1965), p. 15.

In 1928, however, this formulation marked an important new phase in the long process of self-definition in which he had been engaged ever since his entry into English literary society in 1915. It showed that Eliot's tendency to cultural mythmaking had reached a new level of complication and paradox.

As Herbert Howarth has shown, Eliot's tripartite definition was directly derived from a Maurrasian formula: in 1913 an editorial note in the *Nouvelle Revue Française*—to which Eliot was a subscriber—had described Maurras's "three traditions" as *classique, catholique, monarchique*. Eliot had first encountered the writings of Charles Maurras on his visit to Paris in 1910 and the influence of the French monarchist was of crucial importance in his intellectual development. As a man of letters Maurras upheld an ideal of "classicism" that could be much more readily perceived in the French literary tradition than in the English. As a politician and publicist and leader of the *Action Française* movement, Maurras believed in an absolute monarchy as against parliamentary democracy, and strongly supported the Catholic church as an embodiment of the Roman virtues of order and authority and tradition, while rejecting the so-called Jewish or mystical elements in Christianity. Indeed, Maurras was himself an atheist, and it is not surprising that in the end the Vatican found itself forced to condemn such an embarrassing supporter.

Eliot had acknowledged Maurras in "The Idea of a Literary Review" in *The Criterion* in 1926, where he was named with respect, together with Hulme, Benda, and Sorel, as one of the representatives of the antiromantic "tendency" Eliot admired. During 1928 Eliot was engaged in polite controversy in *The Criterion* with Leo Ward, a Roman Catholic pamphleteer who had followed up the Vatican condemnation of the *Action Française* with a documented account of Maurras's anti-Christian tendencies. Eliot certainly got the worst of the argument, which is of interest in revealing the extent of his emotional attachment to Maurras. He replied to Ward's account of Maurras's hostility to Christianity with the testimony: "I have been a reader of the work of Maurras for eighteen years; upon me he has had exactly the opposite effect." In a further installment of the debate he wrote:

I say only that if anyone is attracted by Maurras' political theory, and if that person has as well any tendency towards *interior* Christianity, that tendency will be quickened by finding that a political and a religious view can be harmonious.

I believe that the formulation "classicist, royalist, anglo-catholic" represented an attempt to construct a systematic Maurrasian model, or myth, for the interpretation of English cultural history, which would be an equivalent for Maurras's own versions of the French tradition. The meeting place of these three positions could only lie, for Eliot, in the early seventeenth century. Already, in 1921, he had made clear his admiration for the England of Donne and Lord Herbert of Cherbury and the "undissociated sensibility," though at that time he was concerned only with its literary manifestations. But as we see from the title essay of *For Lancelot Andrewes*, Eliot soon came to have a broader-based regard for late sixteenth- and early seventeenth-century England, as the period of the Anglican *via media* and Hooker and Laud and Bishop Andrewes. In the thought of Maurras, the *grand siècle* in France was one of the few *moments privilégiés* in the history of Western civilization, following the earlier pinnacles of Greece and Rome. Eliot tried to include England before the civil war in the same great phase. As he argues elsewhere in *For Lancelot Andrewes*, in "John Bramhall":

The French Church in the time of Louis XIV (*"il fut gallicain, ce siècle, et janséniste"*) resembled the English Church under the Stuarts in several respects. In both countries a strong and autocratic civil Government controlled and worked with a strongly national Church. In each country there was a certain balance of power; in France between the throne and the papacy; in England an internal balance of power between strong personalities.

However dubious this parallel may be in fact, it shows strikingly how Eliot's mythopoeic view of history was working: if the French had a "classical moment" under Louis XIV, then the English may be allowed one too, if earlier in the century. Hence the oddity of Eliot's announced intention of explaining his allegiance to "classicism" in the unwritten book called *The School of Donne* (presumably based on the Clark lectures which Eliot had delivered under that title in Cambridge in 1926): in the normal usage of English literary history Donne is the last poet that anyone would want to call "classical." But as Eliot disarmingly went on to admit in the preface to *For Lancelot Andrewes*, "classicist" as a term "is completely vague, and easily lends itself to clap-trap."

Of the three words Eliot chose to define his position, "royalist" is certainly the most baffling; no native Englishman, writing as a subject of the impeccably bourgeois George V, could ever have described himself in this way. Nevertheless, for an American admirer of the *Action Française*, who had accompanied his entry into the Church of England by taking out British citizenship, the word had a good deal of emotional resonance if little precise meaning. Here, again, Eliot's defense of Maurras is illuminating:

The *Action Française* insists upon the importance of continuity by the Kingship and hereditary class, upon something which has some analogy to what the government of England was, formerly, at least supposed to be; it would protect the humble citizen against the ambitious politician.

Although Eliot may have been physically a subject of George V, his spiritual allegiance was to Elizabeth and the Stuarts; it was given an elegiac turn years later in the lines from "Little Gidding" about the execution of Charles I.

"Anglo-Catholic" raises fewest problems, once the fact of Eliot's conversion has been accepted. By using this term Eliot was establishing his loyalty to the England of Laud and Andrewes (whom he called "the first great preacher of the English Catholic Church"), and at the same time translating into an English context Maurras's contention about the need for an intimate relation between the national church and the national culture. In the years after Eliot's conversion, speculations were often raised about the possibility of his joining the Roman Catholic church, though it can never have been likely. Although he would have learned from Maurras to regard Rome with great respect, the inherited prejudices of his American ancestry—whether from New England Puritanism or St. Louis Unitarianism—against the religion of Italian and Irish immigrants cannot have been easily brushed aside. And any tentative inclinations toward Rome in the mid-twenties were stopped short by the Vatican's condemnation of the *Action Française*, an event which seems to have deeply shocked Eliot. Thereafter he found himself at home with the Anglican *via media* and in 1931 he made his position clear in "Thoughts after Lambeth":

Whether established or disestablished, the Church of England can never be reduced to the condition of a Sect, unless by some irrational act of suicide; even in the sense in which, with all due respect, the Roman Church is in England a sect. It is easier for the Church of England to become Catholic, than for the Church of Rome in England to become English; and if the Church of England was mutilated by separation from Rome, the Church of Rome was mutilated by separation from England. If England is ever to be in any appreciable degree converted to Christianity, it can only be through the Church of England.

Eliot's declaration of 1928 had the fatal memorability of some of his earlier *aperçus* and was frequently quoted against him. It represented an ambitious attempt to construct a Maurrasian model for his own personal and temperamental allegiances, and it was not long before he realized the unsuitability, not to say the absurdity, of any such project. The influence of Maurras reached its peak in the late twenties—in 1929 Eliot dedicated his *Dante* to him—but thereafter declined, although Eliot always maintained a strong personal regard for Maurras. The polemics of "dynamic classicism" and the heady rhetoric of the *Action Française* were not for long reconcilable with the sobriety of the Anglican churchwarden and guest editor of the *Christian News Letter*.

Eliot's conversion and announcement of new allegiances were not without literary repercussions—for instance, "Stepping Heavenward," a short story by Richard Aldington, who had been one of Eliot's early admirers and for a time assistant editor of *The Criterion*. This somewhat venomous piece describes the life and career of one Jeremy Pratt Sybba, later Cibber, an American historian who comes to London and becomes a dominant force in intellectual life; he is converted to Rome and beatified after his death by the Pope. The parallel between the careers of Cibber and Eliot is rather forced, but the identification of the central character is unmistakable, and a very unpleasant personality is described. Aldington dwells on his quiet but relentless careerism, his snobbery, his pusillanimous behavior, and his inhuman formality of manner. At one time in his life Cibber is an ardent personal follower of Charles Maurras and is known as the Master's Orderly Man: "There was no service from which he shrank, and he was equally proud to buy the Master his packet of Caporal cigarettes and to assist him in denouncing the errors and crimes of the Third Republic." It may be that this story sprang entirely from Aldington's dismay at Eliot's conversion, but the animus it betrays suggests a deeper motive; according to Herbert Read, Aldington developed an "intense jealousy" of Eliot, and this could explain the rancorous tone of "Stepping Heavenward." By the time he wrote his autobiography in 1941 Aldington had recovered a more balanced view of his old friend. There is a more succinct attack on Eliot in a poem by Edgell Rickword:

> Those who are much obsessed by death
> and see the skull beneath the skin,
> may cheat their fear of wanting breath
> with dry philosophy or gin;
> or with the ardours of the birch
> or lure of buxom female form,
> but whose lot creeps into the Church
> to keep its inhibitions warm?

2

As I have remarked, there are signs of Eliot's conversion in such poems as "Journey of the Magi"—which incorporates several lines from a Nativity sermon by Bishop Andrewes—and "A Song for Simeon." But its most profound poetic enactment is *Ash-Wednesday*, which was published as a book in 1930, after sections had appeared in periodicals between 1927 and 1929. Leonard Woolf recalls a session at which Eliot read an early version of *Ash-Wednesday* to the Woolfs and some other friends, inviting their criticism. In fact it became "an examination, not of the examinee, but of the examiners," and only Virginia Woolf, whose critical sense Eliot greatly admired, passed to his satisfaction. *Ash-Wednesday* was shortly preceded by the publication of

Eliot's *Dante*, a short book in the Faber Poets on the Poets series, which is an attractive personal tribute to Dante.

In 1931 Eliot published "Thoughts after Lambeth," which affirmed his institutional attachment to the Anglican communion. The following year this work and *Dante* were both reprinted in his substantial *Selected Essays 1917–1932*, which included the greater part of *The Sacred Wood* and most (but by no means all) of the essays he had written since 1920. The title of the new collection was incorrect, for it contained nothing earlier than "Tradition and the Individual Talent" of 1919. In 1932 Eliot paid his first visit to America since 1915, and during 1932–1933 he delivered the Charles Eliot Norton lectures at Harvard, and the Page-Barbour lectures at the University of Virginia. They were published in book form as, respectively, *The Use of Poetry and the Use of Criticism* (1933) and *After Strange Gods* (1934). The first of these books is subtitled "Studies in the Relation of Criticism to Poetry in England," and although Eliot originally claimed that the lectures were published only because the bequest under which they were delivered required it, he later developed a considerable regard for *The Use of Poetry and the Use of Criticism*, and in his preface to the 1964 edition suggests that he prefers it to his early criticism.

The book is, in fact, rather dull, though it throws out many interesting *aperçus* while elaborating Eliot's earlier argument that there is a necessary relation between poetic achievement and a suitable climate of critical ideas. But he seems excessively conscious of the academic occasion, and the feline urbanity of *The Sacred Wood* has declined into an elaborate and weary politeness, where endlessly fine distinctions are drawn less, it seems, from intellectual necessity than as a stylistic device. This manner has been brilliantly caught in a superb parody by John Updike, which, like all good parody, makes a telling criticism of its subject:

It is our duty, if Western civilization is in any sense to linger on, to differentiate between the excellent, the second-rate, and the fake. These lines do not seem to me to be fake; but they fail to be so, I would suggest, by default. In their presence we experience not even that fear of being hoodwinked which is the *least* with which verse can enrich our lives . . . Indeed the question is real, whether Wordsworth or John

Cleveland has more just claims upon our attention at this moment of history; certainly Cleveland, though the smaller poet, was the larger man.[2]

The best of the lectures is, I think, the one on Arnold; Eliot's need to measure himself against Arnold gives it a peculiar personal force. As I have previously remarked, Eliot always had ambivalent feelings about Arnold, whom he regarded both as mentor and adversary, and in this lecture they are openly manifested. He rejects Arnold's complacently moralistic assumption that "Poetry is at bottom a criticism of life":

At the bottom of the abyss is what few ever see, and what those cannot bear to look at for long; and it is not a "criticism of life." If we mean life as a whole—not that Arnold ever saw life as a whole—from top to bottom, can anything that we can say of it ultimately, of that awful mystery, be called criticism? We bring back very little from our rare descents, and that is not criticism.

Here again Eliot speaks with the accent of the poet who saw the creative act as itself a descent into dangerous depths, and a painful, even sacrificial activity. As R. P. Blackmur remarked of this passage, "The 'abyss' is one of his obsessive images." He is convincing, too, I think, when he attacks the assumption of Arnold and Richards that poetry could take on a religious function: "nothing in this world or the next is a substitute for anything else; and if you find that you must do without something, such as religious faith or philosophic belief, then you must just do without it." In general, the most valuable things in *The Use of Poetry and the Use of Criticism* are Eliot's autobiographical asides and his acute passing comments on his own art, like the reflections on the "auditory imagination" that I quoted in the previous chapter.

The other book which emerged from Eliot's American visit, *After Strange Gods,* was much more contentious. Eliot claims to be writing not as a critic but as a moralist investigating the decline of orthodoxy and the prevalence of error in modern literature. The book shows the development of "tradition" in Eliot's thought from the purely literary concept of 1919 to a fairly complex affair with wide cultural implications. Insofar as he sees

[2] "What is a Rhyme?" *Assorted Prose,* 1965.

"tradition" as the familiar and inherited way of life of a settled and localized community with a strong sense of the past ("a way of feeling and acting which characterises a group throughout generations"), he is describing something which is anthropologically familiar. But in making such "tradition" a desirable norm for humanity he is writing politically. Eliot claimed that such a way of life still existed in the South: he had been much impressed by the manifesto of the Southern Agrarians, and the impulse to flatter his audience at the University of Virginia was, no doubt, a factor in his approach. Adopting for the occasion the role of a New Englander he lamented that he came from a culture which had once possessed "tradition" in abundance, but which had by now almost entirely lost it in the advance of industrialism and material progress. There is a noticeable if diluted flavor of Maurras in this part of Eliot's discourse, as when he compliments the Virginians on being "less invaded by foreign races" than the North: in Maurrasian language they were happily free of the *métèque*.

The notion of tradition, however simplified and mythologized, does at least make sense, which is more than one can say of the other key word of *After Strange Gods*, "orthodoxy." It does not necessarily mean adherence to institutional Christianity, and its relation to actual religious belief is indefinite. James Joyce, who had abandoned Catholic Christianity as soon as he reached manhood, is praised for having an orthodox sensibility, that is, for continuing to show evidence of the thorough Jesuit training he had received in his youth. Eliot is, on the other hand, reluctant to call such an intensely Christian poet as Hopkins "orthodox"; however admirable he may be as a devotional writer, he is not a religious poet in the same sense as Baudelaire! The absurdity of describing Baudelaire as an example of "orthodoxy" is evident, but Eliot continues to cling to the term: he regards it as superior to "classicism" which he had previously employed in the twenties, though one is forced to conclude that it has even less meaning. In essence it seems to imply acceptance of the doctrine of Original Sin as the heart of the Christian religion, and, in effect, more significant than the redemptive power of Christ. For Christian orthodoxy such an emphasis is itself heterodox, and Eliot seems to have derived it largely from the writings of T. E. Hulme, who was not much of a theologian. Eliot's position emphasizes his Jansenistic inability to see any possibility of natural virtue. Man is, in essence, an unredeemed animal, though "tradition" and "orthodoxy" might make something decent out of him. These things, however, are not to be acquired for the asking. As Eliot remarks of Hopkins: "To be converted, in any case, while it is sufficient for entertaining the hope of individual salvation, is not going to do for a man, as a writer, what his ancestry and his country for some generations have failed to do." What then could conversion do for Eliot himself, as a gallicized American *métèque* in England, of mixed cultural heritage? *After Strange Gods* shows the cultural myths that he had for so long pursued in his personal attempts at self-definition being inflated until their chimerical nature is inescapable. The book is not, however, entirely without merit; the passages where Eliot engages in what is in fact literary criticism— whatever else he may have thought of it—of Hardy and Lawrence seem to me to raise questions about these authors which are worth considering. But in its total impression, *After Strange Gods* is crude and incoherent, both in its theological and its literary aspects. All of which Eliot seems to have realized, since he never allowed the book to be reprinted and in effect expunged it from the canon of his works.

The most damaging passage occurs when Eliot is presenting the ideal of a culturally homogeneous community rooted in tradition: "reasons of race and religion combine to make any large number of free-thinking Jews undesirable." These words, and the various slighting references to Jews elsewhere in his verse and prose, point to a regrettable degree of anti-Semitic prejudice on Eliot's part; derived, to some extent, from Maurras, for whom the Jew was preeminently the *métèque*. Such sentiments were sadly common in the pre-Hitler era and on the left as well as the right. This prejudice was, however, sufficiently mild to let Eliot refer more than once with warm admiration to the poetry of Isaac Rosenberg, who had been killed as a private soldier in the British army in 1918, and to praise the way in which it drew on Hebraic tradition. In later years Eliot vehemently denied being anti-Semitic; he told his friend William Turner Levy, "It is a terrible

slander on a man. And they do not know, as you and I do, that in
the eyes of the Church, to be anti-Semitic is a sin." Since Eliot is
quite often charged with being a "fascist" I will briefly consider
the question of his political views. Much depends, of course, on
how one wishes to define "fascist," which tends to be used so
loosely as to have no real meaning at all. Those who regard all
political positions to the right of moderate conservatism as self-
evidently "fascist" will certainly want to apply this label to Eliot,
and within their own terms they will be right to do so. But anyone who hopes to preserve the meaningfulness of political concepts will try to discriminate more exactly.

In an article called "The Literature of Fascism," published in
The Criterion in 1928, Eliot set down his opinions of the original
Italian version of fascism, and on the whole they were not enthusiastic. Although it might suit the Italians, fascism had little to
recommend it for the English. The royalism of Maurras would be
far preferable, he urged, and whatever was positive in fascism
was already present in the thought of Maurras. In his controversy
with Leo Ward he had claimed that "if anything, in another generation or so, is to preserve us from a sentimental Anglo-Fascism,
it will be some system of ideas which will have gained much from
the study of Maurras. His influence in England has not yet begun." For Eliot the Maurrasian combination of a strong king and
a decentralized social order was something quite other than, and
preferable to, the fascist ideal of totalitarian dynamism and a
centralized state, equally removed though both might be from
modern parliamentary democracy. Eliot was not, in fact, opposed
to democracy as such, though the version he favored was restricted and elitist, unlike the liberal model based on universal
suffrage:

From the moment when the suffrage is conceived as a *right* instead of a
privilege and a duty and a responsibility, we are on the way merely to
government by an invisible oligarchy instead of government by a visible
one. But it is another thing to ridicule the *idea* of democracy. A real
democracy is always a restricted democracy, and can only flourish with
some limitation by hereditary rights and responsibilities.

Eliot adds that the United States was more or less democratic in
his sense until the election of Andrew Jackson to the presidency

in 1829. If Maurrasian royalism represented the exotic side of Eliot's political stance, its English aspect lay in the romantic high toryism that he acquired from Whibley. In October 1931 he wrote in *The Criterion:*

The only hope is in a Toryism which, though not necessarily distinct for Parliamentary purposes, should refuse to identify itself philosophically with that "Conservatism" which has been overrun first by deserters from Whiggism and later by business men. And for such a Toryism not only a doctrine of the temporal and spiritual in matters of Church and State is essential, but even a religious foundation for the whole of its political philosophy. Nothing less can engage enough respect to be a worthy adversary for Communism.

Such a toryism, one must add, was a creation of the literary imagination rather than a political possibility, and might well have been expounded by Christopher Tietjens, hero of Ford Madox Ford's *Parade's End.*

Throughout the nineteen-thirties, Eliot's editorial commentaries in *The Criterion* engaged in gloomy, and often obscure reflections about the state of the world. One strangely recurring note is Eliot's concern with communism as the "worthy adversary," a disciplined "orthodoxy" on the other side, and he devotes a remarkable amount of space to discussing the work of Marxist writers. Eliot believed that politics should be grounded in Christian moral principles, and he looked for a Christian mirror image of the dedicated communist militant fearlessly putting his Marxist principles into practice. (This ideal was also shared by the Roman Catholics grouped round the review, *Colosseum.*) It was an illusory ideal, however, since Christian principles, however firmly held, offer little guidance when it comes to making concrete political choices. In fact, sincere Christians can be found at all points of the political spectrum, ranging from the followers of Salazar in Portugal or the free-enterprise Christian Democrats of West Germany to the revolutionary Catholic Marxists of South America. The notion of a uniquely and self-evidently "Christian" approach in politics is chimerical. The conviction that politics should have a Christian basis, combined with the realization that there were no specifically Christian answers to the problems of the contemporary world, seems to have demoralized

Eliot, though an Arnoldian distaste for dealing with the mere "machinery" of public affairs also appears to have been a contributory factor. He adopted a despairing rejection of all visible positions, whether liberal-democratic, fascist, or communist, since all were equally removed from Christian principles. Some of his positive recommendations, like his strong belief in community and decentralization, might be sympathetically regarded by the present-day New Left, while others, like his essentially hierarchical model of society, certainly would not. Other basic positions—his dislike of urban civilization and his belief that the Good Life could be lived only in an agrarian society—might be attractive as ideals but were utopian in actuality. (Eliot, as an inveterate city dweller himself, and a great poet of urban life, disarmingly confessed that he could no more live in the country than he could give up smoking.)

None of these views was in any way "fascist," and contrary to what is sometimes alleged Eliot never at any time said anything in the thirties to indicate his support for the European fascist regimes, unlike, say, Wyndham Lewis. It is true that he also avoided attacking them, and in the light of history this may look like a cardinal sin of omission. Yet his refusal for doing so sprang, I believe, not from sympathy for Germany and Italy but from a refusal implicitly to identify himself with the liberal and left-wing forces ranged on the antifascist side. He was as opposed to capitalism and bourgeois democracy as the Communists, whom he regarded as worthy but absolute ideological adversaries, and since he could see no virtue in fascist totalitarianism, his position was necessarily a lonely and an impotent one. From this point in time it is easy to say that Eliot should have raised his voice against fascist crimes; whatever the deficiencies of democratic nations they were infinitely preferable to the absolute evil of totalitarianism as it emerged in the forties; but the point is worth making that until 1939 Soviet Russia, which many Western intellectuals enthusiastically supported, had shown itself a much more efficiently murderous and oppressive regime than either Italy or Germany, and Eliot's refusal to support either side is worthy of respect. In the July 1937 issue of *The Criterion* he referred to the bicentenary celebrations of the University of Göttingen: "It seems

hardly credible, at the moment of writing, that the motive of the
authorities of Oxford University in deciding not to send representatives to that celebration could have been to express disap-
proval of the German Government." Eliot's elaborately feigned
surprise seems misplaced, for by that time the Nazi hostility to
academic and intellectual freedom had become notorious, though
his motive seems to have been not to defend the Nazi record but
to argue, rather obscurely, that it was not the business of institu-
tions to make such gestures of protest, even though individuals
might. Later in the same editorial he comments on the Spanish
civil war, denouncing the noisy supporters of both the Republic
and General Franco:

The situation in Spain has provided the perfect opportunity for extremists of both extremes. To turn from the shrill manifestoes of the
Extreme Left, and the indiscretions of the Dean of Canterbury, to the
affirmations of Mr. Jerrold and Mr. Lunn, is only to intensify the nightmare.

If Eliot had been a mere aesthete in the thirties he could have ignored the political situation, and concerned himself solely with
literature, as he had in the early days of *The Criterion*. In fact he
was deeply interested in political ideas and the nature of the
good society, and he shared the public concern of many writers of
the time. But his tragic dilemma lay in his inability to maintain a
political position based on Christian principles and Arnoldian
disinterestedness at a time when the extremists of both sides were
dominant.

Eliot's political position was summarized in *The Idea of a
Christian Society* (1939), a series of lectures delivered at Corpus
Christi College, Cambridge. He argues that Western society, having been traditionally Christian, is now, at best, neutral toward
Christianity, and may well be evolving toward a pagan society,
which would entail a return of the religious spirit in a wholly
unwelcome way: "the fundamental objection to fascist doctrine,
the one which we conceal from ourselves because it might condemn ourselves as well, is that it is pagan." Eliot mistrusts the
motive for the democratic opposition to fascism, and he tellingly
observes, "I suspect that in our loathing of totalitarianism, there is

infused a good deal of admiration for its efficiency." There is
some shrewd criticism of the conventional liberal position in this
book, and it is far more temperately and rationally expressed than
in *After Strange Gods.* On one level the book is an implicit tribute
to the Church of England; claiming that in any Christian society
worthy of the name there must be a close and harmonious relation between church and state, Eliot sees the existing role of the
Anglican establishment in British society as an admirable state of
affairs, even though it might not suit other countries. Here as
elsewhere Eliot assumes that the Church of England is the only
valid vehicle for Christian belief, and he ignores the parts played
by Nonconformity and Roman Catholicism in the making of English culture. In a Christian society, he claims, the mass of the people would probably not be consciously committed believers, but
they would pursue a Christian way of life, both in observance and
morality, in accordance with traditionally accepted and inherited
standards. And the leaven in the mass would be provided by a
small group of conscious and educated believers. The Christian
society would not necessarily be pervaded by conspicuous devotion, but its practice would be honored and every opportunity
given for it. The ruling class in such a society would not all be
Christian; indeed, some of them might be unbelievers, but this
would be unimportant provided that the dominant ideology was
Christian. Presumably members of non-Christian sects would
receive some form of limited toleration, and Eliot is tactfully silent on the position of "free-thinking Jews" and other *métèques.*
Having laid down these broad outlines Eliot professes himself
unconcerned with the political forms of such a society, whether
they were those of parliamentary democracy or some other system. Indeed, Eliot seems to assume that such a society, once it
had come into existence would not need politics; but as I have
said, there is no self-evidently Christian position to be taken on
most of the concrete political questions that are likely to arise in
any society. (Christians, like all right-minded people, would op-
pose atrocities or genocide, but that is scarcely a *political* position.) Politics as a necessary response to the problem of balancing
opposed and equally valid social demands, and of coping with
the perennial results of material scarcity and human incapacity,

will always be with us. Eliot's lack of interest in this question is reminiscent of the unreal utopianism of the left. The actual societies which have come close to his ideal have been dictatorships where normal political life has been suppressed, and which have not been conspicuous for social justice or the quality of Christian observance, namely, the Spain of Franco, and the Portugal of Salazar (whom Eliot admired). The Irish Republic is the only democratic instance, and there traditional sanctions are visibly weakening.

A sympathetic Roman Catholic critic, J. M. Cameron, has noted the crucial difficulty in Eliot's position: "A Christian society, in the sense in which Mr. Eliot wishes to use the term, is a theological and not a sociological category." Eliot, in fact, tries to use the term in both senses, so that the "Christian society" sometimes looks like an anticipation of the City of God, and is sometimes no more than an imperfect improvement on the existing system. In his final lecture Eliot engages in one of those bursts of qualification which are a familiar part of the strategy of his prose writings, and which undermines much of what has gone before. He argues that he does not look for a society of saints, but a human order where Christianity is communal before it is individual:

But we have to remember that the Kingdom of Christ on earth will never be realised, and also that it is always being realised; we must remember that whatever reform or revolution we carry out, the result will always be a sordid travesty of what human society should be— though the world is never left without glory.

There is much wisdom here, but the emphasis is very different from the prescriptive note that we find elsewhere; achieving a Christian society seems, after all, to be no more than exchanging one "sordid travesty" for another. Since Eliot wrote, the integralist ideal of an institutionally Christian society has been largely abandoned, except by a few Roman Catholic traditionalists, and most Christian social thinkers accept a neutral and pluralist society as the best soil for religious belief. Eliot never properly resolved the underlying dilemma of *The Idea of a Christian Society;* as a Christian believer he had to regard the church as ultimately a transcendent order, but his temperament and personal myths led

him to place an immensely high valuation on the cultural im-
manence of the church as a social organism—just, indeed, as the
unbelieving Maurras had done. The point has been valuably pursued by Cameron in "T. S. Eliot as a Political Writer"[3] and more
recently by Adrian Cunningham in "Continuity and Coherence in
Eliot's Religious Thought."[4] The most personally revealing passage in *The Idea of a Christian Society* is the conclusion of the
final lecture, where Eliot describes his distress and humiliation
after the Munich crisis of September 1938, and his growing doubts
about the validity of Western civilization. Here he echoes the
great nineteenth-century social critics like Coleridge and Carlyle,
Rustin and Arnold:

Was our society, which had always been so assured of its superiority
and rectitude, so confident of its unexamined premises, assembled
round anything more permanent than a congeries of banks, insurance
companies and industries, and had it any beliefs more essential than a
belief in compound interest and the maintenance of dividends? Such
thoughts as these formed the starting point, and must remain the ex-
cuse, for saying what I have had to say.

3

Eliot's unhappiness at the condition of public life in the thirties
was intensified by a private crisis. While at Harvard he made a
decision he had been contemplating for several years of unhappy
married life, to separate from his wife Vivien. When he returned
to England in the summer of 1932 he did not go back to his house
in London, but instead spent several months living in the Surrey
farmhouse owned by a fellow director of Faber and Faber, Frank
Morley:

It had seemed to Tom least worst [sic] to accept that Vivien's relations
and Enid Faber would do what they could for Vivien in London, and
that he should come to Pikes Farm if he had to know as Dante knew

---

[3] *The Night Battle* (London: Burns & Oates, 1962; Baltimore: Helicon
Press, 1963).

[4] Graham Martin, ed., *Eliot in Perspective* (London: Macmillan & Co.,
1970).

how salt is the taste of another's bread, how hard a path the going up
and down another's stairs.[5]

Eliot was writing little poetry at this time, though some of the
short poems in the "Landscapes" sequence originated in his American visit. He was, however, actively involved, as a director of
Faber, in publishing the work of other poets, notably the new
generation that followed the appearance of Auden's *Poems* under
the Faber imprint in 1930. Although Eliot was not solely responsible for the Faber poetry list, he took on the job of dealing personally with the poets and formed friendships with several of them;
Stephen Spender was one, and he has recalled Eliot's great consideration and concern, and his unruffled tolerance of the criticisms
which Spender, as a Marxist, felt obliged to make of Eliot's ideological position. Eliot was a valuable member of Faber and Faber,
and an immensely hard worker, as Morley testifies:

Of course anybody who did not speak English went to Eliot automati-
cally, as did all correspondence and manuscripts in any foreign language. He had more manuscripts to read than anybody else, and the
odd thing was, he really read them. He was sought after not merely as
a publisher, but as an employment agent . . .[6]

One skill of Eliot's that was particularly prized was his capability
as a blurb-writer, of which Morley comments that "during his publishing career he has turned out so many blurbs as to make it quite
impossible that he should have time or energy left over to write
anything else." Eliot enjoyed the routines of publishing. There was
a certain amount of playful ritual among the directors of Faber
and Faber, including a boyish love of practical jokes, in which
Eliot enthusiastically participated. As he wrote in *Notes Towards
the Definition of Culture*, "the congeniality of any circle of friends
depends upon a common social convention, a common ritual, and
common pleasures of relaxation."

Meanwhile, his long-standing interest in the drama had revived.
In the last of his Harvard lectures he had remarked, "The ideal

[5] Allen Tate, ed., *T. S. Eliot: The Man and His Work* (New York: Delacorte Press, 1966; London: Chatto & Windus, 1967), p. 105.
[6] Richard March and Tambimuttu, eds., *T. S. Eliot: A Symposium* (London: Poetry London, 1948; Chicago: Henry Regnery Co., 1949), p. 66.

medium for poetry, to my mind, and the most direct means of social 'usefulness' for poetry, is the theatre," and soon after his return
from America an unexpected opportunity arose for Eliot to write
for the stage. In 1930 George Bell, Bishop of Chichester, appointed
a young producer, E. Martin Browne, to a new post as director of
religious drama for the diocese. Knowing of Eliot's interest in the
theater and hoping that he would put his gifts at the service of the
church, Bishop Bell invited Eliot as a weekend guest in December
1930. Eliot read *Ash-Wednesday* aloud to the assembled company,
but the meeting was not immediately fruitful. Nevertheless, it had
the important result of introducing Browne and Eliot to each
other. Within a few years Browne was to be Eliot's closest collaborator in the theater, and his book *The Making of T. S. Eliot's
Plays* is a mine of information about the textual and theatrical history of the plays; I am much indebted to it in the descriptive account which follows. During 1933 Browne was working with the
Rev. R. Webb-Odell on a projected pageant of the history of the
church in London, which was intended to raise funds for church
building in new housing areas. Browne prepared a draft scenario,
but was not satisfied with his work, and in September 1933 he renewed his acquaintance with Eliot and invited him to provide the
words for the play. Eliot accepted and enthusiastically took on the
exacting task of providing a script for a largely preexisting story.
He welcomed it, for reasons which he later described in "The
Three Voices of Poetry":

The invitation to write the words for this spectacle . . . came at a moment when I seemed to myself to have exhausted my meagre poetic
gifts, and to have nothing more to say. To be, at such a moment, commissioned to write something which, good or bad, must be delivered by
a certain date, may have the effect that vigorous cranking sometimes has
upon a motor car when the battery is run down. The task was clearly
laid out: I had only to write the words of prose dialogue for scenes of
the usual historical pageant pattern, for which I had been given a
scenario. I had also to provide a number of choral passages in verse, the
content of which was left to my own devices: except for the reasonable
stipulation that all the choruses were expected to have some relevance
to the purpose of the pageant, and that each chorus was to occupy a
precise number of minutes of stage time.

This pageant play was *The Rock*, which was produced by Browne with music by Martin Shaw, at the Sadler's Wells Theatre, London, from May 28 to June 9, 1934. The reviews were respectful, considering the specialized nature of the enterprise, and the notice in the *Times* must have been particularly gratifying to Eliot, for it suggested that *The Rock* had fulfilled his early aspirations for a new theatrical mode which would incorporate both liturgical and popular elements:

Mr. Eliot's pageant play looked first to liturgy for its dramatic form, though wisely imitating also the ready and popular stage modes, such as music-hall, ballet and mime . . . Mr. Eliot . . . has created a new thing in the theatre and made smoother the path towards a contemporary poetic drama.

In 1934, too, Eliot's first attempt at dramatic writing, *Sweeney Agonistes,* was performed in London; it was produced at the Group Theatre rooms by Rupert Doone, who was subsequently responsible for staging the dramatic experiments of Auden and Isherwood, Louis MacNeice, and Stephen Spender. *Sweeney* was repeated in 1935, as part of a series of Group plays at the Westminster Theatre.

After the production of *The Rock* Bishop Bell invited Eliot to write a play for the Canterbury Festival in 1935, and Eliot agreed on the condition that Browne would produce it. His subject—the murder of Archbishop Thomas Becket in Canterbury Cathedral in the year 1170—had a strong dramatic appeal as well as appropriate local associations: for Eliot the martyred Becket was a symbol of Christian witness and fortitude in a time of public violence and political corruption, and his treatment of the theme emphasizes its contemporary significance. *Murder in the Cathedral* is a full-scale liturgical drama, whose intention has been well summarized by Browne: "The purpose of the play was to be the same as that of most Greek tragedies—to celebrate the cult associated with a sacred spot by displaying the story of its origin." The play was first performed in the Chapter House of Canterbury Cathedral on June 15, 1935, with Robert Speaight as Becket. It was immediately acclaimed, and after transferring to London ran for several months, first in the tiny Mercury Theatre and then at the Duchess

Theatre, as well as appearing successfully in the provinces. The *Times* reviewer called it, "the one great play by a contemporary dramatist now to be seen in England." To this day *Murder in the Cathedral* has retained its popularity, and can be reasonably considered the most approachable and theatrically rewarding of Eliot's full-length plays. As Browne records, the play underwent many textual changes in the course of production, and certain excisions were peculiarly important for Eliot, as he records:

There were lines and fragments that were discarded in the course of the production of *Murder in the Cathedral.* "Can't get them over on the stage," said the producer, and I humbly bowed to his judgment. However, these fragments stayed in my mind, and gradually I saw a poem shaping itself round them: in the end it came out as "Burnt Norton."[7]

Thus, Eliot's venture into the theater unexpectedly led him back to the writing of "pure" poetry. In the end "Burnt Norton" became the first of the *Quartets,* but it originally appeared by itself in 1936 as the concluding poem of Eliot's *Collected Poems 1909–1935.*

Following the success of *Murder in the Cathedral* it was predictable that Eliot would receive invitations to write more of the same kind of thing; but given his disinclination to repeat himself in his creative work it was not surprising that he would decline to write more historical or religious plays. He was now determined to write a verse play with a modern setting, though it would utilize a classical myth. Again, one can quote Browne for its genesis:

The seed from which it sprang had been sown long since; as one can see from the epigraph of *Sweeney Agonistes,* Orestes and the Furies' pursuit of him had already a contemporary relevance in Eliot's mind. How it came to be envisaged as happening in a north-country mansion I do not know; but our diary tells us that already on 14 November 1937, Eliot "came to supper and read new play."[8]

The new play, *The Family Reunion,* was the subject of exhaustive discussion between Eliot and Browne and other friends and went into numerous drafts, as Browne duly records. It eventually opened at the Westminster Theatre on March 21, 1939, with Michael Red-

[7] *New York Times Book Review,* November 29, 1953.
[8] *The Making of T. S. Eliot's Plays* (Cambridge: At the University Press, 1969), p. 90.

grave in the leading role of Harry Monchensey: it received a more mixed reception than *Murder in the Cathedral.* Although the reviews praised the distinguished language of the play there were doubts about its theatrical effectiveness.

1939, so black a year in European history, was personally significant for Eliot in several ways. In the February issue of *The Criterion* he announced that he was giving up the editorship; and with a journal which for seventeen years had been so personal a vehicle for his tastes and opinions it was not feasible that another editor could easily take it over. Eliot's reasons, as he explained in his editorial "Last Words," were a compound of personal fatigue and profound depression at the state of Europe. The intellectual community of the twenties had ceased to exist: "The 'European mind,' which one had mistakenly thought might be renewed and fortified, disappeared from view: there were fewer writers in any country who seemed to have anything to say to the intellectual public of another." Eliot looked back with pride on the distinguished writers he had published, but was distressed at *The Criterion's* failure in the later years of its life to preserve its original spirit in a hostile and valueless world: "how obscure and confused my own mind has been, my Commentaries bear painful witness." They were indeed often obscure and confused, and in recognizing the fact Eliot showed the disconcerting honesty and directness that he was capable of in his self-criticism. Eliot sees little light ahead, but he hopes that others will take over the torch, and attempt to preserve literary and intellectual standards:

In the present state of public affairs—which has induced in myself a depression of spirits so different from any other experience of fifty years as to be a new emotion—I no longer feel the enthusiasm necessary to make a literary review what it should be.

Eliot's relief at giving up the burden is palpable. The following month he attended the first night of *The Family Reunion* and delivered his Cambridge lectures on *The Idea of a Christian Society.* Correcting the proofs of the latter work, he added a note dated September 6, 1939, three days after Britain had declared war on Germany, that the possibility of war had always been in his mind while he was writing the book, and "we cannot afford to defer our constructive thinking to the conclusion of hostilities." The book appeared in the following month, and so did another work which revealed a far less familiar aspect of his literary personality: *Old Possum's Book of Practical Cats.* Eliot's gravely whimsical addresses to his favorite animal, composed with great metrical brilliance, showed him a worthy descendent of Lewis Carroll and Edward Lear as a writer of serious light verse. It was not, perhaps, a bad note on which to end a dismal decade.

4

The poetry that followed Eliot's conversion was in no way overtly confessional or propagandist, but it had a new tonality. The irony and the deliberately grotesque and bizarre detail had disappeared, and although the poems were still organized musically rather than logically the transitions and juxtapositions were less abrupt and startling. The Ariel Poems of 1927 and 1928, "Journey of the Magi" and "A Song for Simeon" indicate, as I have remarked, a concern with the Incarnation as a painful rather than a joyous transformation. Considered as poetic structures, they are dramatic monologues of a more straightforward kind than anything Eliot had previously produced. The language has the clarity and openness of texture that we find in his later writing for the theater; they also show Eliot's new tendency to incorporate scriptural and liturgical phrases into his verse. A comparison between these two poems and "Gerontion" is revealing: there is a continuity in tone and feeling, but the Ariel Poems are far less complicated. They are also, one must add, rhythmically less interesting than all Eliot's previous poetry, and read like summaries of experience rather than enactments of it. A third Ariel Poem "Animula" (1929) opens with a line from *Purgatorio* XVI, " 'Issues from the hand of God, the simple soul,' " and ends with a phrase adapted from the *Ave Maria,* "Pray for us now and at the hour of our birth." The poem makes an Augustinian variation on a Wordsworthian theme: the simple soul of the child—rendered with the familiar poignancy of Eliot's treatment of childhood—grows up from play to adult imperatives and spiritual deadness and, ultimately, to the violent shattering of all worldly aspirations. It is a revealing rather than a successful poem, with an unsatisfactorily forced conclusion.

Faced with such relatively minor and unadventurous poems as these an observer in the late twenties might well have endorsed the common assumption that Eliot's conversion had coincided with, if not caused, a sharp decline in poetic force and originality. This assumption could not, however, be easily applied to *Ash-Wednesday* (1930), uncongenial though that work might seem because of its religious themes and its Dantean and liturgical language and imagery. It shows Eliot's constantly surprising capacity for renewing his own art, and is, I think, one of the pinnacles of his achievement, coming not far short of *The Waste Land*. In essence *Ash-Wednesday* is a poem of conversion, beginning at the point of humility and repentence indicated by its title, although it does not provide a comprehensive summary of spiritual struggle and achievement. Rather, it traces the precise emotional trajectory of the experience itself, with all its difficulties and indecisions, which Eliot enacts in the marvelously subtle and expressive movement of his verse; in *Ash-Wednesday* he discovers a whole new range of rhythmical possibilities. One can apply to it Eliot's own description of George Herbert's *Temple:* "a record of the spiritual struggle of a man of intellectual power and emotional intensity who gave much toil to perfecting his verses." The spiritual and the poetic exploration are, in fact, one; F. R. Leavis has said of *Ash-Wednesday,* "poetic technique for Eliot here is a technique for sincerity." The poem does, however, present difficulties, in both its literary and its religious assumptions. The influence of Dante is pervasive, and in its original version the section headings bore titles taken from the *Divine Comedy,* three of them using the Provençal words of Arnaut Daniel in *Purgatorio* XXVI, which had fascinated Eliot ever since he published *Ara Vos Prec* ten years before. Dante was, for Eliot, more than just a literary influence; he was an integral part of his own literary personality, whose poetry had, in Rilke's words, "turned to blood within him." For years he had read Dante with total admiration and a strong sense of identification: after becoming a Christian he would have felt even closer, since he could now participate in Dante's own system of beliefs (even if this participation could never be total, being affected by the inescapable struggle with doubt that Eliot so lucidly described in his essay on Pascal). For the modern reader, the presence of Dante in *Ash-Wednesday* might seem a needless literary intrusion, and Eliot's need to give his religious emotions a medieval embodiment will be equally arbitrary, especially on those occasions when, despite his intentions, they take a form that looks Pre-Raphaelite rather than authentically Dantean.

The poetic quality of *Ash-Wednesday* exists independently of its sources, though it is illuminating to read it with some acquaintance with the *Divine Comedy* and the *Vita Nuova*, if only to observe Eliot's highly idiosyncratic treatment of Dantean effects, to which Mario Praz has drawn attention. Eliot's brilliant essay, "Dante" (1929), describes his own devotion to Dante, and lets us see Dante through Eliot's eyes. It provides a kind of anthology of Dantean "touchstones," with Eliot's own prose translations; in particular, the essay shows how Eliot saw Dante as, above all, a poet of clear visual images and great verbal economy, whose poetry was direct, forceful, and free of needless ornamentation. This was by no means the whole of Dante, as Praz has pointed out, but it was the aspect of Dante to which Eliot was most drawn, and which is strongly influential in *Ash-Wednesday*.

E. E. Duncan Jones, in her excellent essay on *Ash-Wednesday*, has provided the following succinct account of the poem:

It is evident that although in *Ash Wednesday* Eliot follows Dante in many respects, he does not limit the suggestions of his symbols as Dante does, or as his commentators have done for him. Nor does he present the reader with a narrative which embodies his "states of feeling." Nevertheless with some good will, and using the order of Dante's experiences as a guide, it is possible to disengage a "story" from the poem. The sequence begins with a poem of which the centre is the renunciation of a "blessèd face" and voice: this is followed by a vision of spiritual renewal, presided over by a Beatrice-figure who is also the Church, as Beatrice was also Theology; then there comes the ascent of a spiritual stair, with a backward glance at carnal loveliness: and then a scene in a garden or churchyard where "she" appears, transfigured and glorified. One feels, however, that if the poet had attached much importance to the narrative element he would have made it more important. The stress is perhaps rather on the sequence of images: there is, as he remarks in his preface to the translation of St-J. Perse's *Anabase* which was published in the same year as *Ash Wednesday*, "a logic of the imagination as well as a logic of concepts": and *Ash Wednesday* relies as much on the one as on the other.[9]

Mrs. Duncan Jones is right to refer only lightly to the element of "story": if *Ash-Wednesday* is like "Prufrock" in involving us in a particular zone of consciousness and feeling, it differs from the earlier poem in showing marked development, however much this falls short of coherent narrative. Nor has Eliot abandoned the symbolist method: combined with Dantean exactness, it produces the curious sense of precision in vagueness that characterizes *Ash-Wednesday*. Thus, although the successive appearances of the Lady may recall the superimposed significances of Dante's Beatrice, she is also reminiscent of the way in which in *The Waste Land* one character "melts into" another, as Eliot puts it. In *The Sacred Wood* Eliot had expressed his admiration for Dante's large-scale symbolic and hierarchical structure, but he was well aware that he could never hope to reproduce it, and as a poet he never tried to. He was, rather, fascinated by the detail of Dante's imagery, and it was this he was most affected by, as Praz has acutely commented:

The pattern of the images in *Ash Wednesday* seems thus suggested by Dante, but in a very peculiar way. It is as if Eliot had been reading Dante without giving much heed to the meaning, but letting himself be impressed by a few clear visual images: these he rearranged in his own mind just as in a kaleidoscope the same coloured glasses can give a no less harmonious (though different) design than the previous one.[10]

Ash-Wednesday can be enjoyed musically, or as an attempt at what Eliot called the "disciplined dream" of Dante, without much preparation beyond a certain openness toward its governing emotions. When one moves beyond this level, however, it reveals itself as a complex poem which requires a good deal of space to explicate: at this point the interested reader can be referred to the

[9] B. Rajan, ed., *T. S. Eliot, A Study of his Writings by Several Hands* (London: Dobson, 1947; New York: Russell & Russell, 1966), pp. 37–38.
[10] Leonard Unger, ed., *T. S. Eliot, a Selected Critique* (New York: Russell & Russell, 1966), pp. 314–15.

detailed commentaries of Mrs. Duncan Jones, Leonard Unger, and Grover Smith. I shall merely conclude with a few comments on parts of the poem that seem to me of particular interest.

The most striking section is, perhaps, the second, which was in fact the first to be written; in this superbly articulated vision Eliot picks up the theme of dehumanization that we find in his early poems ("I should have been a pair of ragged claws") and transforms it into an exercise in Christian humility, where the protagonist conceives of himself as having been consumed by three heraldic or scriptural leopards, and his scattered dry bones sing "chirping" a litany to the Blessed Virgin. Eliot's sources were in the Book of Ezekiel and a story by Jakob Grimm, but nowhere has he written more personally. As Mrs. Duncan Jones has said, it "strikingly shows Eliot's *stil nuovo*." The section is a self-contained poem which fuses delicate fantasy, assured but unemphatic rhythms, and spiritual insight. The third section of *Ash-Wednesday* is equally moving; here Eliot's already familiar "staircase" image is used to denote a spiritual ascent, where

> the devil of the stairs who wears
> The deceitful face of hope and of despair

looks like an embodiment of what he called, in the Pascal essay, "the demon of doubt which is inseparable from the spirit of belief." The temptation to a carnal backward look is presented in words of haunting beauty and considerable erotic intensity:

> Blown hair is sweet, brown hair over the mouth blown,
> Lilac and brown hair;
> Distraction, music of the flute, stops and steps of the
>   mind over the third stair,
> Fading, fading; strength beyond hope and despair
> Climbing the third stair.

Many readers might not comprehend the rejection of what is so attractively presented; yet the sensibility that can present the scene is certainly not desiccated or bloodless. Negations in poetry, as someone once observed, are often partial affirmations.

These lines incidentally illustrate Eliot's capacity for suddenly evoking an earlier phase of his work. Thus, the four-word line,

"Lilac and brown hair," carries echoes of lines written twenty years before:

> Now that lilacs are in bloom
> She has a bowl of lilacs in her room.
>
> Arms that are braceleted and white and bare
> [But in the lamplight, downed with light brown hair!]

Such effects are frequent in Eliot's poetry and plays, and suggest that an awareness of what he had written in the past may often have been an element in the act of creation. They contribute significantly to the unity of Eliot's *oeuvre*.

The fourth section of *Ash-Wednesday* conveys a fine sense of coolness and withdrawal, and is the most intensely Dantean, being unobtrusively pervaded with images drawn from the appearances of Beatrice in the final cantos of the *Purgatorio*. The fifth section is, in my view, by far the weakest part of the sequence: the overemphatic word-play—despite its source in St. John's Gospel and Bishop Andrewes—and feminine rhymes strike a jarring note. In the final section Eliot returns to the renunciatory note of the opening, though the syntax is significantly different: "Because I do not hope to turn again" has become "Although I do not hope to turn again," suggesting that once the new life has been firmly accepted the possibility of value in the old life can still be recognized. Eliot enlarges on this prospect in some superb lines which draw directly on his boyhood memories of the New England shore:

> And the lost heart stiffens and rejoices
> In the lost lilac and the lost sea voices
> And the weak spirit quickens to rebel
> For the bent golden-rod and the lost sea smell.

Here, unmistakably, we are in the presence of one of the great poets of our language.

The tensions of *Ash-Wednesday* were poetically resolved in "Marina" (1930), the fourth and by far the best of Eliot's Ariel Poems. "Marina" is, in fact, the most exquisitely beautiful of all his short poems, with a unique quality. In invokes the lost and found daughter of Shakespeare's *Pericles,* and the seashore images of part VI of *Ash-Wednesday,* to convey a sense of restoration and harmony; the whole poem presents a "privileged moment" (to use a Bergsonian phrase) of serenity and transfiguration in an immensely skillful concentration of imagery, rhythm, and syntax. It contains a perennial motif of Eliot's poetry—"Whispers and small laughter between leaves and hurrying feet"—and suggests a possible reconcilation between the spirit and the senses, and even, a rare note in Eliot, the possibility of natural blessedness. Eliot's fifth Ariel Poem, "Triumphal March," appeared in 1931, and was later combined with "Difficulties of a Statesman," to appear as *Coriolan* in the Unfinished Poems section of his *Collected Poems*. Leavis has said that the Coriolan poems are "certainly great poetry, and they come as near to great satiric poetry as this age is likely to see," which seems an exaggerated estimate. They are certainly an interesting attempt on Eliot's part at the kind of public poetry that became fashionable a little later in the thirties, and they have something in common with the disapproving surveys in his *Criterion* editorials, where totalitarianism and democracy are found equally wanting. Eliot seems to be symbolizing pagan statesmanship in the figure of Coriolanus, who had appeared at several earlier moments in his poetry: part V of *The Waste Land,* "A Cooking Egg," and the epigraph to the suppressed "Ode" of *Ara Vos Prec.* Against Coriolanus is set the figure of Arthur Edward Cyril Parker, as a representative of mass man, and it seems that the projected work was to show their respectively developing careers. There is some impressive rhetoric in *Coriolan,* but the impact of the satire is, I think, reduced by Eliot's adherence to the method of multiple implication that served him so well in his lyrical and reflective poetry. Thus, in "Triumphal March" a Roman triumph merges with Christ's entry into Jerusalem and the victory parades of 1919: Eliot even transcribes verbatim a list of all the armaments surrendered by Germany after the Treaty of Versailles. The synchronic visions of "Tradition and the Individual Talent" or *The Waste Land* cannot easily accord with the single-mindedness of satire, and *Coriolan* looks like a fragmentary pointer in a direction that Eliot did not feel able to take. In the thirties his creative energies turned to drama, and he wrote little poetry of much stature; the one major exception is "Burnt Norton," which really belongs with the completed *Quartets* as a poem of the forties. However, one critic, John Fuller, has seen the seemingly whimsical "Five Finger Exercises" of 1933 as a piece of semi-serious self-satire on Eliot's part. In the last of them we see Eliot coldly regarding himself in the manner of his hostile critics:

> How unpleasant to meet Mr. Eliot!
> With his features of clerical cut,
> And his brow so grim
> And his mouth so prim
> And his conversation, so nicely
> Restricted to What Precisely
> And If and Perhaps and But.

5

As a theatrical experiment, *The Rock* served the useful purpose of directing Eliot's creative energies once more into dramatic channels, and as a fund-raising spectacle performed before sympathetic audiences it was, no doubt, very effective for its limited occasion. Otherwise, however, there is little to be said for it. In the prose sketches Eliot's writing is limp and uninspired, and the speech of the Cockney workmen building a new church is extraordinarily labored and inauthentic compared with the stylized realism of the pub scene in *The Waste Land*. The only interest of *The Rock* lies in the choruses, which have been preserved in Eliot's *Collected Poems*. Soon after the production in 1934 he denied that *The Rock* could be called a contribution to dramatic literature; it was, he insisted, a revue: "My only serious aim was to show that there is a possible *rôle* for the Chorus." The choruses are something new in Eliot's verse: they are emphatic and rather coarse in texture, exhibiting considerable formal variety but little rhythmic subtlety. There are occasional moments of poetic life that look forward to the *Quartets*, but overall the choruses are excessively didactic, harshly instructing the audience in Christian truth and haranguing them for their godless ways. Eliot later admitted as much in "The Three Voices of Poetry": "it was the second voice, that of myself addressing—indeed haranguing—an audience, that was most distinctly audible."

Eliot used the chorus to far greater effect in *Murder in the*

Cathedral, which is probably the most theatrically successful poetic drama written in English since the seventeenth century: not that there has been much competition, though one should not forget the once very popular historical verse plays of the late-Victorian Stephen Phillips. Much of the impact of *Murder in the Cathedral* is conveyed by the chorus, which participates in the unfolding of the action in a way that looks back to the remote origins of Western drama. The point has been well brought out by David E. Jones in his book on Eliot's plays. He remarks that in Aeschylus the chorus "opens up the spiritual dimension of the action" and that this is essentially what happens in *Murder in the Cathedral,* a play structurally modeled on Greek tragedy: "He has used the chorus to open out the action into its full significance, as nobody else has done since Aeschylus." Mr. Jones quotes from a broadcast talk given by Eliot in 1936, where he says that the Greek chorus "mediates between the action and the audience; it intensifies the action by projecting its emotional consequences, so that we as the audience see it doubly, by seeing its effect on other people." In general this is true of the Women of Canterbury in Eliot's play: in contrast to *The Rock,* these choruses project a real poetic amplification of the action:

> I have smelt them, the death-bringers, senses are quickened
> By subtle forebodings; I have heard
> Fluting in the nighttime, fluting and owls, have seen at noon
> Scaly wings slanting over, huge and ridiculous. I have tasted
> The savour of putrid flesh in the spoon. I have felt
> The heaving of earth at nightfall, restless, absurd.

Such lines make a powerful projection of a disordered collective consciousness; later in the same speech there is a reminder of the pervasive unity of Eliot's work in the phrase, "I have lain on the floor of the sea," recalling "We have lingered in the chambers of the sea" of "Prufrock." The intense but accessible poetic quality of the choruses was undoubtedly one reason for the popularity of Eliot's play, though not all listeners were moved by them. Ezra Pound wrote to James Laughlin from Rapallo:

Waal, I heerd the *Murder in the Cafedrawl* on the radio lass' night. Oh them cawkney woices, My Krissz, them cawkney woices. Mzzr Shakzpeer *still* retains his posishun. I stuck it fer a while, wot wiff the weepin and wailin.

The central situation of the play is compelling: the struggle of the lonely and courageous individual against an unjust and ultimately murderous authority is a common twentieth-century situation, and one which Eliot's synchronous superimposition of the medieval and the modern brings inescapably home to the audience. Again, there is the powerful theatrical appeal of liturgy: in *Murder in the Cathedral* Eliot not only recalled the contemporary drama to its remote liturgical origins, but he deliberately short-circuited the gap between them. Even a sermon, such as forms the center-piece of Eliot's play, can be an effective piece of theater, as was shown in the nineteen-sixties in John Osborne's *Luther*. In *Murder in the Cathedral* Eliot struck a fine balance between the hieratic and the familiar, without ever being deeply obscure, and provided his audience with an interesting combination of the emotions usually felt in church and those customarily aroused in the theater. All of which contributed to the remarkable success of the play. One calls its success "remarkable" advisedly, because in fact *Murder in the Cathedral* is singularly deficient in drama, considered as the enactment of conflict. The political struggle between Becket and the King has taken place long before the play opens, and we are merely witnesses to its violent final stage. The real conflict, of course, takes place within Becket himself and it is aroused by the Fourth Tempter, offering Becket satisfaction in martyrdom for the glory it will bring:

> The last temptation is the greatest treason:
> To do the right deed for the wrong reason.

And yet this temptation cannot be spurned like the preceding ones, since it is not possible for Becket to reject martyrdom, no matter how unsure he may be of his reasons for embracing it. So this temptation, having been posited, is quietly forgotten and Becket moves serenely on to his inevitable death. In essence *Murder in the Cathedral* is a monodrama, with only one character, as Eliot himself has acknowledged: "what dramatic conflict there is takes place within the mind of that character." We are not far

removed from the enclosed consciousnesses of Prufrock or Gerontion, where nothing really happens. Katharine Worth, who refers
to "the deep trance of self-communion in which Becket is engaged
for most of the play" has emphasized the undramatic isolation of
the central character:

> . . . in *Murder in the Cathedral* the isolated elements are meant to co-
> alesce, Chorus and Saint to come together in the redemption of one by
> the death of the other. That there has been an interior happening of this
> kind is declared poetically with such skill as almost to convince us that
> it has happened dramatically too. But it has not. The Chorus are not
> involved in any human relationship with Becket real enough to move
> belief in his having power to affect their lives. They are only a collective
> voice, not living people with a share in the action.[11]

Like *Sweeney Agonistes* before it, *Murder in the Cathedral* seems
to illustrate Eliot's capacity to master dramatic language without
a corresponding mastery of dramatic action. Nevertheless, the play
has proved itself a theatrical success on many occasions, and indicates that good theater is not always the same as effective drama.
David E. Jones has remarked suggestively that it "resembles certain of the vocal works of Stravinsky more than anything in English dramatic art." It may indeed be that *Murder in the Cathedral*
works as a finely scored oratorio rather than a drama.

Becket, like Sweeney in the dramatic fragments of 1926–1927,
was possessed of a graver burden of consciousness than those
around him. So, too, is Harry Monchensey, hero of *The Family Reunion,* where Eliot turns from the hieratic to the naturalistic.
Harry represents Eliot's second attempt on the Orestes theme: indeed the words from *The Choephoroi* about the Furies that formed
the epigraph to *Sweeney Agonistes* are paraphrased by Harry
soon after his first entrance: "Can't you see them? *You* don't see
them, but I see them." In 1923 Eliot wrote in a review of *Ulysses*
in *The Dial,* "In using the myth, in manipulating a continuous
parallel between contemporaneity and antiquity, Mr. Joyce is
pursuing a method which others must pursue after him." *The
Family Reunion* is Eliot's first sustained attempt to do so in the
dramatic medium: a theme from the *Oresteia* is woven into a

[11] Martin, ed., *Eliot in Perspective*, p. 156.

drama set in a mansion in the north of England, where there is a gathering of the members of a rather rundown aristocratic family. The Aeschylean parallel is only brokenly preserved, though it becomes explicit when the choruses of aunts and uncles (a much more marginal affair than in *Murder in the Cathedral*) declaim, in an allusion to lines from *The Eumenides:*

> And we know nothing of exorcism
> And whether in Argos or England
> There are certain inflexible laws
> Unalterable, in the nature of music.

Eliot's interest in Aeschylus was significant and enduring. It was first apparent in "Sweeney Among the Nightingales," with its epigraph taken from the dying words of Agamemnon, and in 1921 Eliot sent Pound what seems to have been a draft translation from Aeschylus, though no more was heard of it. As we have seen, the structure of *Murder in the Cathedral* is Aeschylean, and the story of Orestes and the Furies sufficiently affected Eliot's imagination for him to make two attempts at giving it a contemporary dramatic rendering. (As early as 1919 he referred, in a review of Henry Adams, to "The Erinys which drove him madly through seventy years of search for education.") In "Four Elizabethan Dramatists" (1924) Eliot praises the dramatic concentration of Aeschylus and observes that an ideal production of an Elizabethan drama would be something "like a performance of *Agamemnon* by the Guitrys." The result is not easily imagined, but Eliot was trying to express his desire for a poetic drama that would combine a maximum of stylized emotional intensity with a maximum of what would nowadays be called "contemporary relevance."

In *The Family Reunion* he tried to make such a combination, and the result is hardly a success. Harry Monchensey is, up to a point, dramatically interesting. The audience will be concerned to know whether or not he murdered his wife at sea, and if he did why he is not more repentant about the matter, though they will certainly be baffled by the ambiguity of Harry's relations with his mother Amy, his aunt Agatha, and his cousin Mary. And as in Eliot's earlier dramatic efforts the central defect is a lack of palpable dramatic action. At the end of the play Harry may decide, to his spiritual benefit, to follow rather than flee from the Furies, who have been vaguely Christianized as "bright angels." But it is extraordinarily hard to trace any real connection between his change of heart and what we see enacted on the stage. Eliot was shrewdly aware of these deficiencies and his essay "Poetry and Drama" (1951) contains some remarkably incisive self-criticism. He admits that "I had given my attention to versification, at the expense of plot and character" and that some of the lyrical duets, no matter how moving as poetry, do not help forward the action, but remain apart from it. More importantly, he is aware of the lack of real development: "after what must seem to the audience an interminable time of preparation, the conclusion comes so abruptly that we are, after all, unready for it." He is also dissatisfied with the working out of the Aeschylean parallel: "I should either have stuck closer to Aeschylus or else taken a great deal more liberty with his myth." The Furies are quite unmanageable in practical theatrical terms, he says, and should be omitted from further productions. And even more damning is the conclusion that "we are left in a divided frame of mind, not knowing whether to consider the play the tragedy of the mother or the salvation of the son." It is not easy to disagree with such authoritative criticism, although Katharine Worth has argued that *The Family Reunion* is a better play than its author contends, and has given an interesting account of a student production in London in 1966 that successfully solved the problem of presenting the Furies.

In 1936 Eliot had asserted "the necessity for poetic drama at the present time to emphasise, not to minimise, the fact that it is written in verse." This position was relevant to *Murder in the Cathedral*, though he adopted a diametrically opposed view when he returned to drama in the nineteen-fifties. The verse of *The Family Reunion* partakes both of the unobtrusively naturalistic and the evidently "poetic," and the combination is interesting though not always happy. Some of the poetic passages are remarkably beautiful, even though, as Eliot conceded, they are rather like operatic arias. The perennial motifs of Eliot's poetry are often visible:

> I only looked through the little door
> When the sun was shining on the rose-garden:

And heard in the distance tiny voices
And then a black raven flew over.
And then I was only my own feet walking
Away, down a concrete corridor
In a dead air. Only feet walking
And sharp heel scraping. Over and under
Echo and noise of feet.
I was only the feet, and the eye
Seeing the feet: the unwinking eye
Fixing the movement.

The rose garden and *ces voix d'enfants* and the unwinking eye
were part of the texture of his imagination. Yet such writing, impressive though it is, is something quite other than the "ballet of
words" that Eliot had looked for in his writings about the poetic
drama twenty years before, and which he had promisingly em-
bodied in his unfinished "jazz play" of the twenties. There was no
real way forward from *The Family Reunion* and the hints of Eliot's
earlier experiments were to be developed by such writers as
Beckett and Pinter, who had a sharper dramatic sense but far less
interesting minds.

Eliot's dramatic efforts can be seen as attempts to objectify, in
what he later called the "third voice" of poetry, certain pressing
if obscure personal preoccupations. The exceptional individual
who is separated from those around him by a fatal burden of consciousness and insight is recurrent, and can be expressed in a
criminal, like Sweeney, or a saint, like Becket, or a character who
has elements of both, like Harry Monchensey. The distinction between those who are elected to a peculiar destiny—whether salvation or damnation is immaterial—and the decent but imperceptive
multitude was fundamental to Eliot's apprehension of experience,
and can be seen as a highly personal variation on a major Romantic theme.

V

****

Wartime and the Nobel Prize

1940–1948

THE OUTBREAK OF WAR in 1939 had the effect of shaking Eliot out of the negative and despairing attitude to public events which had possessed him during the nineteen-thirties. In Stephen Spender's words, "the war modified his attitude by convincing him that there was a Western cause to be positively defended. And after the war there was a Germany to be brought back within the Western tradition." The war also had the effect of directing Eliot back to the writing of lyrical and meditative poetry, and of interrupting his career as a dramatist: in the uncertainties and privations of wartime the "first voice" of poetry reasserted itself.

During the first few months of the war he wrote "East Coker," structurally modeled on "Burnt Norton." The new poem appeared in the *New English Weekly* on March 21, 1940. It aroused such interest that it was twice reprinted as a supplement to the magazine, and then published as a booklet by Faber in September 1940. It was only after completing "East Coker" that Eliot conceived the *Quartets* as a set of four poems with the same form. "The Dry Salvages" followed in 1941 and "Little Gidding" in 1942; the sequence was published in book form in the United States in 1943 and in England in 1944. Eliot's earlier assumption that he had written himself out as far as "pure" poetry was concerned had been emphatically disproved.

Nineteen-forty was the year of Dunkirk, the fall of France, and the Battle of Britain, but one sees little sign of these events in Eliot's writing. There is, however, "Defence of the Islands," which strikes an austerely patriotic note: it was originally written to accompany an exhibition of photographs in New York illustrating the British war effort, and Eliot included it in the 1963 edition of his *Collected Poems* with the comment that "its date—just after the evacuation from Dunkirk—and occasion have for me a significance which makes me wish to preserve it." In June 1940, the month of Dunkirk, Eliot went to Dublin to deliver a memorial lecture on Yeats to the Friends of the Irish Academy at the Abbey Theatre. It is a noble tribute, in which Eliot speaks with warmth of his great older contemporary, about whose work he had in the past been sometimes distinctly cool. Much of the fascination of the Yeats lecture lies in the way in which Eliot seems to be discussing not only Yeats's development and achievements but, obliquely, his own. It is the poet of the *Quartets* who writes:

it is my experience that towards middle age a man has three choices: to stop writing altogether, to repeat himself with perhaps an increasing skill of virtuosity, or by taking thought to adapt himself to middle age and find a different way of working.

And Eliot goes on to gloss and extend his celebrated early doctrine of "impersonality" in describing the superior impersonality of the poet "who, out of intense and personal experience, is able to express a general truth; retaining all the particularity of his experience, to make of it a general symbol."

Some of Eliot's wartime experience found its way into "Little Gidding." During the bombing of London in 1940–1941 Eliot served as a watcher on the roof of the Faber office, looking out for fires. He has recalled that after the bombing debris would be suspended in the air, "Then it would slowly descend and cover one's sleeves and coat with a fine white ash."

In July 1941 Eliot wrote to Martin Browne, who had been urging him to embark on another play and had even sent Eliot a detailed suggestion for a play about Simeon: "I am at present struggling to get on paper the fourth of my series of poems and that attempt, if successful, is likely to occupy my spare time for several weeks more." And after that, Eliot added, he had a formidable number of lectures to prepare; nevertheless, he held out the hope that eventually he would turn to drama again, if not precisely to the theme Browne had outlined: "I don't think I shall want to write any more poems in the immediate future and therefore my next attempt at anything interesting to myself will probably be a play." This time Eliot was right about having given up poetry, for "Little Gidding" was the last poem of any importance that he ever published, though it was still to be several more years before he returned to playwriting. At the same time he was continuing to develop his social thinking from the point it had reached in *The Idea of a Christian Society.* In 1940 he expressed a more reserved attitude to Maurras than heretofore, and said of his defense of the *Action Française* in 1928: "my *particular* defence may or not stand; but I believe now that the Pope understood its tendencies better." In September 1941 Eliot engaged in reflections on the French Vichy government which have been subsequently made to appear, by selective quotation, as though he supported the ideology of that government. This was not, in fact, the case. After deploring the Vichy enactment of anti-Semitic laws and hoping that Christian voices would be raised against them in France, Eliot wrote:

The device *Liberté, Egalité, Fraternité* is only the memorial of the time of the revolution: *Famille, Travail, Patrie* has more permanent value. But to substitute the second for the first is to go further than merely to call attention to equal, or even to higher values: it is by implication the denial and repudiation of the first. It suggests the danger of a reaction which might be as bad, or worse than that from which it reacts. To have affirmed Liberty, Equality, Fraternity in that way was, I think, unfortunate: but to repudiate them in this way is at least an equal error.[1]

In 1943 Eliot published a series of articles in the *New English Weekly* under the heading "Notes towards a Definition of Culture" which eventually developed into a book. He was also engaged in ecclesiastical controversy over the projected Church of South India, to be formed by a union of Anglican and Methodist churches. As an Anglo-Catholic Eliot objected to the role of bish-

[1] *Christian News Letter,* September 3, 1941.

ops in the proposed body, considering that the Apostolic Succession was not properly safeguarded, and he expressed his opposition in letters to the *Times* in 1943 and a pamphlet, *Reunion by Destruction*.

The war years in Britain were a period of material hardship, but vigorous artistic, intellectual, and educational activity, to which Eliot contributed by delivering lectures to a variety of audiences. It must have been a considerable burden to him, since he did not find lecturing easy or particularly congenial, and he wrote out his lectures verbatim, often making several drafts. All this was undertaken on top of his regular work as a publisher. Thus, in 1942 he delivered "The Music of Poetry" at the University of Glasgow, and "The Classics and the Man of Letters" as the Presidential Address to the Classical Association. In 1943 he spoke about "The Social Function of Poetry" at the British-Norwegian Institute in London, and the following year he delivered the Ballard-Matthews lectures at University College, Bangor, North Wales, on "Johnson as Poet and Critic." He also addressed the Association of Bookmen of Swansea and West Wales on "What is Minor Poetry?" and delivered "What is a Classic?" to the Virgil Society. In 1942 Eliot made a five-week visit to Sweden in the company of an old friend, George Bell, Bishop of Chichester; the purpose of the visit was to make fraternal contact with Swedish Christians, although Bishop Bell also received communications from the anti-Nazi resistance in Germany and met Dietrich Bonhoeffer.

By his public cultural activities Eliot participated in the sense of community and common purpose of wartime England; he had broken out of the imprisoning and frigid alienation of the thirties. He was still often critical of liberal *idées reçues,* but there could be no doubt that in the face of totalitarianism democracy was by far the lesser evil. Other writers had similar convictions, like the former Marxist C. Day Lewis, who discovered

> That we who live by honest dreams
> Defend the bad against the worse.

Eliot's busy life as man of letters and Christian spokesman brought his name before a larger audience than he had previously commanded, and the *Quartets* were widely read and discussed if not always fully understood: their spiritual assurance and stress on permanent values were welcome at a time of destruction and physical dislocation. The *Quartets* were fairly easily assimilated into the prevalent atmosphere of religious revival, and for a time Eliot was aligned in the public eye with the popular Anglican writers of the so-called Anglo-Oxford group, like C. S. Lewis, Charles Williams, and Dorothy Sayers.

Soon after the war Eliot made his first visit to America in thirteen years, and in New York he saw Laurence Olivier performing in the Yeats translation of *Oedipus Rex,* a highly praised production by the Old Vic company. This performance may have sent Eliot's thoughts back once more to his perennial preoccupation with poetic drama. At all events, after his return from America he was dwelling at length in letters to Martin Browne on possible revisions to *The Family Reunion,* which Browne was about to revive: the immediate postwar theatrical climate was receptive to verse plays, and a number had been successfully put on in London. Eliot's misgivings about *The Family Reunion* were increasing and he became convinced that the play was not really a success. Nevertheless, he eventually decided that there was little he could do to improve it by tinkering with the text, and in the end he accepted Browne's advice to leave it alone. The revived *Family Reunion* was put on in October 1946 at the Mercury Theatre, to a better reception than it had received in 1939. Meantime Browne was urging Eliot, yet again, to write a new play, and this time Eliot seemed finally ready to begin work on one.

Apart from the composition of the *Quartets* the war years and the immediate postwar period had been a period of marking time for Eliot, despite his public activity. But by 1948 it was clear that one phase of his life was ending and another about to begin. A significant personal event was the death of Vivien Eliot, after years of madness and confinement. Eliot's religious principles had never allowed him to consider divorce, but now he was free to marry again if he should ever wish to do so. In the late forties Eliot began to be far more of a public figure than ever before, and to acquire an international reputation. His trip to America in 1946 was followed by many other visits—in 1947 he received an honorary degree at Harvard—often to give lectures or fulfill other academic engagements. In fact Eliot visited America almost every year until his death. In January 1948 he was awarded the Order of Merit, the highest British civil decoration, membership of which is limited to twenty-four persons. "It was presented to me by the King in a very simple way in a very short audience," he told William Turner Levy. For all the simplicity of the occasion it must have been moving enough for the principled royalist who had once raised his hat to a sentry outside Marlborough House. In September 1948 he was back in the United States to take up a place at the Institute for Advanced Study at Princeton, where he hoped to complete his new play. But Eliot had not long been in residence when it was announced in November that he had been awarded the Nobel Prize for Literature. It was a striking sign of international recognition and he was showered with messages of congratulation. Yet the great honor brought with it inconveniences, like forcing him to cut short his time at Princeton in order to journey to Stockholm for the award.

Before returning to Europe Eliot visited Washington to fulfill two engagements. One was to lecture at the Library of Congress on "From Poe to Valery," and the other was to visit his old friend, Ezra Pound, at St. Elizabeth's Hospital where Pound had been incarcerated since 1945 under indictment for treason. Eliot was unhappy about Pound's conditions and he attempted, without success, to get Pound treated with more consideration and to be given more privacy. Julian Cornell, Pound's defense lawyer, who quotes Eliot's letter on the subject, describes him as the most faithful and concerned of Pound's friends: "Throughout Pound's incarceration, Eliot was his faithful friend, his refuge and his strength." The point is worth stressing, since another of Pound's friends, Ronald Duncan, has accused Eliot, in his book *How to Make Enemies,* of being complacent and even indifferent about Pound's fate. In fact, Eliot, who was in close touch with Julian Cornell, seems to have had a much better understanding than Duncan of the baffling legal complexities of Pound's position, and was convinced that foreign intervention would not help. (It was, in the end, that most natively American of poets, Robert Frost, who was largely instrumental in securing Pound's release.)

The Nobel banquet took place at Stockholm on December 10,

1948. Eliot told Robert Giroux that when he received the news of
the award he knew only two things about it: that he would have
to wear formal clothes for the ceremony, and that he would be
asked to crown the Swedish Snow Queen at the Winter Festival.
"I hope they'll combine the two events in a skating rink," he said.
"Then I'll be able to wear ice skates with my tails." Giroux recalls
Eliot's departure:

When he left for Stockholm, the Kauffers and I took him to the airport
where a reporter asked, "Mr. Eliot, what book did they give you the
Nobel Prize for?" "I believe it's given for the entire corpus," he replied.
"When did you publish *that*?" the man wanted to know. When he had
gone, Eliot said to us, "It really might make a good title for a mystery—
The Entire Corpus."[2]

2

November 1948 was also noteworthy in that it saw the publication of *Notes Towards the Definition of Culture,* Eliot's only sustained prose work of the nineteen-forties. It is one of his strangest
books, where profound insights are interwoven with the most superficial observations, and where seemingly firm statements are
then qualified out of existence within a paragraph or so. The
book's excessively tentative title is characteristic; Eliot says many
interesting things about culture but he never succeeds in defining
it. In principle, he is concerned with culture in the broad or anthropological sense, rather than the narrow or Arnoldian sense:
that is to say, the whole way of life of a society, all its inherited
manners, customs, and styles of living; as opposed to "the best that
has been thought and said" and the cultivation of the fine arts. In
practice, however, Eliot slides from one sense of culture to another in a quite disconcerting way. The anthropological use of the
word is descriptive and value-free; any discernible form of social
organization above the merely biological level will have its accompanying cultural modes (indeed, the words "social" and "cultural" are often used interchangeably), however odd they may

[2] Allen Tate, ed., *T. S. Eliot: The Man and His Work* (New York: Delacorte Press, 1966; London: Chatto & Windus, 1967), p. 340.

seem to the observer. And as anthropologists have shown, seemingly primitive peoples can often produce very complicated cultural forms. So when Eliot laments the decline of culture in the twentieth century and contemplates a future "of which it will be possible to say that it will have *no* culture" he cannot be using the word in the anthropological sense, since if organized human life persists at all it is bound to have its accompanying cultural forms. Clearly, Eliot is here using the word in a more particular, value-bearing sense, which is closer to the Arnoldian usage.

Undoubtedly he is aware of the ambiguity, though the subtleties and circumlocutions of his prose do little to resolve it. Yet by examining certain passages one can conclude that Eliot is attempting to move toward a third sense of culture which will go beyond the other two. There is a helpful account in the appendix to the *Notes*, which is a translation of three broadcasts on the unity of European culture addressed to Germany just after the war, where Eliot expresses himself more directly than elsewhere:

By "culture," then, I mean first of all what the anthropologists mean: the way of life of a particular people living together in one place. That culture is made visible in their arts, in their social system, in their habits and customs, in their religion. But these things added together do not constitute the culture, though we often speak for convenience as if they did. These things are simply the parts into which a culture can be anatomised, as a human body can. But just as a man is something more than an assemblage of the various constituent parts of his body, so a culture is more than the assemblage of its arts, customs, and religious beliefs. These things all act upon each other, and fully to understand one you have to understand all.

Eliot is here using "culture" in a holistic or organicist sense as something that pertains to the whole life of a community, and which is more than the sum of its visible aspects. As he says, a man is more than an assemblage of separate organs; the animating principle is what religion and metaphysics have traditionally regarded as the soul. In Eliot's model of society the animating power is religion, and it is this that makes culture more than a collection of disparate elements: in chapter I he writes of the culture of a people "as an incarnation of its religion." He uses this phrase to express the difficult and elusive idea that culture and religion exist with regard to each other in a way that is closer than anything expressed by the idea of "relationship" and yet stops short of actual identity. He arrives at this point in an extraordinarily tortured paragraph:

And both "religion" and "culture," besides meaning different things from each other, should mean for the individual and for the group something towards which they strive, not merely something which they possess. Yet there is an aspect in which we can see a religion as the *whole way of life of a people,* from birth to the grave, from morning to night and even in sleep, and that way of life is also its culture. And at the same time we must recognise that when this identification is complete, it means in actual societies both an inferior culture and an inferior religion. A universal religion is at least potentially higher than one which any race or nation claims exclusively for itself; and a culture realising a religion also realised in other cultures is at least potentially a higher culture than one which has a religion exclusively to itself. From one point of view we may identify: from another, we must separate.

Such a passage illustrates the frequent tendency in Eliot's prose for meanings to collapse and merge into each other as a result of excessive qualification, and which may, as Adrian Cunningham has suggested, have been a permanent legacy of the influence of Bradley (though the tendency was already implicit in Prufrock's complaint, "It is impossible to say just what I mean"). Such a painful pursuit of meanings beyond meaning was much more convincingly carried out in the poetry of the *Quartets.* At the same time, we can observe some of the recurring configurations of Eliot's social thought; the idea of religion-culture (hyphenation, however clumsy, is the best way of indicating what Eliot wants to say) as the whole way of life of a people had been anticipated in the pervasive "tradition" of *After Strange Gods* and the habitual, largely unconscious religious practice of the mass of the people in *The Idea of a Christian Society.* And Eliot's vague gesture toward a relation between a national and a universal church was a return to one of the unresolved dilemmas of the latter book.

J. M. Cameron has justly complained that in *The Idea of a Christian Society* Eliot was confusing the sociological and the theological. In the *Notes* the emphasis is more clearly sociological,

although in a very unspecific way, so that the religion which is in-
carnated in a people's culture does not necessarily have to be
Christian. Insofar as he is writing as a Christian, Eliot's concern
with religion-culture causes him great difficulty in apprehending
religion as transcendent, as something existing apart from its im-
manent manifestation in a particular society. It may be absurd that
"bishops are a part of English culture, and horses and dogs are a
part of English religion," but there it is: "when we consider the
problem of evangelization, of the development of a Christian society, we have reason to quail." Christopher Dawson, the Roman
Catholic scholar who greatly influenced Eliot in the *Notes,* considered that he made needless difficulties for himself precisely because he refused to regard culture and religion as separate entities,
however closely related in particular situations. Eliot's concept of
culture as essentially religion-culture is what underlay his speculation about the possible disappearance of all culture, since he could
not admit the existence of a wholly secular culture. Whether such
cultures can really exist is a matter for anthropologists to pursue: I
suspect that if Eliot had looked at the question from another angle
he might have been unwilling to admit the possibility that a society could exist without religion. Indeed, in *The Idea of a Christian
Society* he specifically attacks the totalitarian powers for setting
up a pagan counter-religion. From a Christian point of view the
Soviet Union is an irreligious society, yet it clearly has a genuine
culture in the anthropological sense, and has a certain amount to
show for itself culturally in the narrow Arnoldian sense. In Soviet
culture, no doubt, the religious dimension is supplied by Marxist-
Leninist ideology.

If Eliot's notion of culture as the incarnation of religion is not
wholly intelligible, his account of the "three senses of culture" is
more readily discussed. The three senses are, respectively, the
culture of the individual, the group, and the whole society: the
culture of the individual and to a lesser extent the group is partly
a matter of deliberate self-cultivation and development, whereas
the culture of the society is a whole way of life and the largely inherited and unconscious assumptions that govern it. In Eliot's ideal
scheme of things—and his prescriptive intentions are apparent—
these three aspects do not exist in mutual separation, but affect

each other to the general good. Eliot speaks not merely of *aspects* but of *levels* of culture, and he projects a vertically extended model of a whole culture which consists of several levels harmoniously interacting. But the top levels are the most complicated and functionally differentiated, where "high" or "minority" culture is customarily produced and received; lower down we have the less conscious levels of traditional and popular culture. But popular culture is beneficially affected by high culture, and vice versa, in a harmonious cycling process, which affects the whole organic culture. This model embodies, in a very abstract way, elements drawn from Eliot's writings about the theater, in which he describes the audience enjoying an Elizabethan play at different levels: at the lowest it could be appreciated for the excitement of the story, and above that for the interest of the characters and situation, and on the highest plane for its poetry and moral and philosophical profundities. At the same time, it would still be one audience watching one play. This scheme also recalls Eliot's outline in *The Idea of a Christian Society* of a community of believers whose belief would be for the most part traditional and instinctive and enacted in behavior, together with a fairly small clerisy of conscious believers, who would be responsible for the spiritual and intellectual direction of the society.

What is new in the *Notes Towards the Definition of Culture* is that Eliot gives this model a fairly specific sociological embodiment in terms of class levels. He projects a system of checks and balances; a measure of social mobility prevents the system from hardening into the fixities of a structure based on caste, though too much mobility would cause disintegration. The family is the primary channel for passing on culture, and a class system is valuable since it is based on inheritance and so preserves a certain continuity of values; elites based solely on merit and particular attainments are liable to be atomistic and not helpful to cultural transmission, and so need to be kept in check by an inherited class system. Much of this seems true; it is certainly the case that the family is the main channel of primary socialization, however important secondary influences may be at a later stage. It is for this reason that the social mobility derived from freedom of educational opportunity provides such frequent cases of cultural shock, as has been illustrated in many recent English novels and plays. Eliot anticipated by several years Michael Young's exposure of the evils of a pure meritocracy. Nevertheless, it is an excessively simple model which leaves out a vast amount of social reality. To quote Raymond Williams's study of the *Notes:*

In particular, the exclusion of the economic factor—of the tendency of function to turn into property—leaves the view of class narrow and misleading. Eliot seems always to have in mind, as the normal scheme of his thinking, a society which is at once more stable and more simple than any to which his discussion is likely to be relevant.[3]

The notion that only a fairly small number of people in a society is capable of producing or advancing "high" culture, in the sense of art or thought, and that probably not a very much larger number is capable of genuinely—as opposed to conventionally—receiving it, seems to me not unreasonable, particularly if one also maintains that such high culture must be related to the broader culture of the community, and not exist in isolation. What is less evident is that this minority can be placed in a hierarchical social model in the way that Eliot recommends: Matthew Arnold was, I think, being more realistic when he, too, saw English society divided into layers, but with the barbarians at the top and the philistines in the middle, neither of them noticeable for their cultivation. As on earlier occasions, Eliot seems to be extrapolating from an idealizing outsider's view of English society.

In fact, Eliot does not absolutely need his metaphor of social levels. As Terry Eagleton has recently observed, there is a point in the book, when Eliot is discussing regionalism, where he remarks that "a national culture, if it is to flourish, should be a constellation of cultures, the constituents of which, benefiting each other, benefit the whole." The image of a constellation offers a "horizontal" alternative to the "vertical" image of levels used elsewhere; we would then have a differentiation of cultural functions without necessary subordination. This is, as Eagleton points out, the model projected by Raymond Williams in his own socio-cultural writings; Williams, like Eliot, is insistent that culture is a question of a

[3] *Culture and Society* (New York: Columbia University Press; London: Chatto & Windus, 1958), p. 236.

whole way of life, and not merely the activities of an elite, though he writes from an ideological position diametrically opposed to Eliot's. In discussing regionalism Eliot also describes the socially creative role of conflict, which contrasts strikingly with the static image of hierarchical levels that he projects elsewhere in the book: in sociological terms a model of functional integration is briefly replaced by one that is conflict-based, but Eliot does not follow up these implications.

Although *Notes Towards the Definition of Culture* is an uneven and sometimes contradictory book, it is an important example of the kind of socio-cultural criticism regularly produced by British men of letters since the early nineteenth century, and it has proved fruitful in its influence on other writers in the same tradition, notably Raymond Williams. Since I have quoted passages where Eliot's meaning collapses in an unfortunate way, I will also refer to the wry and penetrating remarks that he often throws out in passing, as when he observes: "A local speech on a local issue is likely to be more intelligible than one addressed to a whole nation, and we observe that the greatest muster of ambiguities and obscure generalities is usually to be found in speeches which are addressed to the whole world." And there are some shrewd comments in the "Notes on Education and Culture" which need to be pondered by educational progressives, however unacceptable they may find Eliot's basically elitist position; for instance, his insistence that socialization and self-development in education may often be in conflict, and that it does not necessarily ensure happiness:

to be educated above the level of those whose social habits and tastes one has inherited, may cause a division within a man which interferes with happiness; even though, when the individual is of superior intellect, it may bring him a fuller and more useful life.

Again, Eliot anticipates a common theme of recent literature. There is, too, a somewhat bitter wisdom in his reflection that "it is possible that the desire for education is greater where there are difficulties in the way of obtaining it—difficulties not insuperable but only to be surmounted at the cost of some sacrifice and privation." Eliot's notes on education are, however, fragmentary, and are affected in places by the ambiguity about the meaning of culture that occurs elsewhere in the book; he expanded some of his arguments in the lectures on "The Aims of Education" that he delivered at the University of Chicago in 1950, and which were printed in *To Criticize the Critic*. His views on education are sympathetically discussed by G. H. Bantock in *T. S. Eliot and Education* (1970).

3

Four Quartets, which Eliot wrote between the ages of forty-seven and fifty-four, are a striking illustration of one of the three choices—and certainly the hardest—that he described in his Yeats memorial lecture as open to the middle-aged writer: namely, to adapt himself to middle age and find a different way of working. Eliot himself thought the *Quartets* his major achievement and so do many of his critics. This is not my own view, although I recognize that sections of them contain some of his finest and most moving poetry; other sections, however, include some of the flattest and least interesting verse that he ever published, and the whole work seems to me to be somewhat less than the sum of its parts. In one sense the *Quartets* continue the process of spiritual struggle and exploration that Eliot embarked on in *Ash-Wednesday:* they, too, are poems of religious experience that avoid being overtly confessional. But the *Quartets* differ significantly from the earlier sequence; whereas in *Ash-Wednesday* Eliot had relied on a haunting and elusive "music of images" and on the soft, quasi-hypnotic deliberations of the "first voice," in the *Quartets* he combines these elements with a deliberately abstract and philosophical poetry which is new in his work. It is not philosophical in the sense that it attempts to versify preexisting ideas, but in making poetry out of the actual process of thinking rather than its results. Some, at least, of this succeeds brilliantly; what is less welcome is the assertive presence in the *Quartets* of the "second voice" of poetry, where Eliot addresses the reader in an exhortatory way that is too reminiscent of the choruses from *The Rock*. The "third voice" of the created dramatic character, which had given a peculiar force to Eliot's early poetry is quite missing, reserved now, no doubt, for the plays. On the surface the *Quartets* look much simpler than *The Waste Land*, despite the local difficulty of the philosophical passages: there are very few phrases in foreign languages and obscure allusions, and there is a complete absence of the jazzy transitions that had given such a startling flavor to the earlier poem. If the *Quartets* are difficult, then they are difficult in a fairly familiar and traditional way, which has not deterred admiring readers. Reinhold Niebuhr, for instance, regularly used them as devotional reading.

As the title suggests, the *Quartets* invoke the ideal of musical form that had attracted Eliot ever since he wrote the "Preludes" and the "Rhapsody on a Windy Night" at the beginning of his career, and his 1942 lecture on "The Music of Poetry" provides a useful background to the *Quartets*. Indeed, it has been suggested that Eliot had one or more specific string quartets in mind as models, and works by Beethoven and Bartók have been suggested. However this may be, the point is worth making that the quartet is a more intricately organized form than the prelude or the rhapsody, and in the *Quartets* Eliot attempts to stiffen and support the articulations of pure musical expression with a regular and predictable form, based on a five-fold division. This division may, as Herbert Howarth suggests, have been derived from Beethoven's Quartet in A Minor Op. 132; but I suggest that its more immediate source was *The Waste Land*. The genesis of "Burnt Norton" lay in Eliot's visit to a country house of that name near Chipping Camden in Gloucestershire in the summer of 1934. Whatever poetry arose from that experience originally went into *Murder in the Cathedral*, but Eliot had to remove it in production and then, as he said, "these fragments stayed in my mind, and gradually I saw a poem shaping itself round them: in the end it came out as 'Burnt Norton.'" As we have seen, Eliot's poetic impulses usually produced fairly short passages of isolated intensity, and the problem of assembling them into larger wholes was a matter of some deliberation and conscious strategy. Needing a model for the construction of "Burnt Norton," Eliot seems to have turned to *The Waste Land*. C. K. Stead, to whose account of the *Quartets* in *The New Poetic* I am greatly indebted, has analyzed their five-fold structure in the following way:

1. The movement of time, in which brief moments of eternity are caught.

2. Wordly experience, leading only to dissatisfaction.
3. Purgation in the world, divesting the soul of the love of created things.
4. A lyric prayer for, or affirmation of the need of, Intercession.
5. The problems of attaining artistic wholeness which become analogues for, and merge into, the problems of achieving spiritual health.

This analysis can also be applied to *The Waste Land* in the following way:

1. "The Burial of the Dead." This section is obviously about movement in time; the seasons bringing change and the reluctance of the buried to come alive again. There are no moments of eternity here, but the moments of nostalgic beauty associated with Marie's childhood and the girl in the hyacinth garden form a secular equivalent.
2. "A Game of Chess." This is very patently about dissatisfaction with wordly experience.
3. "The Fire Sermon." This section culminates on a note of ascetic purgation.
4. "Death by Water." A brief lyric, which though not a prayer, contains an invocation and a warning: "O you who turn the wheel and look to windward."
5. "What the Thunder Said." In my reading of *The Waste Land* this section is certainly concerned with problems of artistic wholeness and spiritual health: "Shall I at least set my lands in order" and "These fragments I have shored against my ruins."

In extending Stead's analysis in this way I have not attempted to say anything new or profound about either *The Waste Land* or *Four Quartets*, but have tried to show that in writing, or rather assembling, "Burnt Norton" Eliot used the earlier poem for his model, however many differences there were in texture. (There are, in fact, a few verbal parallels also: the "hyacinth garden" of "The Burial of the Dead" becomes the "rose-garden" of part I of "Burnt Norton" and the phrase "heart of light" appears in both; and there are the London place names in the third section of each poem.) The critical conclusion one can draw is that whereas in writing almost all his poems up to *Ash-Wednesday* Eliot had been able to relate the separate parts by a courageous reliance on his own feelings and "ego rhythm," extended in the case of *The Waste Land* by his trust in Ezra Pound's judgment and understanding of his own deepest intentions, when he came to "Burnt Norton" he deliberately used one of his own earlier works as a kind of template. Then, a few years later, when he continued the sequence "Burnt Norton" itself served as the formal model for "East Coker" and the rest. There was no reason why he should not have done this, but it was a new departure in Eliot's poetry, and it inevitably resulted in the presence of the manipulatory will that Stead has observed at work in the *Quartets,* and in the necessity for low-pressure linking passages. As I have previously remarked, Eliot was capable of expressing the most intense moments of experience, but had little capacity for sustained structure. In the early poems the juxtaposition of separate images was one effective strategy for dealing with this limitation: the *Quartets* are a determined attempt to articulate a larger structure in a more traditional way, but inevitably they are something of a formal compromise. Eliot arrived at the aim of composing a fairly long personal poem, which would bring together several elements—philosophical, religious, poetic, and autobiographical—but he was not able to write it out directly in the manner of, say, *The Prelude.* If *The Waste Land* was originally a set of short poems which mysteriously coalesced to form a single entity, something of the reverse tendency is at work in the *Quartets,* which is presented as a unified poem but which is, I think, constantly tending to fall apart into twenty separate sections, of very unequal poetic merit, and which is held together only by the exigencies of the imposed musical form. To some extent, *Four Quartets* mimes one of its major themes: the tension between time, which is sad and waste and mostly unredeemable, and eternity, which breaks through at rare moments of significance and beauty. The contrast between mere activity and extension, without intrinsic meaning, and the privileged moment, is perhaps the most profound structural element in Eliot's sensibility, and it reveals itself in many forms, both in his poetry and plays, and in his prose writings.

The title of "Burnt Norton" merely records the occasion of a particular experience, but the other three are personally important to Eliot: East Coker is the Somerset village from which Andrew Eliot departed to America in the seventeenth century (and in whose parish church Thomas Eliot's ashes now lie); the Dry

Salvages refers to a group of rocks off the Massachusetts coast, where much of Eliot's boyhood was passed; and Little Gidding, the name of the Huntingdonshire village where Nicholas Ferrar founded a religious community in the seventeenth century, again recalls a period that was of central emotional and imaginative importance to Eliot.

In 1936 D. W. Harding described "Burnt Norton" as a newly created concept which would include and replace such worn counters as "regret" and "eternity." I doubt if this approach is philosophically valid, yet it offers a helpful perspective in which to read "Burnt Norton." Certainly the beautifully controlled and suasive opening seems to move through and beyond everyday meanings in a far more convincing way than the parallel attempts in Eliot's prose. It contains some of Eliot's finest poetry, a true musicalization of thought which modulates without hesitation into the sensuous presence of "the dust on a bowl of rose-leaves." We are led on by the same firm and delicate movement into the rose-garden to hear the birds and the children's voices and to contemplate the empty pool. Eliot does not often recapture this precise fusion of thought and feeling; more often there is a division between the sensuous and lyrical on the one hand, and the abstract and reflective on the other. He approaches it again in the fifth section of "Burnt Norton," though I am less impressed than some critics by Eliot's willingness to dwell directly on the difficulty of his undertaking, as in the lines describing how "Words strain, / Crack and sometimes break."

Time is, of course, the villain of the *Quartets,* and the evil of living in time is at the heart of the poem. The difficulty is stated with attractive humility and directness at the end of section II of "Burnt Norton." But in the third section the note becomes more querulous and Eliot seems to be revisiting one of the familiar reaches of his imagination, the abode of the wretched souls who were neither living nor dead in *Inferno* III:

> Only a flicker
> Over the strained time-ridden faces
> Distracted from distraction by distraction
> Filled with fancies and empty of meaning

> Tumid apathy with no concentration
> Men and bits of paper, whirled by the cold wind
> That blows before and after time,
> Wind in and out of unwholesome lungs
> Time before and time after.

So far—unlike other critics—I have not found it difficult to be tolerant of Eliot's antihumanism, his frequently superior or disapproving attitude to his fellow human beings: I see this as the expression of feelings which were not merely personal to Eliot but which are much more widely shared than we like to admit and which so, paradoxically, relate his poetry to the generality of human behavior, however reprehensible they may be morally. But I am less inclined to accept Eliot's readiness, here and elsewhere in the *Quartets,* to give this state of mind a Christian sanction.

The *Quartets* are, indeed, often described as a great Christian poem, and in this context I refer to the opinions of a critic who is also a theologian, William F. Lynch, S.J. The essence of Fr. Lynch's argument is that for the Christian salvation occurs *in* time, in the everyday flux of human life, not by attempting to escape from it. Whereas in Eliot

it is hard to say no to the impression, if I may use a mixture of my own symbols and his, that the Christian imagination is finally limited to the element of fire, to the day of Pentecost, to the descent of the Holy Ghost upon the disciples. The revelation of eternity and time is that of an *intersection.* . . . It seems not unseemly to suppose that Eliot's imagination (and is this not a theology?) is alive with points of *intersection* and of *descent.* He seems to place our faith, our hope, and our love, not in the flux of time but in the *points* of time. I am sure his mind is interested in the line and time of Christ, whose Spirit is his total flux. But I am not so sure about his imagination. Is it or is it not an imagination which is saved from time's nausea or terror by points of intersection?[4]

This, for all its gentle tentativeness, seems to me to imply a cogent criticism: no doubt the author of *After Strange Gods* would have been interested in the suggestion that his imagination was less orthodox than his mind. Fr. Lynch goes on to remark, most sug-

---

[4] *Christ and Apollo* (New York: Sheed & Ward, 1963), pp. 170–71.

gestively, that in the *Quartets,* "Everything that is good is annunciation and epiphany (and we may note here the altogether understandable poetic passion for epiphany in our day)." In other words, Eliot has translated into Christian terms an underlying disposition both of his own sensibility and of modernist aesthetics in general. Fr. Lynch continues the argument:

There seems little doubt that Eliot is attracted above all by the image and the goal of immobility, and that in everything he seeks for approximations to this goal in the human order. "Love is itself unmoving." There is the violin, and we are the music while the music lasts, and the perpetual stillness of the Chinese jar, and the caught measure of the dance that does not seem to advance as the dance should.

Here, perhaps, we have a clue to Eliot's perennial difficulty in writing for the theater; despite the fact that his dramatic *writing* is superbly articulate, his basic orientation toward states of stillness and immobility has made it difficult for him successfully to project dramatic *action.* Lynch glosses Eliot's phrase "Love is itself unmoving" by remarking that St. Thomas "tells us that God is act, and that everything is perfect in so far as it is in act." It is arguable that the religious influences at work in the *Quartets* are as much Oriental as Christian. Fr. Lynch concludes, against the general argument of the *Quartets,* that it is not possible to leap, even momentarily, out of time toward eternity, since it is only by living more fully in time that redemption can be found.

No, what we must do is go along with the time-ridden faces. For they are at least on the right track and dealing with the right fact. We are constitutionally committed to the structures of temporality, and the major reason for most of the pain therein, for the boredom and the terror, is that at the moment we are historically committed to but one level of it. Jumping out of our human facts will not help at all, and will produce nothing but further strains. The only answer, as in every case, would seem to be to deepen the fact and its possible levels, to enter more deeply into it.

If, as I believe, there are manifest strains in the work it may well be for the reasons that Lynch suggests, and because of the real difficulty that Eliot found in bending his imaginative inclinations to what he knew were the objective demands of Christian belief.

As I have said, *Four Quartets* tends to fall apart rather readily into its constituent sections, despite the imposed intricacy of form, and I shall conclude this discussion by briefly describing those places—or "moments"—where Eliot's creative imagination is most satisfyingly at work. In "Burnt Norton," in addition to those lines I have discussed, there is the exquisite though cryptic lyric in section IV, which recalls the purely musical qualities of *Ash-Wednesday:*

> Time and the bell have buried the day,
> The black cloud carries the sun away.

In "East Coker" the first section is a finely rendered account of the coexistence of past and present, which unobtrusively incorporates a variety of literary and historical allusions. It contains some very beautiful notations of direct experience:

> In a warm haze the sultry light
> Is absorbed, not refracted, by grey stone.
> The dahlias sleep in the empty silence.
> Wait for the early owl.

There is much that is excellent on a lower level in sections II and III; the autobiographical directness is admirable, but the writing is marred in places by a slightly stiff rhetoric and overrepetitiveness. I can see no merit in the overingenious lyric, "The wounded surgeon plies the steel," in section IV, and I find section V frankly dull, with a tendency to lapse into what John Fuller has called "evasive bluster."

"The Dry Salvages" is the least satisfactory of the sequence, though at the same time it contains some of its best lines. The opening lines are poor, in a weakly sub-Whitmanesque fashion. Yet the writing suddenly picks up at the words, "The river is within us," and from there to the end of the section we have a magnificently sustained sequence, with a vivid evocation of the New England coast, beginning "The salt is on the briar rose, / The fog is in the fir trees." The sestina in the next section opens with a fine image that interestingly recalls the motifs of Eliot's undergraduate poems:

> Where is there an end of it, the soundless wailing,
> The silent withering of autumn flowers
> Dropping their petals and remaining motionless.

But the attempt to sustain the pattern through the remaining stanzas of the sestina fails and the writing becomes clumsy and forced. In the remainder of the poem I admire only the lyric of section IV, a suave prayer to the Virgin, rather in the manner of *Ash-Wednesday*, and the rhythmically interesting first dozen lines of section V, "To communicate with Mars, converse with spirits."

In "Little Gidding" the opening lines project a superb fusion of thought and feeling and observed physical scene:

> The brief sun flames the ice, on pond and ditches,
> In windless cold that is the heart's heat,
> Reflecting in a watery mirror
> A glare that is blindness in the early afternoon.

I have referred already to the lyric at the opening of section II, which makes a memorable emblem out of the fact and aftermath of the bombing of London. The lines which follow, beginning "In the uncertain hour before the morning," are at once a technical tour de force and some of the most directly personal poetry that Eliot has written. It is characteristic that when he wishes to write most personally he uses Dante as a model and a point of departure: one recalls his observation in "Tradition and the Individual Talent" that a poet can be at his most individual when "the dead poets, his ancestors" speak most openly through him. In form, these lines are an astonishingly successful attempt to provide an English equivalent to Dante's style, or at least that aspect of it which most appealed to Eliot, the grave, sparse, direct, and at the same time energetically moving manner. He later wrote, "This section of a poem—not the length of one canto of the *Divine Comedy*—cost me far more time and trouble and vexation than any passage of the same length that I have ever written." The setting is a London street just after an air raid, and the poet meets another, a fellow poet who is also something of an alter ego. The "familiar compound ghost" is partly Brunetto Latini, Dante's old teacher, from *Inferno* XV, and partly Swift, but primarily Yeats, who tells Eliot in harshly moving words of "the gifts reserved for age." In this passage, suggests Richard Ellmann, Eliot felt himself finally reconciled with Yeats, after lifelong differences: "it brought about his rapprochement with the poet who had always been formidably present in his consciousness. True friendship was only possible after Yeats was dead, and could be sifted down to those elements which Eliot found congenial." The section ends with a convergence of significant images:

> "Then fools' approval stings, and honour stains.
> From wrong to wrong the exasperated spirit
>   Proceeds, unless restored by that refining fire
>   Where you must move in measure, like a dancer."
> The day was breaking. In the disfigured street
>   He left me, with a kind of valediction,
>   And faded on the blowing of the horn.

The "refining fire," previously invoked at the end of *The Waste Land*, is associated with Arnaut Daniel in *Purgatorio* XXVI, and the dancer with Yeats; while the horn, one of the ancient properties of European poetry—from Roland to de Vigny's *J'aime le son du cor, le soir, au fond des bois*—merges into the siren blowing the "all clear" signal.

After this "Little Gidding" moves through a phase of didacticism, and then returns to its point of departure, Nicholas Ferrar's community, where Charles I had sheltered. From the darkness of the Second World War Eliot looks back to the English civil war, the cataclysmic event that had destroyed the mythic Laudian England that meant so much to him; he now conceives all the dead as ultimately reconciled, "folded in a single party," whether King Charles on the scaffold, or Milton "who died blind and quiet." He carries the note of reconciliation and union through to the final section, where he expresses some of his most deeply held convictions, the importance of tradition and community, and the interpenetration of the living and the dead:

> We die with the dying:
> See, they depart, and we go with them.
> We are born with the dead:
> See, they return, and bring us with them.

In the final lines Eliot moves to an impressive though perhaps overdeliberate conclusion, drawing together motifs from what has gone before, including the persistent and poignant image of "the children in the apple-tree." At the end he invokes the medieval mystic, Dame Julian, and finally the rose and the fire from the end of the *Paradiso*. At this point Eliot virtually concludes his career as a poet—though not as a dramatist and critic—with a fitting allusion to Dante, the poet who had guided him, as Virgil had guided Dante himself, in his progress through the hell and purgatory of his own imagination.

VI

✦✦

Comedies and Second Marriage

1949–1965

ELIOT'S LONG-AWAITED new play, *The Cocktail Party,* was staged at the Edinburgh Festival in August 1949, directed by Martin Browne with Alec Guinness as Sir Henry Harcourt-Reilly. *The Cocktail Party* was a great success at Edinburgh, and the acclaim was repeated when it opened at the Henry Miller Theater, New York, in January 1950; the London opening at the New Theatre in May had a somewhat more mixed reception. Curiously, in both cities, the "popular" papers were more enthusiastic than the "quality" press; but by now the play had aroused so much interest that its success was assured, and it ran for several hundred performances in both New York and London. It was a commercial success, not just a *succès d'estime,* and made a substantial amount of money. For a time it seemed that Eliot's aspiration, cherished for over thirty years, of restoring poetic drama to the popular theater had been fulfilled.

The success of *The Cocktail Party,* following on the Nobel Prize, brought Eliot a new degree of fame: he was now talked about in circles where his achievement as poet and critic meant nothing. The ultimate accolade, perhaps, came with a cover story in *Time* magazine on March 6, 1950. There is no reason to doubt that Eliot enjoyed his success, but the accompanying publicity was certainly trying to one of his reserved temperament. As he complained to William Turner Levy, "No one thinks of me as a poet any more, but as a celebrity. . . . Everybody wants you to meet their friends. Huge cocktail parties. No time for talk." Eliot's austere mode of living was, however, unchanged, and another of his friends, Ronald Duncan, in some spirited but malicious recollections, has accused him of being mean with money in small ways, even if generous in large ones (Eliot defrayed the losses on Duncan's play *Stratton* after it failed). According to Duncan, Eliot, though plagued with bronchitis and asthma, refused his friends' advice to "go south in the winter," saying he could not afford it:

Eliot began to affect many signs of premature old age. His stoop began to be accentuated, his umbrella trailed, he even started to cup his hands at remarks he could hear perfectly well. The elation he had at receiving the Nobel Prize and particularly the Order of Merit, was short-lived.[1]

Eliot's health was certainly not good; he had a mild heart attack in 1951 and attacks of tachycardia, or rapid heart beat, in 1954 and 1956. He also had to enter a London nursing home on one occasion for treatment for athlete's foot, which called forth a satirical comment from one of his oldest acquaintances, Wyndham Lewis: "If I had the money, and acted as a magnet to many people as you do, I believe I should often flee into a nursing home, and I should sometimes say that it was because of my feet, sometimes my knee, and sometimes higher up."

Despite his poor health, Eliot continued the lecturing activity he had begun during the forties. Harold Nicolson in his diary entry for November 19, 1953, describes Eliot delivering "The Three Voices of Poetry":

The lecture takes place in Central Hall, and I have never seen such a crowd for any literary lecture. They told me that there were more than 2,500 people there, and they remained silent throughout. . . . I had to propose a vote of thanks this evening, but the audience were so obviously moved by Tom's lecture that I did it in ten words.

But this was insignificant compared to the audiences that Eliot commanded in America. The climax was reached on April 30, 1956 in Minneapolis, when he delivered the Gideon D. Seymour lecture on "The Frontiers of Criticism" in the University of Minnesota's

[1] *How to Make Enemies* (London: Rupert Hart-Davis, 1968), p. 332.

Williams Arena to an audience that was reported in *Time* as consisting of 15,000 people (Eliot later discovered the correct figure was 13,523), and for a fee that William Turner Levy discreetly describes as the largest ever paid for a literary lecture. Eliot had not known that he was to address such an enormous audience, and as he later put it, "I felt like a very small bull walking into an enormous arena." It was undoubtedly a symbolic moment in the institutionalizing of literary culture; but as Eliot remarked to Levy, "I do not believe there are fifteen thousand people in the entire world who are interested in criticism."

Encouraged by the success of *The Cocktail Party*, Eliot began work, in his slow and deliberate fashion, on another play; once more, there were many drafts to be hammered out in discussion with Browne, who reproduces them in his book. This play, *The Confidential Clerk*, opened at Edinburgh on July 25, 1953, to a quite warm reception, and then transferred to the Lyric Theatre on Shaftesbury Avenue, where it ran for several months. Not all the reviews were friendly, but *The Confidential Clerk* was generally welcomed as an entertaining and adroitly constructed piece of artificial comedy. In February 1954 it opened at the Morosco Theater on Broadway: as with *The Cocktail Party* the critics were divided, and, once again, Eliot's most enthusiastic admirers were those writing for the "popular" papers. The play did well in New York, but less well than *The Cocktail Party;* in Browne's words, "New York likes the new thing, and this, however glamorously, was Eliot over again . . ." In 1956 Eliot began work on his last play, which was originally called *The Rest Cure* but became, finally, *The Elder Statesman*. Like Eliot's other postwar plays it opened at the Edinburgh Festival—in August 1958—and was directed by Browne and presented by Henry Sherek; in September it transferred to the Cambridge Theatre in London. This time the critics were respectful but not enthusiastic, and several of them were uneasy about its lack of theatrical vitality. Kenneth Tynan, for instance, wrote:

Towards the end, to be sure, he casts over the play a sedative, autumnal glow of considerable beauty, and here and there a scattered phrase reminds us, by its spare precision, that we are listening to a poet. On the whole, however, the evening offers little more than the mild pleasure of hearing ancient verities tepidly restated.[2]

It ran for only two months in London, and this time there was no New York production. The apparent breakthrough of *The Cocktail Party* had not been followed up.

Most of Eliot's literary criticism of the forties and fifties, together with a few earlier pieces, was collected in *On Poetry and Poets* in 1957. This volume provides an opportunity to consider the final phase of Eliot's criticism; he himself conducted a survey of his own critical career in "To Criticize the Critic," delivered as a lecture at Leeds in 1961. The opening phase, which was substantially limited to the years 1919 to 1921, when he wrote the essays later collected in *The Sacred Wood* and *Homage to John Dryden,* represented what Eliot called "workshop criticism." It was the work of a young poet who was attempting to reform the practice and traditions of English poetry, and who was prepared to use any amount of polemical sharpness and wit in his attempt to dislodge a somnolent literary establishment. As we have seen, the attempt was only too successful, and within a very few years Eliot himself was enshrined, or imprisoned, within a new establishment that had turned his early *aperçus* into iron laws. After the ideological digression marked by *After Strange Gods,* Eliot's late criticism is marked by its acceptance of the cultural status quo, an excessive sense of occasion, and a weary formality of manner, somewhat lightened by what W. W. Robson has called "a poised and quizzical urbanity." There is a complete lack of the spirited iconoclasm of the early criticism, and in his Leeds lecture Eliot protested, reasonably enough, that it was neither possible nor appropriate to sustain such a manner for many years. The best essays in *On Poetry and Poets* are those where Eliot continues the spirit of his early "workshop criticism" by dwelling on the problems that were of direct concern to him as poet and dramatist, such as "The Music of Poetry," "Poetry and Drama," and, above all, "The Three Voices of Poetry," which is immensely helpful in understanding the development of Eliot's poetic career. And there is "The Social

[2] Quoted in E. Martin Browne, *The Making of T. S. Eliot's Plays* (Cambridge: At the University Press, 1969), p. 341.

Function of Poetry" which relates his literary and his social criticism. An essay such as "Milton I," which was first published in
1936, is very much a survival of the early "workshop criticism";
the burden of Eliot's objection to Milton is that the latter's way of
writing was not reconcilable with the practice of writing good
English poetry in the twentieth century, which we can understand as Eliot's kind of poetry. (His personal and ideological distaste for Milton is also a contributory factor.) Eliot's essay offers a
very partial view of Milton, and it has not been found generally
convincing. Nevertheless, it is a workmanlike piece of literary criticism, which tries to make its point by particular reference to "the
words on the page"; the same thing can be said about another
piece surviving from the thirties, the sharp but judicious essay on
Byron. In the later critical pieces, there is the admirable "Johnson
as Critic and Poet," where Eliot writes warmly of a writer for
whom he felt an intense personal affinity.

When we turn to "Milton II," written in 1947, all the short-
comings of Eliot's later manner become apparent. This essay is
often referred to as a refutation of his early Milton essay, but it is
not at all clear that this is so. It is an obscure piece, which certainly does not contradict directly what Eliot had written eleven
years before; indeed, it directly endorses Johnson's severe criticisms of Milton. But in contrast to the earlier essay it pays little
close attention to the text of Milton. What Eliot seems to be saying
is that the qualities he had previously analyzed as faults can be
safely tolerated as idiosyncrasies, since now "poets are sufficiently
liberated from Milton's reputation, to approach the study of his
work without danger . . ." Milton can be allowed to remain as a
great eccentric and even, perhaps, a great Englishman: "the Civil
War of the seventeenth century, in which Milton is a symbolic
figure, has never been concluded." The kindest judgment on Milton II" is that it represents a continuation of the conciliatory gesture made in "Little Gidding" to "one who died blind and quiet."

"Milton II" was originally delivered as a lecture to the British
Academy, and shows Eliot's extreme sense of occasion. The same
thing is even more true of what is surely the most grotesque essay
in On Poetry and Poets, "Goethe as the Sage." The scattered references to Goethe in Eliot's earlier criticism are, at best, lukewarm;

indeed, in "What is a Classic?" included in the same volume, there are complaints about Goethe's work; he refers to its partiality and the impermanence of some of its content and "the germanism of the sensibility," remarking that "Goethe appears, to a foreign eye, limited by his age, by his language, and by his culture." Nevertheless, having been awarded the Hanseatic Goethe Prize for 1954, Eliot was under the obligation of preparing a speech of thanks and appreciation of Goethe, which he delivered at Hamburg University in May 1955. It is a strangely rambling and even incoherent performance, in which Eliot refers in an embarrassed and apologetic way to his own doubts and reservations about Goethe, but without ever quite withdrawing them. He proceeds with all the evasiveness and obliquity of which he was master, and with plentiful padding, largely to bypass Goethe's poetry, and to concentrate on Goethe's virtues as sage and great European figure. It must have been distinctly mystifying to the original audience. Ronald Duncan has given his own account of the background to this lecture:

Once when he was stooping almost double with asthma and cold, he told me that he was busy writing a paper on Goethe as he had to go to Germany to receive the Goethe Prize and an honorary degree. He already had over twenty.

I thought his visit was unwise at the time and I had never been able to be sympathetic to Goethe after I had read that he had not even acknowledged Schubert's letter when he had sent the poet his settings of his poems.

"Isn't it a bit of a grind for you to write about Goethe?"

"It is. I can't stand his stuff."[3]

The Goethe lecture was an extreme case; but other essays in *On Poetry and Poets* give the impression of laboriously spinning out points which, though sound in themselves, could have been made more succinctly. Indeed, I think that much of the unsatisfactoriness of Eliot's late criticism arises from the fact that it was delivered in the form of lectures, which he wrote out beforehand. In order to fill an hour's lecturing time he had to enlarge his reflections to seven or eight thousand words, regardless of the actual

[3] *How to Make Enemies,* p. 384.

extent of the material. As I have suggested, as a poet Eliot could more easily achieve intensity than extension, and the same thing was true of his prose writing. It is significant that much of Eliot's really valuable criticism was written in the form of review articles for the *Athenaeum* or *Times Literary Supplement,* where reasons of space made him compress what he wanted to say into a fairly small compass: the resulting style, though mannered, was also pithy. In preparing lectures Eliot was subject to precisely the opposite pressure, with unfortunate results. It is significant that two of the best and best-written pieces in *On Poetry and Poets,* "Milton I" and "Byron," were published as articles, not delivered as lectures.

On Poetry and Poets was dedicated "To Valerie." The lady in question, Valerie Fletcher, had been Eliot's devoted secretary for several years: they were married on January 10, 1957. All those who knew him have testified to the transformation that his second marriage brought about in Eliot: a bleak story came, at last, to an unequivocally happy ending. Robert Giroux's account can be taken as representative:

In retrospect, the most striking single aspect of the years (nearly twenty) during which I was privileged to know him as a friend is the contrast between the rather sad and lonely aura that seemed to hover about him in the earlier period, and the happiness he radiated in the later one. "Radiant" may seem an odd word to apply to T. S. Eliot, yet it is an accurate description of the last eight or so years of his life, and this was due of course to his marriage in 1957 to Valerie Fletcher. More than once in those years I heard him utter the words, "I'm the luckiest man in the world."[4]

A more sardonic impression was conveyed by one of Eliot's oldest friends, Aldous Huxley, who, after a visit to London in 1958, reported that Tom Eliot "is now curiously dull—as a result, perhaps, of being, at last, happy in his second marriage."

Eliot and his wife continued to make frequent visits to the United States, where he enjoyed picking up the threads of his own origins. He told William Turner Levy that he was grateful for the

---

[4] Allen Tate, ed., *T. S. Eliot: The Man and His Work* (New York: Delacorte Press, 1966; London: Chatto & Windus, 1967), p. 335.

privilege of living in two cultures, and that each was more interesting because of the contrast with the other: "Thoughtfully, Tom
concluded, 'In some ways I am very American; yes, ah . . . and in
some ways'—he glanced down at his umbrella and smiled—'very
British!' " As so often with Eliot one has the impression of a quietly
but deliberately assumed role and manner, ranging from the sober
elegance of the poet and bank clerk of 1917 to the conscious vale-
tudinarianism observed by Ronald Duncan in the late forties, and
finally to the genial impartiality of the Anglo-American elder
statesman of letters. Eliot's failure to go abroad for his health, of
which Duncan had complained, was now corrected, and during
the last years of his life the Eliots wintered in the West Indies.

Critics have seen indications of Eliot's marriage in *The Elder
Statesman,* but the only specific literary consequence is the poem
"A Dedication to My Wife," which is placed at the end of the 1963
Collected Poems, and which first appeared, in a truncated form,
as a prefatory verse to *The Elder Statesman.* As a poem it is of no
great literary interest or merit; as a personal document it is poignant. When Eliot writes in praise of "The breathing in unison / Of
lovers whose bodies smell of each other" the result is a trifle mawk-
ish. But it both recalls and makes a decisive separation from the
fastidious young poet who had been acutely conscious of "female
smells in shuttered rooms" and of the feline smell of "Grishkin in a
drawing-room"; and also, perhaps, from the gloomy moralist who
once wrote "that Baudelaire has perceived that what distinguishes
the relations of man and woman from the copulation of beasts is
the knowledge of Good and Evil . . ." Later in the poem Eliot
seems to be consciously adapting for new purposes one of the
perennial motifs of his poetry: "No sullen tropic sun shall wither /
The roses in the rose-garden which is ours and ours only."

"In my end is my beginning." Eliot's sensibility and memory
showed a constant tendency to circle back, often in unexpected
ways, to the persons and places and interests which had been important to him at earlier phases of his career. Thus, in 1955 he
payed his final tribute to Charles Maurras, in a lecture on "The
Literature of Politics": "I think of a man whom I held in respect
and admiration, although some of his views were exasperating and
some deplorable—but a great writer, a genuine lover of his coun-

try, and a man who deserved a better fate than that which he had
in the end to meet." Both the intonation and the elegiac sentiment
recall the lines from "Little Gidding" beginning, "If I think of a
king at nightfall." And in 1962 Eliot published a short, pamphlet-
length study of George Herbert in the Writers and Their Work
series, issued by the British Council and National Book League.
It gave Eliot the opportunity, not only to record his devotion to
one of the most attractive of English poets, but to revisit for the
last time a favored realm of his imagination and memory: the
England of the early seventeenth century, the age of the "undissociated sensibility" and the first Anglican establishment, of Donne
and George Herbert and his brother, Lord Herbert of Cherbury,
and of Herbert's friends, Lancelot Andrewes and Nicholas Ferrar
of Little Gidding.

In the last few years of his life Eliot formed a new acquaintance
that may seem surprising until one remembers his often-recorded
admiration for great comedians. This was Groucho Marx, whose
fan he had been for many years. In fact, Ronald Duncan recalls
once arguing with Eliot about the respective merits of Charlie
Chaplin and the Marx Brothers; Eliot felt that the world was
divided between those who liked the one or the other, and that
there could be no agreement between them; he was a firm ad-
herent of the Marx Brothers. Eliot and Groucho were in correspondence in 1961, and exchanged photographs; Groucho's comment, on receiving Eliot's picture, was, "I had no idea you were
so handsome. Why you haven't been offered the lead in some sexy
movies I can only attribute to the stupidity of the casting directors." Their subsequent entertaining correspondence is printed in
The Groucho Letters. Eventually a meeting was arranged when
Groucho was in London in June 1964; extending an invitation to
dinner at his flat Eliot wrote:

The picture of you in the newspapers saying that, amongst other reasons, you have come to see me has greatly enhanced my credit in the
neighbourhood, and particularly with the greengrocer across the street.
Obviously I am now someone of importance.

According to Groucho's account, he tried to talk about Shakespeare and Eliot's poems, while Eliot wanted to discuss *Animal*

Crackers and *A Night at the Opera*. But he was gratified to find that he and Eliot had three things in common: "(1) an affection for good cigars and (2) cats; and (3) a weakness for making puns . . . He is a dear man and a charming host."

Eliot had had a long and severe illness in the winter of 1962–1963 and was slow to recover. But in December 1963 he and his wife were in New York for the last time, en route for Nassau; William Turner Levy was distressed at his appearance. Yet his spirits remained high, as was apparent during his dinner with Groucho Marx, who nevertheless formed the impression that his host was "not long for this world." Martin Browne, dining for the last time with Eliot in September 1964 found him "very frail." Bad weather at Christmas caused a further deterioration in his health, and he died peacefully on January 4, 1965.

There were many personal tributes, as well as formal memorial notices, though no one has said more in fewer words than Robert Giroux: "To me he was a great human being, quite aside from being a great artist." Among the mourners at the memorial service in Westminster Abbey was one who must have known Eliot longer than anyone else present. Ezra Pound, then in his eightieth year, had traveled from Italy to pay his last tribute to an old friend. It was fifty years and four months since Eliot, newly arrived in London, had presented himself at Pound's flat, together with the manuscript of "Prufrock." Now a great age had ended. Pound wrote in Allen Tate's memorial volume:

His was the true Dantescan voice—not honoured enough, and deserving more than I ever gave him . . .

Am I to write "about" the poet Thomas Stearns Eliot? or my friend "the Possum"? Let him rest in peace. I can only repeat, but with the urgency of 50 years ago: READ HIM.

2

Eliot's verse comedies of the nineteen-fifties mark the last phase of his career as a creative writer; and they conclude a lifelong preoccupation with the problem of writing poetic drama, already apparent in 1920, when he wrote:

The composition of a poetic drama is in fact the most difficult, the most exhausting task that a poet can set himself, and—this is the heart of the matter—it is infinitely more difficult for a poet of today than it was for a poet of no greater talent three hundred years ago.[5]

We have seen Eliot's subsequent elaborations of this aim: the insistence that poetic drama should be both stylized and capable of appealing to a wide audience; that the dramatic and the poetic should be one, and that poetry could find its highest fulfillment in the theater, though a modern audience, like an Elizabethan one, might appreciate what was offered at different levels of understanding; and that the poetic drama should utilize and transform popular dramatic forms. And we have seen Eliot's successive attempts to take up this most difficult and exhausting of tasks. First, *Sweeney Agonistes,* the fragmentary "jazz play" of the twenties, where he brilliantly makes use of the popular modes of the music hall and the minstrel show. Then, the Christian ritual drama of *Murder in the Cathedral* which found its original audience in an ecclesiastical setting, and which was written in the conviction that poetic drama should emphasize, not minimize, the fact that it is written in verse. Next came *The Family Reunion,* Eliot's attempt to enact an Aeschylean theme in a modern setting, which is still a deliberately "poetic" drama, written in a variety of verse forms and with heightened moments of metaphorical intensity.

The Family Reunion is uneasily poised between the stylized and the naturalistic, and when Eliot again took up dramatic writing, ten years later, he moved decisively toward naturalism, and a blank verse that no longer emphasized its nature as such but was so formally unobtrusive as to be for the most part indistinguishable from prose. The audiences in Edinburgh, London, and New York that found *The Cocktail Party* a rewarding theatrical experience were no doubt relieved by what they got; despite Eliot's reputation as a difficult modern poet and dramatist there was little obscurity to trouble them, and virtually no obvious "poetry," and this was precisely what Eliot intended. In the fifties he preserved his original aim of bringing together poetic drama and the popular theater, but his concept of both these entities had changed: the

[5] *Athenaeum,* May 14, 1920.

poetic element was reduced to a flexible and lucid blank verse that faithfully reproduced the cadences of the speaking voice and avoided metaphorical concentration; while the popular theater was no longer seen as the music hall or the minstrel show, but as the realistic "well-made play," traditionally enjoyed by audiences on Broadway and Shaftesbury Avenue. Thirty years before Eliot had regarded the conventional naturalistic drama as the enemy of theatrical progress and made it a target for his critical invective; in the fifties, however, he attempted to make use of it for his own purposes. From the point of view of the ordinary theater-goer, *The Cocktail Party* is, undoubtedly, a very well made play indeed; it is skillfully constructed, with a reassuringly familiar setting, a nicely balanced range of characters, and an intriguing plot developed with appropriate suspense and mystification. There is a degree of high comedy, notably in the exchanges between Julia and Alex, while the presence of moral, religious, and philosophical profundity is lightly signaled, without being too portentously asserted; all this was in direct contrast to the rather heavy-handed changes of gear in *The Family Reunion*. And, for the first time in Eliot's dramatic work, things actually happen in *The Cocktail Party:* Lavinia Chamberlayne leaves Edward and is persuaded to return to him, and both of them become aware of their essential mediocrity and make a conscious effort to live as well as they can with each other, which, by the end of the play, seems to be succeeding. Celia Coplestone, on the other hand, who is one of the spiritually elect, gives up the inauthentic social round of cocktail parties and trivial adulteries and goes off to become a nursing missionary in a savage part of the world. And there she is cruelly martyred. The party that ends the play shows us a clearly different community from the one that opens it.

To say that *The Cocktail Party* is an entirely naturalistic play would be an exaggeration. There is, for instance, the curious moment of ritual formality when the usually comic Julia and Alex, together with Sir Henry Harcourt-Reilly, the distinguished psychiatrist (a version of the miracle-working Hercules in Euripides' *Alcestis*, which was Eliot's point of departure for *The Cocktail Party*), assemble together and engage in a libation and prayers for Edward and Lavinia and Celia. Eliot does not, however, strike an overtly Christian note, either here or elsewhere in the play, so that the religious feelings appear no more than magical and vaguely mystifying. Even Celia's atrocious death is presented as the fulfillment of a particular pattern of spiritual fulfillment rather than as a clear act of Christian witness. Eliot was evidently determined to avoid any hint of preaching. Nevertheless, much of the play reflects themes already very familiar in his work, notably the division between those burdened with consciousness and a sense of high destiny, like Celia, and those, like Edward and Lavinia, who have to be content with an existence of limited opportunities and awareness. Eliot does his best to be fair to the latter way of life, which is, after all, the common lot of the mass of humanity, but he finds it hard to be enthusiastic:

> They do not repine;
> Are contented with the morning that separates
> And with the evening that brings together
> For casual talk before the fire
> Two people who know they do not understand each other,
> Breeding children whom they do not understand
> And who will never understand them.

Edward learns to accept such a life—"In a world of lunacy, / Violence, stupidity, greed . . . it is a good life"—but not before he has expressed his own sense of spiritual alienation, in one of the few heightened passages in the play. The words appear to be a refutation of Sartre's *l'enfer c'est les autres,* and they look back to part V of *The Waste Land,* "We think of the key, each in his prison," with echoes of Dante's Ugolino and Bradley's *Appearance and Reality:*

> There was a door
> And I could not open it. I could not touch the handle.
> Why could I not walk out of my prison?
> What is hell? Hell is oneself,
> Hell is alone, the other figures in it
> Merely projections. There is nothing to escape from
> And nothing to escape to. One is always alone.

In the final scene of the play Reilly gives Edward and Lavinia advice that recalls and transposes the central argument of "Tradition and the Individual Talent":

You will have to live with these memories and make them
Into something new. Only by acceptance
Of the past will you alter its meaning.

Celia is martyred, and Edward and Lavinia must learn to live
with their memories, both of her (she had been Edward's mis-
tress) and of their own pasts. The two facts remain disconnected
on the plane of action, and Eliot does not suggest any possibility
of integrating them, for martyrdom cannot itself be a meaningful
concept in the inauthentic world of the dramatic convention he
has here adopted. Nor, by implication, can it be for the audience
that is at home in such a world. Eliot may have intended to use the
naturalistic drawing-room comedy for his own purposes, but its
inherent conventions seem to have exerted a stronger pressure on
him than he was prepared for. Clearly Eliot enjoyed the technical
challenge of writing within this convention and the result is, in
formal terms, extremely adroit. But conventions are, in themselves,
a mode of meaning, and Eliot's meanings in *The Cocktail Party* are
correspondingly impoverished. In terms of Eliot's early passion for
a revivified poetic drama, where poetic metaphor and dramatic
action would be two aspects of the same effect, as is supremely
the case in Shakespeare; for a "ballet of words," where modern
meanings would be conveyed with the formal intensity of dancing,
The Cocktail Party, and *a fortiori* its two successors, are abdica-
tions. Much of the verse seems to serve only as a kind of notation
to assist the actors, and the same end could have been equally
achieved in well written theatrical prose. Eliot's decisive mistake
was undoubtedly to exaggerate the centrality and potentialities of
the rather tired mode of naturalistic theater that he at length
adopted, after spurning it for so long. The irony is that he did so
just before the advent of Beckett as a dramatist and the delayed
impact of Brecht in the English theater showed the immense possibilities of an expressive and non-naturalistic drama, even without
the obligation of being formally poetic. Helen Gardner, in a vigorous but not very convincing defense of Eliot's comedies has tried
to present them as living works in a central tradition of English
stage comedy that runs through Congreve and Wilde; she denies
that the "well-made" drawing-room comedy of the early twentieth-

century theater is no longer viable even if currently out of fashion. Professor Gardner may be right, but she seems to be confusing social comedy as a perennial theatrical mode with a particular naturalistic version of it; the former may well go on, even if in unimaginable forms, but the latter has surely had its day. Significantly, she defends Eliot's comedies simply as plays, stressing their excellence of characterization, construction, and dialogue, and the seriousness of their inner meanings, rather than as poetic drama.

The Confidential Clerk has a mythic underpinning in Euripides' Ion, but its vehicle is not so much the drawing-room comedy as the Victorian melodrama, that dealt in mysterious entanglements of identity and children lost in infancy and found again in adult life. Eliot might, indeed, have done better to have presented the play as a frankly Victorian period piece, but references to air travel prevent one reading it in this way. It is certainly a long time since such creatures as "confidential clerks" were to be found in the offices of financiers, though they might still have existed when Eliot began work in the City in 1917. One does not, admittedly, look for a full representation of contemporary life and manners in an artificial stage comedy; if one compares The Confidential Clerk with Sweeney Agonistes, which vividly conveys the idioms and rhythms of its setting and period, one can see how far Eliot had lost touch with the world he was writing about, and was content with weaving patterns in a theatrical void. For one reader, at least, The Confidential Clerk is an irredeemably trivial work. There is little more to be said for Eliot's last play, The Elder Statesman, which takes its part of departure in Oepidus at Colonus, just as its two predecessors had in plays by Euripides, and in much the same perfunctory manner: none of these myths had the same pressing significance for Eliot that the Oresteia had in the writing of Sweeney Agonistes and The Family Reunion. The Elder Statesman does not even have the virtue of being technically well constructed, and the story is no more credible than in The Confidential Clerk. Such interest that the play possesses comes from Eliot turning once more to problems he had attempted to resolve in earlier works: the intractable Furies of The Family Reunion appear now as real characters, in the predatory Gomez and Mrs. Carghill, figures from Lord Claverton's early life who return to plague him when he is near death. As Raymond Williams has pointed out, Claverton's monologues convey feeling in ways that recall Eliot's early poetry. Such lines as

> But waiting, simply waiting
> With no desire to act, yet a loathing of inaction.
> A fear of the vacuum, and no desire to fill it

look back to "Gerontion." From his earliest days, Eliot had been drawn to the persona of an old man; in this play, produced in his seventieth year, the figure has acquired a greater existential significance. Kenneth Tynan's observation that toward the end Eliot casts over the play "a sedative, autumnal glow of considerable beauty" is a remark one can endorse. What is new in the play is the frank assertion of the value of human love, even if in accents that are still tentative and unpracticed.

It is, by now, a common opinion that Eliot's theatrical development in the fifties was a move in the wrong direction, after the promising dramatic experiments of the twenties and thirties. Predictably, one hears such views from those who are out of sympathy with Eliots' aims and achievements as a writer. It is more significant and surprising to find doubts expressed, in however qualified a form, by one who for over thirty years was Eliot's closest theatrical collaborator. At the end of *The Making of T. S. Eliot's Plays*, E. Martin Browne reflects:

I feel that, by adopting this pattern of ironic social comedy, Eliot placed upon his genius a regrettable limitation. He tied himself to social, and still more to theatrical, conventions which were already outworn when the plays were written. Perhaps they reflect an unconscious reversion to the drama that Eliot must have seen as a young theatregoer before 1914. At any rate, the result was that, while he was working successfully to free his dramatic verse from the exhausted post-Shakespearean forms, he was submitting his dramatic form to the same kind of constriction.

And to do so, he put his poetry, as he says, "on a thin diet." We have seen the progressive diminution of poetry in these plays, quite deliberately achieved. The poet's skill is still supremely evident in the choice of language, and his inspiration often peeps through it; but too much of his energy is devoted to the correct expression of unimportant social niceties. The comedy is often delightful, but one pays too great a price for it in prolixity; the comedy of *Sweeney* is more concise, and its comic form is an evident reflection of the depths beneath.

For Browne, the essence of Eliot's dramatic achievement was in the ritual vision expressed in *Murder in the Cathedral* and, however imperfectly, in *The Family Reunion*. There is, certainly, a promise and a possibility in these plays that is lacking in *The Cocktail Party* and its successors. Browne is making the same essential criticism of Eliot as has been more sharply formulated by Raymond Williams and others: that Eliot took with excessive seriousness the trivial manifestations of the late naturalistic theater, and the social modes and assumptions that went with them. And this points not merely to a failure of literary and dramatic judgment on Eliot's part, but to the tendency, so often manifested in the last part of his life, to be content with the status quo.

It is reasonable to assume that Eliot would have resisted this judgment on his last plays, to which he devoted so much effort, and its larger corollary that his lifelong concern with establishing a modern poetic drama was ultimately without successful issue. Yet he might have accepted its truth, however reluctantly, knowing as he did that

> every attempt
> Is a wholly new start, and a different kind of failure.

3

Eliot's penetration and capture, first of the British cultural establishment, and then of large areas of literary orthodoxy in the English-speaking world, was not deliberately striven for. It resulted from the fortuitous appearance of his example and precepts at a time when literary taste was in need of reorientation just after the First World War, and when the academic growth of English studies was able to take up and use Eliot's timely critical discoveries and his emphasis on tradition. His success, once it came, was rapid and complete, though there remained pockets of resistance, notably in Oxford. Indeed, it now looks to have been too rapid, and the inevitable reaction, which began some years before Eliot's death, has been marked on both sides of the Atlantic. In the United

States, Eliot is increasingly rejected as a "paleface" and a seeker after alien masters and cultures, in contrast to the true tradition of American poetry, which runs from Whitman via Pound, in his native rather than his European aspects, to Williams and Olson and Ginsberg. In England, on the other hand, Eliot is often regarded as an outsider and a modernist by the kind of middle-aged taste that is inclined toward the insular tradition of Hardy and Betjeman and Larkin. (Young readers, on the other hand, are much taken up with the current American models in poetry). There exists, in both countries, a conventional notion of Eliot as bloodless, pedantic, and overerudite, that was curiously anticipated in his own account, written in 1919, of Henry Adams, the "sceptical patrician":

He was much more refined than the equivalent Englishman, and had less vitality, though a remarkably restless curiosity, eager but unsensuous. And his very American curiosity was directed and misdirected by two New England characteristics: conscientiousness and scepticism . . . Against the naive, Adams represents the in some ways precociously and immaturely sophisticated American . . . The Erinys which drove him madly through seventy years of search for education—the search for what, upon a lower plane, is called culture—left him much as he was born: well-bred, intelligent and uneducated.

Whether or not this is a fair description of Henry Adams, Eliot's personal involvement in it is unmistakable: Adams, in this account, shared some of Eliot's temperamental and cultural characteristics, and provided a warning of what he might have become, lacking genius. In fact, it bears much the same relation to Eliot that James Joyce's characterization of the failed, genteel man of letters, Gabriel Conroy, in "The Dead," does to Joyce himself.

Eliot goes on to indicate the qualities that Adams lacked, in some sentences which reveal a theme later worked out in "The Metaphysical Poets":

It is probable that men ripen best through experiences which are at once sensuous and intellectual: certainly many men will admit that their keenest ideas have come to them with the quality of a sense-perception; and that their keenest sensuous perception has been "as if the body thought." There is nothing to indicate that Adams's senses either flowered or fruited: he remains little Paul Dombey asking questions.[6]

[6] *Athenaeum*, May 23, 1919.

Eliot compares Adams unfavorably with Henry James, "who was not, by Adams's standards, 'educated' but particularly limited; it is the sensuous contributor to the intelligence that makes the difference." And so it was with Eliot; what set him apart from the hesitant desiccated figure that he drew of Adams was precisely the quality of his sensuous perceptions, his awareness of the abyss and the deepest terrors and desires, and his familiarity with the lonely, painful act of creation. As a poet Eliot was solitary and unaffected by being culturally institutionalized. If he is less significant now as a force for literary orthodoxy, this is irrelevant to his true stature as a poet; when the cultural idol has been displaced the voice of the poet may be heard more clearly. If that voice is to go on being listened to, as I believe it will, the present decline in Eliot's reputation may be both inevitable and salutary. Future readers will acknowledge Eliot's genius, but they will see different things in him from his first readers, and from ourselves. All of which, we may be sure, he would have calmly understood and welcomed. Tradition is always being rewritten: "We have not reached conclusion. . . ."

A Select Bibliography

There is an immense amount of biographical and contextual information in Herbert Howarth, *Notes on Some Figures Behind T. S. Eliot,* particularly about Eliot's family background and education; this can be supplemented by the account in Kristian Smidt, *Poetry and Belief in the Work of T. S. Eliot,* and by Helen Gardner's article, "The Landscapes of Eliot's Poetry," *Critical Quarterly,* Winter 1968. Eliot himself touched briefly but illuminatingly on his early life in *The Use of Poetry and the Use of Criticism* and in "American Literature and the American Language" in *To Criticize the Critic.* For an account of Eliot at Harvard, see Conrad Aiken's memoir in *T. S. Eliot: A Symposium* (ed. Richard March and Tambimuttu), and his fictionalized autobiography, *Ushant.* Eliot recalled his year in Paris in *The Criterion* "Commentary" for April 1934, and a further account is quoted by E. D. H. Greene in *T. S. Eliot et la France.* There are impressions of Eliot as a graduate student by Bertrand Russell in *Ottoline* (ed. Robert Gathorne-Hardy) and *The Autobiography of Bertrand Russell,* Vol. I.

For Eliot's early London career see the letters of Ezra Pound (ed. D. D. Paige), Wyndham Lewis (ed. W. K. Rose), and Aldous Huxley (ed. Grover Smith). See, too, Wyndham Lewis's *Blasting and Bombardiering* and his memoir in *T. S. Eliot: A Symposium;* also *The Autobiography of Bertrand Russell,* Vol. II; Richard Aldington, *Life for Life's Sake;* Brigit Patmore, *My Friends When*

Young; Michael Holroyd, *Lytton Strachey,* Vol. II; Osbert Sitwell, *Laughter in the Next Room;* and Herbert Read's memoir in *T. S. Eliot: the Man and His Work* (ed. Allen Tate).

There are accounts of Eliot in the twenties and thirties in several contributions to the volumes edited by March and Tambimuttu, and by Allen Tate; notably by Frank Morley in both collections, and by I. A. Richards, Herbert Read, Bonamy Dobrée, H. S. Davies, and Stephen Spender in the latter. See also Spender's *World Within World,* Leonard Woolf's *Downhill All the Way,* and Arnold Bennett's *Journals,* Vol. III. There are interesting quotations from Eliot's correspondence with John Quinn in B. L. Reid, *The Man from New York.* The last part of Eliot's life is recalled in Robert Giroux's memoir in the Tate collection; in Ronald Duncan, *How to Make Enemies;* and William Turner Levy and Victor Scherle, *Affectionately, T. S. Eliot.*

Eliot's work in the theater is recorded by E. Martin Browne in *The Making of T. S. Eliot's Plays;* David E. Jones, *The Plays of T. S. Eliot,* documents many of Eliot's opinions about the drama as well as examining his practice as a playwright. Eliot's political and social ideas are discussed by J. M. Cameron in *The Night Battle* and by Raymond Williams in *Culture and Society,* and his attitudes to education are summarized by G. H. Bantock in *T. S. Eliot and Education. Eliot in Perspective,* edited by Graham Martin, contains several valuable essays on particular aspects of Eliot's work: by Richard Wollheim on Eliot's study of F. H. Bradley; by Katharine Worth on Eliot in the theater; by Adrian Cunningham on Eliot's religious development; and by John Peter on his editorship of *The Criterion.* Sharply opposed views of Eliot's achievement as a critic, and particularly of "Tradition and the Individual Talent," are expressed by F. R. Leavis in *Anna Karenina and Other Essays* and by F. W. Bateson in "T. S. Eliot: 'Impersonality' Fifty Years After," *Southern Review,* July 1969.

Critical studies of Eliot's poetry are so numerous that I can do no more than mention a handful of names. One must acknowledge, first, the important early essays, such as those by E. M. Forster in *Abinger Harvest,* by F. R. Leavis in *New Bearings in English Poetry,* and by Edmund Wilson in *Axel's Castle;* and such a pioneering book as F. O. Matthiessen's *The Achievement of T. S.*

Eliot. Grover Smith's *T. S. Eliot's Poetry and Plays* is the most exhaustively informative work about the allusions, references, and contexts of Eliot's poetry. There are several useful collections of essays on Eliot's work, such as *T. S. Eliot, A Study of his Writings by Several Hands,* ed. B. Rajan; *T. S. Eliot, A Selected Critique,* ed. Leonard Unger; and *T. S. Eliot, A Collection of Critical Essays,* ed. Hugh Kenner. Major poems are discussed in *A Collection of Critical Essays on The Waste Land,* ed. Jay Martin; *The Waste Land: A Casebook,* ed. C. B. Cox and A. P. Hinchliffe; and *Four Quartets: A Casebook,* ed. Bernard Bergonzi. In writing the present book I have found myself most deeply indebted to the chapters on Eliot in C. K. Stead's *The New Poetic* and to Hugh Kenner's *The Invisible Poet.* And finally I must acknowledge the timely assistance I got from the second edition of Donald Gallup's magnificent work, *T. S. Eliot: A Bibliography.*

The most comprehensive collection of T. S. Eliot's poetry is the *Complete Poems and Plays,* which includes the works published separately in *Poems Written in Early Youth, Collected Poems 1909–1962,* and *Collected Plays.* His prose writings currently available include *Knowledge and Experience in the Philosophy of F. H. Bradley, The Sacred Wood, For Lancelot Andrewes, Selected Essays, The Use of Poetry and the Use of Criticism, The Idea of a Christian Society, Notes Towards the Definition of Culture, On Poetry and Poets,* and *To Criticize the Critic.*

INDEX

Index

DATE DUE